Treating Sexual Addiction

A Compassionate Approach to Recovery

Dr. Kevin Skinner, LMFT, CSAT-S

Published by:

KSkinner Corp.

199 N. 290 W. ste. 150

Lindon, Utah 84042

Library of Congress Control Number: 2019920384

Author's note: Throughout this book most of the stories come from individuals who have completed my online assessment or shared their stories with me as a counselor. This work would not have happened if they hadn't been willing to be vulnerable enough to open up and share their stories and challenges with me. I honor those who have been willing to come forward and say, "I need help."

In order to protect the confidentiality of all clients and research participants, names and personal identifying information have been changed. In some cases, the author has also taken the liberty to combine cases to illustrate specific points.

This book should not replace medical or professional advice.

Dedication

It takes a lot of support from others to write a book. This book is dedicated to my wife and children who have encouraged and supported me throughout my long days and nights of writing. It would not have been possible for me to write this without their support.

I would also like to thank the many therapists who have read chapters from the manuscript and provided me valuable feedback. I honor you and the work you are doing.

Finally, over the past 25 years, I have witnessed so many men and women who have suffered in silence due to their sexual behaviors. As they have reached out for support and help, I have seen them face their demons. Their courage and willingness to say, "I need help," has inspired me. I have learned so much from these individuals as they have engaged in their hero's journey. I know their challenges have not been easy to overcome, but I respect them for never giving up. This book is dedicated to those who have reached out for help and those who will come after you who are looking for answers to the real-life challenges of sexual addiction.

Contents

Introduction 7

PART ONE
Treating Sexual Addiction, Taking Your First Steps Toward Recovery **15**
Chapter One: Modeling Your Recovery After What Works 17
Chapter Two: Getting to the Root of the Problem. 31
Chapter Three: Understanding Your Story. 46

PART TWO
Developing the Foundational Skills for Long-Term Recovery **57**
Chapter Four: Creating Your Recovery Plan 58
Chapter Five: Succeed in Crucial Moments. 73
Chapter Six: The Power of Being Vulnerable 82
Chapter Seven: Compassion: The Secret of Successful Recovery 95

PART 3
How to Address the Barriers that Prevent Recovery **107**
Chapter Eight: Addressing Loneliness, A Silent Driver of Addiction 108
Chapter Nine: Letting Go of Your Shame 123
Chapter Ten: The Healing Power of Emotional Regulation 144

PART FOUR
Improve the Quality of Your Life **159**
Chapter Eleven: Building Healthy Habits 160
Chapter Twelve: Creating the Moments that Will Change Your Life 173
Chapter Thirteen: How to Establish Meaningful Support for
  Long-Term Recovery. 181
Chapter Fourteen: Loving Your Way Through Addiction Recovery 196

Thank You. 216
References and Notes 217
Appendix A: Family History/Genogram 230
Appendix B: Outlining Your Recovery Plan. 232
Appendix C: Five Things To Do Before You Relapse 236
Appendix D: Sexual History Timeline. 238
Appendix E: Key Life Inventory 240
Appendix F: Recommended Readings and Other Resources 243
Online Courses. 246

Introduction

When Jacob sat down, it was clear he didn't want to be in my office. He had already seen two other therapists and was feeling like nothing would help him. His wife was ready to leave him, and I was his "last" chance. As I looked at him, it was clear he was worn out. He was losing everything. He was facing scrutiny at work because he wasn't performing. His business partner was threatening to buy him out. His wife was tired of giving him chances, and his children no longer trusted him. He wasn't sure it could get any worse.

Before our meeting, I had him take several assessments that were related to his sexual behaviors, sexual history, and mental health. It was evident by looking at the results that his sexual acts were controlling his life. He was depressed and had moderate levels of anxiety. He also reported very low on the life satisfaction scale that I had given him.

There are many professionals in my field that still question whether sexual behaviors can be addictive. However, if they had asked Jacob whether he thought he was a sex addict, he would have given them a look of disbelief that they could even ask such a stupid question. He would ask them to look at his life and how out of control he felt. He was on the brink of losing everything because he couldn't stop acting out sexually.

As we began talking, it was clear that he wanted my help. He hadn't found any success in his previous attempts at becoming sober, and he wasn't sure I could help either. In his past attempts at recovery, he had talked with his religious leaders, attended 12-step groups, and met with other therapists. The more we spoke, however, the more it became apparent that he had been making token efforts, but his overall day-to-day commitment to the recovery process had not been consistent. In other words, he'd been going through the motions but never really engaged in his recovery journey.

After reviewing his assessments, I asked if he believed he could succeed. He gave me a look I will never forget. He was scared, and it showed. He was also angry—angry at himself, angry at his wife, and angry at life in general. He didn't know if he could stop. He had been viewing pornography and having affairs for most of his marriage. His sexual behaviors had controlled him for so long that he honestly didn't know if recovery was a possibility for him.

It was at this point that I looked at him and said, "I have been doing this for more than 20 years. I have seen individuals just like you rise from the ashes and reclaim their lives. I have studied the healing and recovery process, and I know you can succeed. My experience tells me you are a fighter. After all, I am your third counselor, and you have reached out to others for support. Perhaps the most critical question you need to address is, 'Are you ready to pay the price?'

"Healing is possible," I went on, "but it will always come with a price. It will take time, and you will have to commit to learning new ways of thinking, feeling, believing, and behaving. It will require a strong commitment, and there will be days where you feel like nothing you do is helping. In the end, your recovery will be life-transforming. Recovery is so much more than just stopping your behaviors. If you are going to heal truly, we have to help you improve the quality of your life. Perhaps most important will be learning to develop a better, more meaningful relationship with your wife and children. Would you like that?"

He replied earnestly, "Yes, I do want that. I want to stop. And, if at all possible, I want to save my marriage. I want my children to trust me again."

For much of my twenty-five-year career, I've had the privilege of working with individuals like Jacob, who have been trapped in destructive life-altering sexual habits (e.g., having multiple affairs, visiting prostitutes, etc.). I have observed the lives of individuals who are caught in an addictive loop. They have tried a few things to stop acting out, but nothing has stuck. I have seen the chaos these addictive habits have created. Most of those I have worked with are lost individuals whose lives have been out of control. Sadly, many have never been taught how to heal, nor have they been given the right tools to make their healing possible. They live for years with shame and guilt, wondering what's wrong with them. They struggle to realize their real value and worth. Unfortunately, nobody has helped them understand the process of change so they can experience a better way to live. I have found almost all who seek my help want to be free from the chains of addiction. They just don't know where to start.

During the past few years, I have helped individuals from around the world discover how to heal and reclaim their lives from sexual addiction. I have studied what successful people do in their journey to recovery. I have witnessed my clients change the quality of their lives and make significant life-altering changes. I hope that, as you read this book, you, too, will see a path to recovery and reclaim your life. However, I don't want it to end there. I want you to improve the quality of your life. My hope is that you will be better at relationships, find more joy in your work, and find that your overall satisfaction with life increases—that's what real recovery looks like to me.

Is Sex Addiction, Real?

Before we continue, we must address an important question: Is there such a thing as sex addiction? In our society today, many question whether a person's sexual behaviors can be addictive. Most people agree that drugs and alcohol can be addictive, but there is much debate about whether an individual's sexual acts can become so out of control as to call them "addictive."

I believe that using the term "addiction" should not be taken lightly. Therefore, in using it to describe one's sexual behaviors, it is essential that we understand and agree on the definition and its accompanying symptoms. Indeed, it is a bold claim to say that one's sexual behaviors are addictive. Furthermore, because we are all sexual beings, we have to ask ourselves difficult questions, e.g., what is normal, healthy sexual behavior? And what is too much sexual behavior? In other words, what determines if one has a sexual addiction?

Let's start by defining "addiction." According to the American Society of Addiction Medicine (ASAM), "Addiction is a primary, chronic disease of brain reward, motivation, memory, and related circuitry. Dysfunction in these circuits leads to characteristic biological, psychological, social, and spiritual manifestations. This is reflected in an individual pathologically pursuing reward and/or relief by substance use and other behaviors" (1).

Historically, when we observe any addictive behavior, the following five characteristics manifest themselves:

1. Inability to consistently abstain;

2. Impairment in behavioral control;

3. Craving or increased "hunger" for drugs or rewarding experiences;

4. Diminished recognition of significant problems with one's behaviors and interpersonal relationships; and

5. A dysfunctional emotional response.

According to ASAM, "Like other chronic diseases, addiction often involves cycles of relapse and remission. Without treatment or engagement in recovery activities, addiction is progressive and can result in disability or premature death" (2). The five core characteristics, as defined by ASAM, is the definition I am referring to when I use the word "addiction." By using the same symptoms across behaviors (e.g., drugs, alcohol, sex), we will have a shared definition. Now, with a shared definition and description of the symptoms, we must ask ourselves if individuals who seek professional help for their sexual acts are exhibiting these same symptoms? If they are, then we would appropriately say that sex addiction is real.

Based on my clinical experience with hundreds of individuals seeking help for their unwanted sexual behaviors, I have observed each of these symptoms in my clients. One man's description of what pornography did to him is a painful example of how sexual behaviors, as seemingly harmless as pornography, can alter one's life. His story describes the power of his battle well.

He wrote, "You can spend so much time looking at it (pornography) that it becomes a part of you without you realizing it. You devote more time to it than your own family, and you don't even like it (the addiction). Then, one day you look up from the screen, and your kids are grown, and your wife gives you one-word answers with no eye contact, and you start adding up the money, and it's over $300,000 through 40 years. You miss out on what matters and hurt loved ones in the process, and you did it with your choice to be with something you despise. It basically took my life from me."

Whether it's pornography, prostitutes, massage parlors, or engaging in other unwanted sexual behaviors, I hope to help you reclaim your life. Whether you call your sexual behaviors addictive or not, if they've had a negative impact on your life (e.g., creating problems at work or in your family life), there is hope and healing is possible. Help is available. You do not have to be defined by your past. You don't have to engage in sexual activities you want to stop. You and your life are worth so much more than what you have ever done sexually.

This book is divided into four sections. In the first section, I share with you what some refer to as the "science of addiction recovery." Dr. Alexandre Laudet from the National Development and Research Institutes believes that great strides have been made in understanding how to best treat addictions (3). In essence, Laudet and others studying the recovery process have been able to identify what leads to a successful recovery. This book will build upon their model and will also incorporate valuable insights from Dr. Patrick Carnes's task model. Dr. Carnes has spent his life educating others about sexual addiction and helping individuals heal through his clinical work (see Appendix F for a list of his books). Together, these two models are powerful and can help you in your journey to recovery.

Building upon the foundation of what works, I hope to help you build a recovery plan. We will apply the same principles that have worked for thousands of individuals to help you deal with your unwanted sexual behaviors and other potential addictions you may be experiencing.

In Chapter One, I introduce you to the ten categories of recovery capital. These ten areas are what researchers have discovered as the components of recovery. After many years of studying what works in recovery, researchers have observed that people who succeed in recovery score higher in each of these ten categories. In applying this model, you will be doing what others have done who have succeeded. The main idea is to build your recovery capital. The more capital you have, the more likely your efforts will lead to success. At the end of this chapter, you will be invited to take the Sexual Addiction Recovery Capital Scale. This short quiz will help you to establish your current baseline level of recovery capital.

In Chapter Two, you will learn how to get to the root of your problems. A few years ago, my neighbor asked me to take out a rose bush from her yard. I dug down about one and a half feet and couldn't see any more roots. The next year that rose bush came back. I realized that I had not dug deep enough to get all of the roots. If you don't get to the deeper roots of what is driving your behaviors, they will likely come back.

In Chapter Three, the focus will be on helping you to understand your story. There is always a story of how individuals get stuck in their sexually acting out behaviors. In this chapter, we will help you identify how your story was written and help you to explore how the story developed. Often your sexual acts are just the tip of the iceberg. In order to succeed, you will need to look at what's beneath your iceberg. In most cases, when you look deeper, you will find some of the reasons you haven't been able to succeed. Your awareness of what's below the tip of the iceberg will help you prepare for long-term recovery.

The chapters in Section Two will help you to develop the foundational skills that I believe are required for long-term recovery.

In Chapter Four, you will learn how to create an effective recovery plan. Often when I talk with individuals about their strategy for recovery, many do not have a plan at all. In this chapter, you will learn how to create a personalized recovery plan.

The focus of Chapter Five is to help you to succeed in crucial moments. In my clinical experience, I have observed clients who, even with well-established plans, can give in and relapse. What I have come to understand is that even the best plans can fail during crucial moments. During these times, when the cravings are high, and you are feeling stressed, you are at the highest risk for relapse. In this chapter, I am going to prepare you to succeed in your most vulnerable times.

In Chapter Six, I discuss the power of being vulnerable. The recovery process will require you to learn how to be open and vulnerable. This chapter will help you to develop insight into how you can start rebuilding trust with the people you care the most about.

The final chapter in this section addresses self-compassion. Learning to develop this form of self-love may make this the most critical chapter in this book. The ideas found here will help you to discover the "real" you. You will need the concepts in this chapter as you go through your healing and recovery journey. After years of observing successful clients, I have come to believe that self-compassion is the single most crucial part of recovery. When you develop self-compassion, your ability to heal will be accelerated.

In the third section, you will learn how to address some of the most common barriers individuals face in their recovery journey. The hope is that, by helping you remove the obstacles, your chance of success will significantly increase.

In Chapter Eight, the focus is on helping you to address the loneliness that often comes with addiction. Research on the role of loneliness in driving sex addiction will also be shared.

The focus of Chapter Nine is addressing your shame. Unresolved shame is a powerful driver of addictive behaviors. This chapter will provide you with a new model for resolving your shame and help you to learn how to let go of your shame.

In Chapter Ten, the final chapter in section three, we address how to deal with difficult emotions. This is what professional counselors call "emotional regulation." You probably think of it as dealing with your stress. No matter what we call it, if you can learn to regulate difficult emotions (stressors), you will be much more effective in your efforts. In this chapter, you will learn about emotional regulation and how to apply it in your recovery process.

In the fourth and final section, the focus is on helping you to improve your overall quality of life. Recovery is much more than just stopping your sexual behaviors. Recovery is about living a life full of joy. It is about improving the quality of your life.

In Chapter Eleven, we discuss the importance of building healthy habits. Because healthy habits lead to healthy lives, we explore how seemingly simple habits can lead to powerful and profound changes in your life.

The focus of Chapter Twelve is to help you understand how certain moments or events can be game-changers. You will discover how key moments can change your life and lead you toward long-term healing and recovery. Some moments are defining. You will learn about these moments and how you can put them to work in your life.

In Chapter Thirteen, the focus is on helping you to find meaningful support in your recovery journey. In the recovery capital literature, developing a positive social network is consistently listed as one of the most essential parts of recovery. In this chapter, we discuss how to find the necessary support you will need in recovery. It is important to understand that not all support is the same. Learning who can help and who cannot help is an integral part of healing and recovery.

Chapter Fourteen is titled "Loving Your Way Through Addiction Recovery." I have found that learning to love self, others, and society is a powerful solution that aids in the recovery process. The tools provided in this chapter will help you to improve your relationships with the key people in your life. If you are married, you will learn how to be better in your marriage. If you are single, you will learn how to be better in your relationships and, if you choose, more prepared for a significant relationship. When you learn to love your way through the recovery journey, your life will be enriched because you will be better at finding and creating true intimacy. You will be better at making love.

Are you ready to get started?

Part One

Treating Sexual Addiction

Taking Your First Steps Toward Recovery

Chapter One

Modeling Your Recovery After What Works

Almost nothing works the first time it's attempted. Just because what you're doing does not seem to be working, doesn't mean it won't work. It just means that it might not work the way you're doing it.

(Bob Parsons)

"I have tried everything. I have been to other counselors, talked with my church leaders, attended countless 12-step groups. You name it; I have probably tried it. What makes you think this time will be any different?" This was the question Charles, my new client, raised to me in our first session. I replied, "Honestly, I don't know if what I have to offer you will be the catalyst that changes your life so you can be the 'real' you. However, what I do know is that the model I use is based on the science of recovery."

"What do you mean?" Charles asked.

"For years, addiction professionals and much of society have looked at addiction from a pathological perspective. In other words, our field focused on simply stopping the unhealthy behavior such as drug use or alcohol abuse. During the past few decades, we have learned to focus on how to achieve long-term recovery rather than focusing on stopping the behavior alone. Now the goal for recovery is to help you to improve your overall quality of life. It is not enough to just stop the unwanted behavior; the focus of recovery is shifting to help you improve in all areas of your life. Furthermore, over the years, researchers have identified the key behaviors that lead to recovery. By engaging in these activities, your chances of recovery can significantly improve."

Charles gave me a curious look and reluctantly asked, "If what you say is true, why didn't my other counselors talk with me about this?"

My response was, "These ideas are relatively new to the field of drugs and alcohol, and the field of sexual addiction is still hardly even recognized (the term 'sexual addiction' wasn't used until the late 70s), and even today there are many skeptics."

I continued, "The model I use is based on the idea of 'recovery capital.' You need to understand that my focus will be on helping you to build your recovery capital and not just on stopping your sexual behaviors. The focus of recovery using this model is not on seeing your behaviors as pathological. Instead, our focus will be on helping you to build internal and external assets that are required to initiate and sustain long-term recovery (1).

"Let me give you an example. Most individuals, when they attempt recovery, may try one thing, like attend a 12-step group. When they continue acting out, they think to themselves, 'Well, that didn't work,' and they stop going to their meetings because they are ashamed that they aren't making progress."

I turned to Charles and asked, "What would happen if that same individual began doing multiple actions that could lead to recovery at the same time? For example, in addition to attending a 12-step group, what would happen if the same person also began talking with a friend, found a sponsor, attended counseling, and established an accountability team? In addition, imagine that this same person also developed more meaningful relationships and dealt with the root causes that drive his unwanted behaviors. What do you think the odds of this person succeeding would be?"

Charles looked down for a second, reflecting on what I had said, and responded, "I think the chances for success would improve a lot."

I looked Charles in the eye and said, "If you let me help you build your recovery capital, and you do the work, I firmly believe you can succeed like the thousands of individuals who are using this model to recover. Does this interest you?"

He looked at me and said, "Where do we start?"

Understanding Your Recovery Capital

More often than not, individuals begin their recovery journey, much like Charles. They reluctantly seek help for their sexual behaviors. Embarrassed, ashamed, and feeling hopeless, they come to counseling, wondering if they can ever succeed. I often find that they have tried many things. They have told themselves repeatedly that they were done acting out only to find that they can't quit on their own. They have been attempting to stop and failed so many times that they genuinely question whether recovery is possible for them.

So why haven't they succeeded?

The simple answer is that they haven't put everything together at once. It's not like they haven't been trying, but rarely have they tried all of these recovery ideas together. For example, by attending a single 12-step group meeting once a week for a few months, they are only making a minimal effort, which only places a small deposit in the bank of recovery. We wouldn't expect to get rich from a small deposit once a week. However, if we deposited money into our account every day for weeks, months, and years, we would create a significant amount of recovery capital. Our investment would continue to grow over time, and we would eventually see the benefit of making daily investments.

Building recovery capital is what happens when key elements (e.g., attending a group, connecting to others in your community, sleeping well, exercising, coping well with stress, etc.) behind recovery happen at the same time and are added upon for an extended period of time. As the capital begins to grow by making daily deposits, these activities turn to long-term recovery habits. As resources increase, so does hope and a belief that recovery is possible. Based on years of observing individuals who have succeeded in the recovery process, researchers have discovered a simple truth: The more recovery capital you have, the more success you will have in your recovery efforts.

In order to help you understand your current level of recovery capital, there is a short assessment you can take. I will provide a link for you to take it at the end of the chapter. The next part of this chapter will explain each of the ten categories the researchers have identified as key components of recovery. Researchers have split the ten categories into two parts: 1) personal recovery capital, and 2) social and lifestyle recovery capital.

We will review both parts and the five subcategories under each part and then invite you to take the Sexual Addiction Recovery Capital Scale (SARCS), so you can see your current level of recovery capital.

Personal Recovery Capital

Personal recovery capital has five subcategories: 1) recovery experience; 2) psychological; 3) physical; 4) risk-taking; and 5) coping. Let's look more in-depth at what makes up each category.

1. *Recovery Experience*: The items under "recovery experience" focus on your sense of having a purpose in life and your progress in recovery. For exam-

ple, one item asks if you are engaging in activities and events that support recovery. Another item asks if you have a network of people to assist you in recovery. Finally, you are asked about your view of the future and if it makes you feel optimistic. These seemingly simple things are what researchers have discovered as the elements that drive successful recovery.

2. *Global Health (Psychological):* This subcategory focuses on your ability to concentrate and cope with stress, your level of happiness, your appearance, and the hope you have for your future. Your responses to the items in this section will help to identify how well you are dealing with day-to-day stress. Because stress has been linked to increased risk for relapse, this is an important area to understand. As you develop effective ways to cope with stress, you will naturally make progress toward recovery.

3. *Global Health (Physical):* The questions in this subcategory explore how you deal with daily tasks, how your physical health relates to your ability to work, whether you have enough energy to complete tasks, if you can get around, and whether or not you are sleeping well.

    In his book, Willpower, Dr. Roy Baumeister suggests that, when individuals are low in energy, they tend to revert back to old habits. He calls this being "ego depleted." Baumeister suggests that "If you're trying to resist temptation, you may find yourself feeling the forbidden desires more strongly just when your ability to resist them is down. Ego depletion thus creates a double whammy: Your willpower is diminished, and your cravings feel stronger than ever" (2). Improving in this area will increase your ability to sustain long-term recovery.

4. *Risk-Taking:* The items in this subcategory explore your willingness to take responsibility for your actions, your desire to not hurt or damage others, and if you have the privacy you need to succeed. It also looks at your financial stability. You will learn from the items in this category about your desire to take accountability for your actions, your awareness of how your behaviors influence others, and if you are experiencing financial stressors.

5. *Coping and Life Functioning:* Do you eat healthily? Do you look after your health and well-being? Do you meet your obligations and try to avoid letting people down? Are you comfortable interacting with professionals and others who can help in the recovery process? The items in this subcategory explore essential habits that will influence your ability to function in daily tasks.

When you complete the online assessment, you will see a graph like the one below: The five categories listed are referred to as "Personal Recovery Capital." You can see the five categories with a bar chart indicating your personal answers.

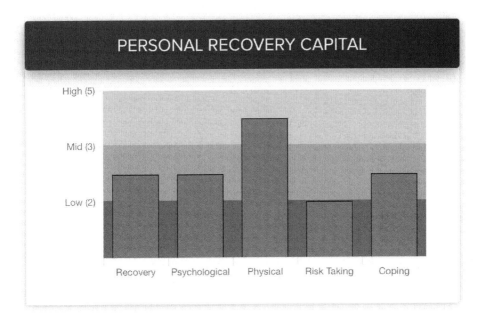

The next part of recovery capital will help you to explore your current level of social interactions and lifestyle choices.

Social and Lifestyle Recovery Capital

The five categories under social and lifestyle recovery capital are: 1) sexual behaviors and sobriety; 2) citizenship and community involvement; 3) social support; 4) meaningful activities; and 5) housing and safety. Here's more about each of these subcategories.

1. *Sexual Behaviors and Sobriety:* The items in this subcategory look directly at your current level of sobriety. For example, are you currently clean from engaging in unwanted sexual behaviors? Do you feel in control of your sexual desires? These are just a couple of important questions that are addressed. Usually, at the beginning of recovery, individuals score lower in this area, but, as they develop a recovery plan (see Chapters Four and Five) and implement their plan, their scores in this section go up.

2. *Citizenship and Community Involvement:* One of the more exciting findings in

the field of addiction recovery is that feeling a part of a community and getting involved is helpful in the recovery process. The researchers who developed the idea of recovery capital found that being a part of a bigger community and being a good citizen helped individuals maintain sobriety. The items in this subcategory will identify your level of involvement in your community.

3. *Social Support:* Social support has consistently been found to be one of the critical ingredients of recovery capital. If you have excellent social support, you will be able to turn to individuals in your time of need. In contrast, if you are feeling isolated or alone, the likelihood of relapse increases. Regarding this, Dr. John Cacioppo wrote, "When we are lonely, we not only react more intensely to the negatives, we also experience less of a soothing from the positives. Even when we succeed in eliciting nurturing support from a friend or a loved one, if we are feeling lonely, we tend to perceive the exchanges as less fulfilling than we had hoped it would be." (3)

4. *Meaningful Activities:* One of the common elements behind lasting change is that individuals working on recovery begin participating in meaningful activities (e.g., sports, educational training, self-improvement, career development). The items in this subcategory help you identify the extent that you are engaging in meaningful activities and events.

   As individuals improve in this area, they often find that they are enjoying life more fully. They realize how much their addictive behaviors have deprived them of enjoying sporting events, developing a new talent, or improving their career opportunities. You will find that the more meaningful activities you engage in, the less prone you will be to return to unhealthy habits that have been robbing you of finding sustained joy and happiness.

5. *Housing and Safety:* One area that can easily be overlooked in the recovery process is your living environment. In an effort to identify potential barriers to recovery, the items in this subsection explore your perception of your living space, if you are proud of your home, and if you feel safe and protected where you live.

   In many instances, your living environment can be a major trigger that can cause a relapse. It is usually within an individual's home that he or she encounters stress in relationships, loneliness away from the world, and burdens of keeping up with household tasks. It is also where many individuals act out. The items in this section will address if your living environment is helpful or not to your recovery. If not, it will be essential for you to identify strategies on how to improve the climate in your home.

This completes a review of the Social and Lifestyle Recovery Capital section. When you take the Recovery Capital Scale, you will see a graph like the one below. The graph is an example of what your report will show once you have completed the assessment. In the graph, you can see that, in all five categories, the recovery capital was very low.

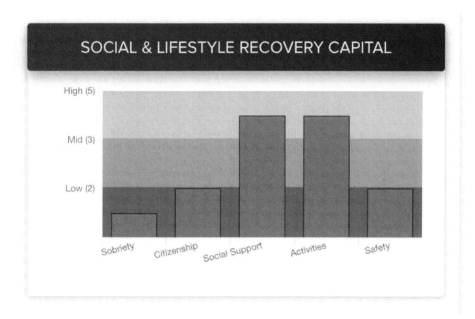

This indicates that this client would need to work on each area of the social and lifestyle recovery capital in order to improve his or her chances of succeeding. Usually, individuals in the beginning steps of the recovery process score low in many of the categories. The average score for individuals coming through our clinics throughout the United States and Canada is a little over 32 out of 50 before they begin treatment (see Research on the SARCS, 2019). As clients start to build their recovery capital, they will be able to see measurable progress.

One important part of Charles's life was his spiritual beliefs. He wanted to incorporate his spiritual life into his healing and recovery program. While none of the ten categories listed above include spiritual recovery capital, I found some exciting literature that describes spiritual recovery capital for individuals who believe in a higher power.

Spiritual Recovery Capital

Because it has been challenging to quantify the extent that spirituality aids in the addiction recovery process, more often than not, spirituality has been left out of recovery literature. However, there is now a growing body of research that includes the power of using spirituality in the recovery process. In fact, "scientific literature strongly supports the notion that spirituality and religiousness can enhance health and quality of life (QOL). In a review of 200+ studies, positive relationships were documented with physical and functional status, reduced psychopathology, greater emotional well-being, and improved coping." (4) Furthermore, it has been argued that "If religious and spiritual involvement can act as a protective factor, it should come as no surprise that it could act as a means of ridding oneself of an addiction." (5)

Based on this research and my clinical work with those who use spirituality in their recovery, I have included spiritual capital as one of the elements to assess your progress in recovery. If you would prefer not to include spirituality in your healing and recovery, feel free to disregard the parts in this book where spirituality is discussed. If spirituality is important to you, I believe you will find the addition of spiritual recovery capital a critical component to add to your long-term recovery plan.

If you would like more ideas on building your spiritual recovery capital, you can find additional resources at https://bit.ly/treating-sex-addiction under the section titled: Spiritual Healing and Recovery.

Summary of Recovery Capital

When individuals achieve high levels of personal, family/social, and community recovery capital, their chances for a successful recovery increases significantly (6,7). Unfortunately, for clients like Charles, they begin on the road to recovery with very little recovery capital. In Charles's case, he had been fighting internal battles (e.g., I'm a terrible person, nobody would want me) and powerful unwanted desires by himself for years. Then, when he did attempt to seek help, those he met with gave good suggestions, but they simply were not enough for him to succeed, i.e., he didn't have enough recovery capital. When he failed, his shame and sense of helplessness increased. What most individuals and even some professional therapists do not realize is that a significant investment of time and energy is required to succeed in building recovery capital skills.

Furthermore, because recovery from sexual addiction usually involves family members who are experiencing a deep sense of betrayal, there is often limited support from loved ones. In Charles's case, he had no idea whether his wife would hang around while he worked on recovery. He felt alone. These thoughts triggered a lot of fear and made his recovery attempts seem daunting.

As Charles expressed his worries, I encouraged him to focus on what he could control at this moment. I wanted him to understand that change is a process and not an event. I needed him to trust the process. I told him that real recovery is a journey that takes more than a week or a month. True healing is a process that creates a new being, someone who forgets about time and instead focuses on living a more full and joyful life. It may take years, but that journey will be worth it. That was my promise to Charles, and it is the same promise I offer you.

As we were about ready to finish our first session, Charles asked me what he should do about his wife, children, and others he had let down. I explained that, because he had kept his behaviors a secret from them for so long, they would not be able to trust him at this point. In fact, they might be skeptical of his efforts. I asked him to focus on what he could control: his recovery efforts in this early stage. In addition, I encouraged him to, instead, focus on seeking help from others who could support him while he rebuilt the trust of his wife and children. The idea of seeking support from others was uncomfortable to him, but, as we reviewed what successful people do in recovery, he understood that it would be critical for his long-term healing. I explained that we would discuss how to rebuild trust with his wife and children, but for now, he would likely need to find recovery support in other areas, like finding a sponsor and establishing an accountability team.

I told Charles that he would need to be patient with his wife, even when she was upset and angry with him. I told him that if he wanted to help his wife, he would need to learn how to listen to her without becoming defensive. I let him know that, in order to rebuild lost trust, he would have to genuinely try to understand her suffering, which he might not be fully able to do right now because of his own shame. I let him know that we would be focusing on how he could reduce his shame.

I felt it was important for Charles to understand that recovery would take patience and that it would be hard work. I let him know that building up his recovery capital would take time and that he would be best off realizing that recovery is more like running a marathon than it is a sprint. I share this with my clients because it is not uncommon for them to want to speed up the process. They often want a short path to recovery. I have found that, when clients have overly optimistic expectations, their hopes are dashed when they experience intense cravings, have a slip, or relapse. These challenging times often lead to feelings of hopelessness and discouragement. For this reason, I emphasize to my clients that how long recovery takes should not be a focus during their recovery. Instead, when clients accept that time doesn't matter as much as practicing and implementing recovery skills, real recovery begins to happen. Going back to the marathon analogy, most people can't run a marathon without significant training. Healing and recovery require a similar type of training as running a marathon.

When clients focus on implementing recovery capital, they naturally change how they think, feel, believe, and behave. As they begin to experience the benefits of implementing the mindset of increasing their recovery capital, they realize that change can be an enjoyable process. Eventually, they discover that their recovery journey is one of the most difficult and yet one of the best things that they have ever done. They realize that, while challenging, the change they experience is a blessing to their life. Perhaps just as important, they see how their change influences every part of their life. They are better at relationships, are more productive at work, feel more confident, and experience more peace. They realize that engaging in the recovery process is a blessing to them, their loved ones, and, if they are parents, to their children.

Assessing Your Recovery Capital

After outlining the idea of recovery capital, I told Charles it would be a good idea to review his baseline level scores so we could see where to start our work together. Before clients like Charles come to my office for the first time, I send them a link to take a variety of assessments. One of the assessments is the Sexual Addiction Recovery Capital Scale (SARCS). In our next appointment, we discussed his results in-depth. As we reviewed them together, it was clear to both of us that there were many areas of recovery capital that he could improve upon.

You can see how he scored in the chart below (higher scores indicate more recovery capital).

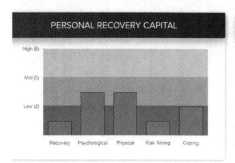
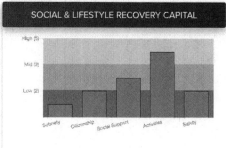

In reviewing his scores, Charles observed the many areas of his life that were being influenced by his sexual behaviors. His sexual desires and actions were affecting his health, opportunities for wealth, self-worth, important relationships, social interactions, and his spirituality. In our review, he realized that he scored in the low or midlevel range for all but one of the categories. As we discussed these results, he said, "I feel overwhelmed and feel like I will never be able to overcome my challenges." I explained to him that results like his were actually prevalent in the early stages of recovery.

He replied, "I feel that I am incapable of doing all of these things."

What I told him is important for you to understand as well. I said, "Let's begin by focusing on just one area of your life. You don't have to change everything all at once. In fact," I continued, "it is imperative at the beginning of recovery work to avoid overloading yourself." This made sense to him.

Finding the right starting point for Charles was important. For example, he wasn't ready to open up to his extended family or friends. He felt like that would be too hard. However, he was willing to start an educational group at my center, meet with me, and talk with his religious leader. We developed a plan where he agreed to get a sponsor and develop a team to whom he would be accountable for his daily progress.

As expected, at the beginning of recovery, he was discouraged by how difficult it was. His wife was often angry and upset. He tried to remember my suggestion that he learn to listen rather than get upset and fight back, but that proved to be difficult for him. He wanted her to see his progress and that he was trying, but she didn't. He reported that his cravings were low, but he felt like he wasn't making much progress. In an effort to deepen his understanding of the change process, I shared the following information with him, which is realistic and hopeful about healing and recovery.

Most professionals now agree that it takes time to rewire the brain and develop new neuropathways. As individuals focus on building their recovery capital, the process is usually slow and requires patience. In fact, there is a common consensus among professional therapists that addictive habits can take three to five years to overcome. Therapists estimate that this is the time required to effectively rewire the brain, which occurs when new habits replace unhealthy older habits (i.e., patterns). Recent research regarding alcoholism and relapse supports this claim. After five years of abstinence, a recovering alcoholic has approximately the same chances of lifetime relapse as a randomly selected member of the general US population (8).

After sharing this information with Charles, I said, "As you go through the recovery process, remember that each time you add to your recovery capital, you are developing new habits and patterns that will help you heal. If you attempt to rush the process, you will be less likely to succeed. However, by patiently learning to think, act, and feel differently, you will build up your resources, and you will gradually experience changes that you never thought possible when you started down the path toward recovery."

If you have struggled to make progress in your recovery, please remember that the answer to why you struggle to make progress most likely is not because you are not trying. Instead, if you are like most people, you simply have not been utilizing all of the necessary resources for recovery. If you have felt that recovery is too hard, or if you have come to believe that you don't have enough willpower, or that there is something wrong with you, I invite you to push the pause button on your self-judgment, instead, let's increase your recovery capital. Let's replace your shame and self-limiting beliefs with the thought that perhaps recovery is possible.

You may be thinking about how alone you feel and how nobody seems to know what you are going through.

Rest assured that I have been through this journey with many clients. I have seen individuals who are on the brink of losing everything, rebound, and metaphorically go from bankruptcy to great riches. One client recently shared his experience in recovery with me.

I began working at Addo in 2017 to overcome a two-decade pornography addiction. I had lied to my wife for ten years about my addiction. When I finally began to disclose my addiction, she took our four children and left. That same week, I started a 7 a.m. men's Foundation group with you. I remember sitting in the first class, and you said, "If I could show you what people with lasting sobriety do to achieve freedoms from addiction, would that interest you?" Yes! This is what I'd been looking for. For some reason, the things you taught me resonated more than anything else that I had tried to overcome or control my addiction. The next 12 weeks were life-altering for me.

I learned things in Foundations, tactical things that made sense in my everyday life: boundaries, emotional attunement, empathy, COAL Approach (see Chapter 10). I practiced these regularly until they became normal parts of my life. They began to change the way I thought about my addiction, but, more importantly, they changed the way I thought about who I was.

I'm writing to say thank you. As of today, I'm 689 days sober. And not just bordering on sobriety, fully living a free life. I'm not afraid of my addiction anymore. I'm not naive to think I'll never relapse again, but I've built skills and routines that prevent me from being in a place where that is likely.

My marriage is stronger than it's ever been; my relationship with my children is better than it's ever been. Thank you for what you've taught me. But, even more so, thank you for what you've helped me find: a self-belief that I am valuable, unstoppable, and full of worth."

It is this type of story that can be yours. Remember that there is always hope, as long as you are trying. There is even more hope if what you are trying is what has worked for thousands of individuals. When you combine the right knowledge with the right behaviors, great things can happen.

Finally, I know that you are used to carrying the burden of your battle on your own. For years, you have put on a brave face and acted like everything is okay. However, inside your mind, you have likely been fighting an intense battle. By trying to show others that everything is okay in public while fighting an internal struggle inside, you have experienced a lot of stress. Eventually, all of that stress catches up to you. However, in starting this book, you are saying, "I want help." I applaud you for reaching out. Regardless of the reason, you are seeking help now, you no longer have to live with sexual addiction. It is time to let go of the shame and hidden behaviors and discover the real you again.

As you get to know me through this book and my online resources, you will discover that I believe in you and your ability to recover. You may feel emotionally and spiritually broke, but you are not. Up to this point, you have likely not had the information and necessary tools to succeed. As you implement the strategies outlined here, you will build your recovery capital and learn how to invest in the bank of recovery.

Get Started: Take the Sexual Addiction Recovery Capital Scale (SARCS)

Are you ready? Let's get started so that you can begin your journey to recovery. I'm going to do the same thing with you that I do with my clients. Let's start by evaluating your current level of recovery capital. By helping you assess where you currently are, we will be able to help you identify what steps you will need to take in your journey toward recovery. As you go through the recovery process, please remember that there isn't just one behavior or thing that needs to change. Instead, you will eventually alter many parts of your life. In recovery, you will be a different person. You will think, act, behave, and believe differently. While I don't know what recovery will look like for you, I do know that you will be more confident, less lonely, less depressed, less anxious, less stressed, and your overall quality of life will significantly improve.

You can take the Sexual Addiction Recovery Capital Scale (SARCS) by visiting this website: https://bit.ly/treating-sex-addiction.

So, how did you score in each of the ten key categories?

I encourage you to review your scores carefully. You can also retake the test in four to six weeks to measure your progress. Now that you have your baseline scores, it is time to help you make sense of your story and how you got into this situation in the first place. Following that, we will turn our attention to helping you create a recovery game plan. This plan will include strategies on how you can improve in each area over time.

Chapter Summary

There is a growing body of evidence that suggests that individuals who build their recovery capital in ten specific areas are more likely to succeed in recovery. As you build your recovery capital in both personal and social/lifestyle areas, your life will be more balanced, and you will experience an improved quality of life.

Support Resources: (found at https://bit.ly/treating-sex-addiction (under Chapter 1)

- How to Interpret Your Recovery Capital Results

Chapter Two

Getting to the Root of the Problem

*From the cradle to the grave, human beings are hardwired to
seek not just social contact but also physical and emotional proximity to special others who are deemed irreplaceable.*
(Susan Johnson)

During my 25-year career, I have observed thousands of individuals struggle
with addiction, anxiety, divorce, depression, grief, loss, abuse, all kinds of trauma,
and countless other painful experiences. If there is a common root to the suffering
behind these issues, it is this: Those who suffer the most do so alone; they do not
have others in whom they can trust to share the most difficult parts of their lives.

Victor L. Brown once wrote, "The lives of most people are histories of their
search for intimacy, of their attempts to be socially, physically, and emotionally
close to others" (1). This desire begins in the mother's womb, continues throughout
our most formative years, and goes on into our adult years. In other words, our
desire to bond with others in meaningful ways is a significant part of being human.

However, our first bonds established in early childhood can significantly influence the way we attempt to form relationships in preadolescent, adolescent, and
adult years. When our relationship with our primary caregiver is nurturing, we feel
safe and connected. We feel a sense of being able to depend on a loved one, which
creates a secure base (2). Conversely, when we experience relationship distress, and
our primary or basic needs are not met, we form insecure attachment bonds that
encode patterns of distrust and insecurity into our relationships. Dr. Susan Johnson
described it this way: "If others have been perceived as inaccessible or unrespon-
sive, or even threatening, when needed, then secondary models and strategies are
adopted" (3).

31

A few years ago, I was discussing ideas for effective clinical work with Dan Oakes, a colleague, when he shared with me a model that describes the critical importance of establishing healthy relationships. Based on that conversation and the works of Drs. Stephen Porges and Susan Johnson, the model below, explains why having our most basic needs met is so important. It also addresses how our overall health and well-being may be negatively influenced when these needs are not met.

I know you may be thinking, "What does all of this have to do with my recovery?" I invite you to let me explain the model and encourage you to give it serious thought. You likely didn't just develop addictive tendencies from nowhere. There is always a story behind unwanted behaviors. Over my years as a therapist, this model has helped many of my clients understand their own story. It has also helped them identify how addiction entered into their lives. As we go through this model, I hope you will see the relevance of all of our life experiences and how certain life events, especially those during our most formative years, can significantly alter the rest of our lives.

Our Most Basic Needs

When we are young, we are dependent upon our primary caregivers, as we have basic needs that we cannot meet on our own and have limited ways to communicate our needs. Regarding this early phase of development, Dr. Stephen Porges wrote: "Social engagement depends, rather, on how well we can regulate the muscles of our faces and heads via pathways linking the cortex with the brainstem (i.e., corticobulbar pathways). These are the muscles that give expression to our faces, allow us to gesture with our heads, put intonation into our voices, direct our gaze, and permit us to distinguish human voices from background sounds (4)." Noting simple facial gestures and detecting a tone of voice are critical elements for communication in our early human development.

Dr. Porges continues to explain the importance of this by writing: "This process of identifying familiar and trustworthy people and evaluating the intentions of others based on 'biological movements' of face and limbs seem to be located in the temporal lobe of the cortex. If neuroception identifies a person as safe, then a neural circuit actively inhibits areas of the brain that organize the defensive strategies of fight, flight, and freeze. Slight changes in the biological movements that we see can shift a neuroception from 'safe' to 'dangerous.' When this shift occurs, the neural systems associated with prosocial behavior are disrupted, and the neural systems associated with defensive strategies are triggered" (5).

This suggests that, even in our infancy, we determine if our environment is safe; if it is safe, then we social bond and connect to our caregivers and others. Some of the primary ways that we determine whether we are safe include

- making eye contact;

- vocalizing with an appealing inflection and rhythm;

- displaying contingent facial expressions; and

- modulating the middle-ear muscles to distinguish the human voice from background sounds more efficiently. (6)

It is important to understand what Dr. Porges is suggesting about our safety, i.e., we socially bond with others when these basic needs are being met. However, he found that even slight changes in a tone of voice or a negative facial expression can put us on the defense; as such, we naturally go into protective mode. (7) Imagine what happens when a crying child is told to shut up or witnesses one parent yelling at the other parent. This kind of environment can instantly put a child into safety mode where it protects the self and does not desire social bonding. If this happens frequently, the infant will struggle to connect with others.

In contrast, when a tender parent takes a child into his/her arms, sings a lullaby, or provides comfort when the child is hurting, the child feels nurtured and relaxes due to the safe environment. Naturally, this child will desire connection and bonding in relationships. Furthermore, as this child develops and grows, s/he will likely be more comfortable expanding connections with others.

The stark difference between these two cases illustrates how basic needs can significantly alter how we see "self" in relationship to others. The environment in which we grow up can significantly influence our physical development and mental well-being (8).

The Power of a Nurturing Environment

What happens next is what makes this model so important to understand. When we have our basic needs met, we naturally develop confidence in others because we believe that they are safe and reliable. We explore and become more creative because we are allowed to extend our safe zone. We have fun, become more playful with others, and develop a healthy curiosity for life and what is happening around us. This leads to social confidence and an increased sense of worth.

When these needs are not met, we develop an insecure model of attachment in relationships. The typical outcomes include avoiding closeness with others, dismissing others' attempts to be close, and we become more prone to be sensitive to negative messages from others. (9) We also become more prone to develop a relationship style that is consistent with protection, caution, and fear. As humans, when our basic needs are not being met, we naturally do not feel safe.

The model below illustrates the ideas described above. I have also included two other critical basic needs that Dan Oakes shared with me: healthy touch and nourishment.

Attachment Model

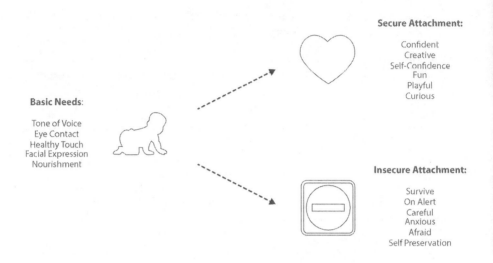

This attachment model helps explain why some individuals grow up confident in their relationships, while others are hesitant and reluctant to bond. It also brings up some critical questions that need to be addressed:

- First, what are the social and relational outcomes of individuals who grow up in a secure environment in contrast with those who grow up in an insecure environment?

- Second, how do people cope when their basic needs for connection are not being met?

- Third, can we learn to form healthy bonds later in life if we didn't have these needs met when we were in our most formative years?

When I present this model to my clients who are dealing with addictions, relationship problems, and other mental health challenges, they often share with me some of the painful experiences they had while growing up. Many come to realize that they didn't just stumble into their sexually acting-out behaviors or their relationship problems. Instead, they discover that some of their current challenges stem from early childhood experiences; in some cases, they see unhealthy patterns that are generations old.

It is not uncommon for individuals to identify multiple generations of relationship problems, addictions, and other issues. They see the generational transmission of unhealthy coping mechanisms due to the lack of connection and healthy relationships. When our most basic needs for connection are missing, we don't cope well. I help my clients explore their past—not to blame or accuse their parents— but instead to understand their story.

Often, as we discuss the past, we transition through time looking at patterns of addiction, trauma, abuse, neglect, and mental health challenges. We also identify patterns of resilience and strength that clients found in their parents and grandparents. This awareness is often helpful to my clients, as it puts into perspective the challenges and strengths that their family has had for generations.

When my clients gain a better understanding of their history, it often takes away some of the shame they have felt. Many came to me thinking that there was something wrong with them. When they see the difficult challenges that stem from generations of unhealthy attachment and connection, their difficulties begin to make more sense to them. Their perception of their sexually acting-out behaviors and other unhealthy habits begin to change in good ways. It is usually at this point that I tell them that many in their family who have come and gone before them didn't figure out how to deal with these unhealthy patterns. However, by coming and seeking help now, this is a chance to break the cycle. I let my clients know that they can do something that hasn't been done in generations of time in their family: They can become a chain breaker. If your family has such patterns, I believe you, too, can create the change that is necessary to shift from addiction into intimacy. In doing so, you will replace addiction with more meaningful relationships and lasting bonds.

Now let's look at a case study to illustrate the power of this attachment model.

The Importance of Being Soothed

Johnny learned at a young age that he would have to fend for himself. His parents were good people. They worked hard and took care of him the best they could, given their busy schedules. When I asked him about which parent he was closest to, he said, "I'm not really close to my parents. I love them and everything, but we just aren't that close." When I asked him about that, he said, "We just aren't that type of family." I asked, "So who comforted you as a boy when things were difficult at school, or something bad happened to you?"

35

He responded, "I was alone most of the time. They really did love me, but they were busy providing for our family." I asked, "What was that like for the younger you?" Johnny said, "I learned to take care of everything by myself. I grew up quickly because I had to. It was a badge of honor in my family."

"So, if you didn't have someone to comfort you when things were hard, what did you do?" His reply to this question helped both of us to understand his current sexual behaviors better. He said, "I discovered pornography when I was 12 or 13 years old. I would view it almost every day after school. I did that for years. Then, when I got into high school, I wanted to do what I was seeing done in the videos I was watching, and I started pushing girls for sexual favors. The first time I did that, the girl told her friends what I asked her to do. I was so embarrassed that I didn't talk to girls for a long time. I turned back to pornography, but not long after that happened, I discovered I could meet people from some of those online sites. I began looking for random hookups. I have been doing that for years now."

From this discussion, Johnny realized that he had learned to self-soothe when he was alone and when he felt rejected. Each time these two feelings would come to the surface, he would seek out a sexual experience to comfort him. Unfortunately, even when he got into a committed relationship, when things were difficult, he would revert back to the same behaviors. This caused a lot of conflict in his relationships. He sought my help because his wife had given him an ultimatum: get help, or their marriage was over. He put his relationship at risk because of his inability to stop acting out.

When I introduced Johnny to the attachment model for a healthy connection, he started understanding why he had been acting out. He realized that he would often act out when he was feeling embarrassed, rejected, ashamed, or alone. He especially wanted to escape when his wife was upset at him.

One question he had related to his relationship about how to deal with his wife. He asked, "What do I do when my wife is angry and upset? I don't know how to respond when she is yelling and telling me how bad I am." He continued, "She yells at me all the time, accuses me of never loving her, and when she is really upset, she threatens to leave me and take the kids with her."

My response to Johnny and many others is this. Right now, your wife doesn't know how to see you. She sees how you have hurt her, and it makes her angry. Underneath her anger is deep hurt and insecurity. Usually, when people are angry, it is because they feel that they have to fight to protect themselves. They don't want to be hurt again.

I then told Johnny that I wasn't sure if his relationship would work out, but I did reassure him that there were things he could do to increase his odds of repairing his relationship (see the video on rebuilding trust—(https://bit.ly/treating-sex-addiction). I told him that if he wanted to succeed, I would provide him with specific ideas that he could try in an effort to give his relationship a fighting chance. I also cautioned him that right now, he would need to focus on his own healing because he wasn't prepared to truly understand his wife's anger.

He was surprised by my response, which I explained by asking him a question: "How do you typically respond when your wife gets angry?"

His response was, "I don't know what to say. Sometimes I say, 'I'm sorry.'"

I then asked, "How does she respond to that?"

He said, "She doesn't believe me."

And when she doesn't believe you, how do you respond?

He said, "I get upset and ask if she is ever going to forgive me, or I leave the room because I don't think I can do anything to regain her trust."

I then said to Johnny, "That is what I mean by you don't know how to respond." You want to, but you don't yet know what to say or how to say it. I told Johnny that I would explain how to be more effective in his communication with his wife, but first, he needed to develop other skills, which I discuss in the chapter on emotional regulation. (If you can't wait to learn how to respond more effectively to your spouse, skip ahead to Chapter 14, Loving Your Way Through Addiction Recovery. I am also including a video I recorded titled, "Helping Your Betrayed Spouse Heal.")

I told Johnny that I would help him to respond more effectively when his wife was upset. I also said to him that as he learned how to self-soothe in healthy ways, he would develop the skills necessary to respond more effectively to his wife. I explained that, rather than acting out sexually when he was feeling the need to escape, if he could develop positive self-soothing strategies, he would be more likely to succeed in response to his wife. The initial focus of his healing, I explained, was to help him understand his (attachment) story and then develop effective self-soothing strategies.

Finally, I explained to Johnny that there are two primary ways to be soothed. The first is self-soothing, which can be done in many ways. Here's a list of ideas I have seen others use:

- Listening to music that calms the mind
- Going for a walk
- Praying or meditation

- Exercise
- Reading a good book

The second method we can use to soothe our minds is through others. This can be especially difficult if we haven't been able to trust or rely on others throughout our lives. However, a valuable recovery skill is learning to allow others into our lives to help soothe us during difficult times. This is called "co-regulation." In essence, co-regulation is when we accept help from others so that they can help us deal with difficult emotions.

Examples of effective co-soothing strategies include

- Talking with a sponsor
- Reaching out to a friend
- Confiding in a religious leader
- Going to lunch with a coworker
- Going on a run or on a bike ride with a friend or family member

The idea of having others help us regulate difficult emotions during challenging times is powerful. This is because, when we are in active addiction, our brains can easily be hijacked, and we need extra support to avoid relapsing. After reviewing these ideas with Johnny, he asked me, "Do I have to talk about this with others? I can't imagine doing that. My whole life, I have taken care of my own needs." My response was simple: "Successful people in recovery report that having support is one of the most important things they did to sustain their recovery efforts." If you want to succeed, model your recovery after those who have already been down this road.

I can't emphasize enough the importance of establishing meaningful support in the recovery process. Recovery is more than achieving sobriety; it is learning to develop meaningful relationships. It has been my experience that healing and recovery are directly tied to learning how to create connections and interactions with others in ways that meet our basic human needs. I, therefore, believe that recovery requires friendship, fellowship, and loving-kindness.

Because each of us has to learn soothing strategies, I have created a short list of questions to help us evaluate our current soothing strategies. I give this assignment to my clients; I even use it myself periodically to assess my own life (I invite you to stop and do this assignment now):

Assignment

1. What are my positive/healthy, soothing strategies?

2.   What are my negative/unhealthy soothing strategies?

3.   Do I have people I can turn to to help me deal with difficult emotions and experiences? If yes, who? If not, try to think of at least one person from your past that brought you comfort during a difficult time. How did they comfort you? If you cannot think of anyone who has comforted you, I am so sorry. As you read through the chapters in this book, I hope you will find new strategies to build a support team around you.

Some of the healthy coping strategies I have seen include:

- I turned to my friends to fill that void
- I played sports
- I got involved in drama and the arts
- I worked as hard as I could so I could get out of my parents' home
- I got a job

Some of the unhealthy coping strategies I have heard over the years include:

- I used to get into a lot of fights
- I started drinking at an early age
- I turned to pornography
- I had meaningless sexual encounters
- I got lost in video games

When I ask clients about how they deal with stressful situations, many report that they have used both good and bad strategies. The critical point here is that we all have coping strategies for when we feel disconnected from others and society and for when things go wrong in our relationships. The question is: When our most basic needs are not being met, how will we respond? If we have learned to cope using unhealthy responses, the challenge is to identify healthy behaviors and establish meaningful relationships that can help soothe us.

The Barriers to Establishing Meaningful Attachment Bonds and Connections

Some stories and life events may seem ordinary; when we look at the details; however, they can leave a deep imprint on our lives. Such was the case of Brad. His parents divorced when he was around the age of six or seven. He ended up living with his dad because his mom was in no condition to take care of him due to her drug addiction. Not long after his parents divorced, his dad remarried. His new stepmom was nice initially, but he said that he always felt awkward around her. When I asked what she was like, Brad said, "To this day, I still don't understand why she did this, but she would often walk around the house in the nude." Brad added, "It was common for me to see my dad and stepmom having sex in the living room. On one occasion, I just sat and watched them. They didn't seem to care or even acknowledge that I was there." There were no boundaries in Brad's home.

Not long into their relationship, Brad started observing more and more intense fighting. One night, it escalated to the point where Brad was scared his dad was going to hurt his stepmom. Over time, his dad became so caught up in his work that he didn't come home until late at night. Brad thought his dad was super busy, but his stepmom told him that he was probably having an affair and that he better not turn out like his dad.

When Brad's dad was home, it seemed like the fighting was constant. By this time, they had had two children together who took up a lot of time as well. As Brad got older, he began having more conflict with his dad, and his stepmom grew distant and became preoccupied with the addition of his new siblings. His new brothers seemed to get all of the attention. Brad felt alone.

While Brad's story might not seem too out of the norm for today's culture, there are common elements that he experienced in his childhood that could create significant challenges for him in his adult years. Researchers have revealed that adverse childhood experiences such as a parent's divorce, substance misuse in the home, witnessing or experiencing violence at home, or being abused can all influence our lives as adults. These findings are startling and essential for us to understand.

Dr. Vincent Felitti and Robert Anda, in their landmark study on the influence of adverse childhood experiences, discovered that the more adversity one faces in childhood, the more likely one will face both physical and mental health problems as an adult)(10). He or she is also likely to have significant relationship problems (11, 12, 13).

In their initial research, Fellitti and Anda tried to determine each patient's level of exposure by asking if he or she experienced any of the ten categories listed below before the age of 18.

1.   Emotional abuse (recurrent)

2.   Physical abuse (recurrent)

3.   Sexual abuse (contact)

4.   Physical neglect

5.   Emotional neglect

6. Substance abuse in the household (e.g., living with an alcoholic or a person with a substance-abuse problem)

7. Mental illness in the household (e.g., living with someone who suffered from depression or mental illness or who had attempted suicide)

8. Mother treated violently

9. Divorce or parental separation

10. Criminal behavior in the household (e.g., a household member going to prison)

Each category of abuse, neglect, or dysfunction experienced counted as one point. Because there were ten categories, the highest possible ACE score was 10. Researchers discovered that higher scores play a significant role in the following areas:

- Addiction (alcohol, drug, smoking, obesity)

- Depression, anxiety, suicide, and PTSD

- Unintended pregnancy, HIV, STDs

- Cancer, diabetes

- Education, occupation, and income

[See the following resource (14) for research on each of these bullet points.]

Let's explore this information and compare it with Brad's story. Based on the information we have about Brad, we know that he experienced the following ACEs:

1. His biological mother was unavailable as a mother due to drug addiction

2. He felt unloved in his home growing up (emotional neglect)

3. He witnessed anger and violence between his dad and stepmom

4. His stepmom struggled with high levels of anxiety

5. His stepmom was treated violently by his dad

6. His parents divorced

Brad's ACE scores would have been six. Remember above I said it might seem like Brad had some hard things happen to him, but I questioned if these things were out of the ordinary. The answer is, absolutely, yes. Based on research, he is at high risk for both physical and mental health challenges. Research suggests that individuals who score this high are in danger of dying earlier than the general population, sometimes by as much as 20 years (15). Yes, that statistic is correct. When individuals experience a significant trauma in their childhood, it influences every aspect of their lives, and it puts them at higher risk for early death.

I hope, at this point, you may be thinking about your adverse childhood experiences (ACEs). I would encourage you to take the Adverse Childhood Experience Test to help you better understand yourself (See Resources below). Due to my observations as a therapist and reading about the significant impact that these experiences have on each of us, I included the ACE for all of our clients at our Addo Recovery agencies.

In the past year, more than 450 individuals seeking help for their sexual behaviors have completed the ACEs at our centers. In the graph below, you can see how our clients from throughout the United States and Canada compare with the general population.

ACE Comparison

Number of Adverse Childhood Experiences (ACE Score)	General Population (n = 17,337)	Clients Seeking Help for their Unwanted Sexual Behaviors (n = 468)
0	36.1%	34.8%
1	26.0%	23.7%
2	15.9%	13.5%
3	9.5%	9.0%
4 or more	12.5%	19.0%

As can be seen, the differences in the percentages are between 1 and 2 percentage points until we get to the four or more categories. The individuals seeking professional help for their unwanted sexual behaviors are more likely to score a four or higher on the ACEs. In essence, if we lined up 100 people from the general population, about 12.5% would score a four or higher on the ACEs. In contrast, if we identify 100 of our clients, 19% of individuals seeking counseling support for their unwanted sexual behaviors would score a four or higher.

Due to the significant physical, mental, and relationship health challenges associated with ACE scores, it is vital for all of us to understand and evaluate our scores. If your score is high, there are things that can be done to help offset the potential effects of adverse childhood experiences. I will talk about these strategies in later chapters. In particular, you will want to review Chapter Nine, Compassion: The secret of successful recovery, and Chapter Ten, Utilizing the Power of Emotional Regulation.

Making Sense of Your ACE Scores

Perhaps you are wondering what your childhood experiences have to do with your current sexual behaviors. That's a fair question. It is possible that the relationship between your ACE score and your current sexual behaviors have little in common. In fact, in my preliminary research, where I evaluated ACE scores and sexual compulsivity, I found that there is only a small correlation between ACE scores and current sexual activities (16).

However, there is a relationship between some of the individual ACE responses and current sexual behaviors. For example, individuals who grew up in a home where they felt like no one in their family loved them or thought they were important or special reported higher scores on the sexual addiction screening tool. Also, individuals who grew up with a parent who experienced depression or another mental illness reported increased levels of sexually acting-out behaviors. In addition, individuals who experienced sexual abuse as a child reported slightly higher levels of sex compulsivity.

(Note: These are early findings and have not been published. To see all of the results from this preliminary study, visit (https://bit.ly/treating-sex-addiction) Section: Research.

Regardless of your personal score on the ACEs, it has been my experience that clients who make the most progress in their recovery from sexual addiction are willing to step back and evaluate possible issues that stem from their childhoods. Based on the findings of researchers, it is important that individuals with higher ACE scores develop strategies to help them deal with the distress of their childhood. By learning how to process their difficult experiences and develop healthy coping strategies, they will become more confident in their ability to combat the negative impact of such experiences (17).

I spend a great deal of time educating individuals about ACE scores because all individuals should understand the importance of protecting our children and how their lives have been influenced by adverse childhood experiences. The research findings are too significant to simply ignore.

It is also essential to help individuals who have higher ACE scores to understand the strategies that can be used to help neutralize the powerful negative experiences they had in the early years of their lives. Unfortunately, far too many individuals do not realize how seemingly ordinary experiences (i.e., parents' divorce, living with someone who is an alcoholic) can trigger unhealthy coping mechanisms such as sexual addiction.

I have observed that, when some of my clients were going through some of the most difficult adverse childhood experiences, they simultaneously discovered their sexuality. Sometimes it started with just rubbing themselves. In other cases, they were playing doctor with a neighbor. Still, others were sexually abused by someone older than them. And at other times, they discovered pornography and used it to comfort themselves during difficult times. Regardless of how their sexual behaviors started, many found comfort in their own way by turning to sexual behaviors. The powerful combination of trauma and sexual discovery often created negative outcomes in their adult years.

Finally, if we are going to help you get to the root of what drives your addictive behaviors, we have to explore all of the potential possibilities of what has been driving you to act out the way you do. My desire is to help you gain a deeper understanding of your whole story.

If, as you are reading about the influence of ACEs on people's lives, you realize that your score is high or that the adverse childhood experience you went through is having a negative impact on you today, please know that answers are available. Throughout this book, I will provide suggestions to help you respond to adverse childhood experiences (see video: Responding to Your ACE Score under Chapter Two at https://bit.ly/treating-sex-addiction).

If you experienced even one or two ACEs, be cautious about saying that it was just a couple of experiences and that it isn't that bad. Sometimes in life, one event can change our lives for years. Further, having an ACE score of two or more doubles someone's likelihood of developing an autoimmune disease (18).

If you are fortunate, and you didn't experience any ACE scores, that is a good thing. It means there are fewer things you will need to address in your healing and recovery.

Chapter Summary

By getting to the root of your problem, your chances of recovery go up. In this chapter, the focus has been on helping you to understand how your early relationships may have influenced you. When we do not have healthy connections with the key people in our lives, we are more likely to turn to unhealthy coping mechanisms. Throughout our lives, we seek human intimacy; when it is not available; however, we try to comfort ourselves in ways that can prevent us from achieving true intimacy.

When individuals experience adverse childhood experiences, they become more prone to develop physical and mental health challenges as they get older. These adversities can increase the likelihood of turning to sexual activities to cope. My hope is that this chapter has raised your awareness of the potential challenges early experiences may have had upon you.

Author's Note: Over my years in counseling, I have had many people tell me that they had a wonderful childhood. They report that their parents weren't perfect but still good. They scored a zero on the ACEs and were typically confused about how they got so caught up in their specific sexual behavior. My answer to this question is this: We can have wonderful parents, but that doesn't mean we know how to utilize their support while growing up. Here's a short story that illustrates this really well.

Eric grew up in a good home. His parents were loving and caring. He felt their love, and they supported him in his sporting activities and other events. However, at a young age around age 10, he discovered that he could access pornography on the Kindle that he played his games on. Over the next few months, his curiosity led him to seek pornography out more often. By the time he was going through puberty, he was staying up later and later at night while his parents were asleep. They didn't realize he had a problem until he was 16 years old when he finally had the courage to tell them. By that time, he had lived with his secret for six years and had developed a daily pattern of viewing pornography. I personally believe living with that kind of secret for so long is traumatizing all by itself. It separated him from feeling close to his family, although they were available to him. One definition of trauma is that it creates a separation from self, others, and society. Clearly, his sexual secret created problems for him, even though he had loving and caring parents.

In Chapter Three, the focus will be on exploring your personal story in-depth. You will learn how your first sexual experiences may still be guiding your actions today.

Chapter Three

Understanding Your Story

We all have a life story. We are the only ones who have lived through our unique experiences. The challenge we face is to stop, look into the mirror, and explore the life of the person who is looking back at us?
(Dr. Kevin Skinner)

What are the circumstances that made you pick up this book and begin reading it? Perhaps another way of saying that is, "How did you get here today?" When I run groups at my center, I usually begin by asking participants, "What is it that brought you to the group, at this moment in time?" Often the question leads to comments like, "I want to stop my sexual behaviors" or "I want to learn new skills so I can overcome this problem." While these are great reasons, I encourage my groups to dig deeper. Together, we spend much of the first session exploring their history. I often say, "Let's go back in time to your first exposure to pornography or your first sexual experience." That experience, I tell them, is likely what started you down the path that got you here today. We continue by discussing subsequent sexual experiences that reinforced that first experience.

In this chapter, we will explore four ideas that can help you understand your own story and make changes that can last a lifetime. First, we start this chapter by seeking to understand how your first sexual experience may have influenced your life. Second, we will identify how to understand your story more in-depth. We will explore how other things like ADHD or depression, may be contributing to your sexual behaviors. Third, we will identify the role that your family's history may have in your current sexual practices. Fourth, we will look beyond the sexual behaviors you have been engaging in and invite you to look at the thought patterns that may be contributing to your sexual behaviors.

Your First Sexual Experiences

Throughout my career, I have observed that an individual's first sexual experience can determine a lot about the challenges he or she will face while growing older. We know, for example, that early exposure to drugs and alcohol can make individuals more prone to be drug or alcohol dependent as they get older (1). While we do not have a lot of research on the influence of early sexual experiences on adult sexual activity, it would be fair to say that there is a strong relationship.

One of the common patterns that I have observed is that, when individuals are prematurely exposed to sexual behaviors, they have to make sense of their experience. For example, how can a six-year-old understand someone older touching them sexually? Or how can an eight-year-old make sense of hard-core pornography? The innocent mind typically cannot understand why these experiences bring up intense emotions (e.g., arousal, curiosity, fear, shame).

In some cases, because of the intensity of emotions and overall curiosity, individuals will often return to what they experienced to try it again. In my research with thousands of individuals who completed my online survey, I found that a majority of them returned to pornography a few weeks after their first exposure (2).

Often our first sexual experiences leave a deep imprint upon our minds. It is easy to understand why. Think about the first time you rode a bike, drove a car, or kissed someone. Usually, the more emotionally intense an activity or experience, the more our mind wants to give it attention. Our minds are used to ordinary things, but when experiences are novel, our brain says, "What is happening here? I should pay close attention to this." When something is so powerful, as is our sexuality, we pay close attention.

Here's a story that illustrates the power and complexity of a first sexual experience.

If you were sitting in one of the groups I run for individuals seeking help for their unwanted sexual behaviors, you would see that I often ask for a volunteer to share his/her story. Together, we would walk through some of the key life events that influenced this person and ultimately brought him/her to our group. I hope that by helping people understand their own story, they will begin to have more self-compassion and also a better idea of the challenges they will face as they start their healing and recovery process. As I ask the questions and the clients respond, together, we discover the depth of their stories. On one such occasion, I found myself surprised by the candor and pain of a man in his late twenties.

"A few simple clicks changed my life," Brandon said, as we discussed how pornography had changed him. When he was 11 years old, he overheard some boys at school talking about how they had typed in a specific word into the Google search engine and found a pornographic website. Curious, he went home and typed in the same word he had heard the boys talking about at school. Initially, he was surprised at the images he found. His heart was racing, and he was feeling emotions that he had never felt before. He viewed it for a while and then shut it off. He felt bad about what he had seen and yet was also feeling something physical going on inside of himself that he liked. He didn't know what was happening to him. He was confused by this experience. He didn't know what to do or to whom to turn.

In our discussion, he told the group and me that his mom was quite protective of him because his older brother had been involved in drugs at a young age. She wanted him to avoid drugs at all costs. She also told him not to be like his brother. He wanted her acceptance, so he tried his best to stay out of trouble. Somehow, he knew inside that his mom would not approve of him viewing pornography.

His relationship with his dad was strained. Not only was his dad gone a lot, but when he was home, he didn't have time for him. When they did talk, it was usually about something he was doing wrong. He wasn't getting good enough grades, forgetting to mow the lawn, or leaving his room a mess. His dad offered no support.

Brandon also reported that his parents would often fight. He would hear their arguments after bedtime. Usually, it was about how much his dad was gone. On one occasion, Brandon overheard his mom accuse his dad of cheating on her. The fighting that night was especially bad. In the end, he was sure that his dad was being unfaithful to his mom.

He felt like he couldn't turn to his parents when things were difficult for him. So, after being exposed to pornography, there was no way he wanted to talk with them about it. He grew more curious about the images he had seen, so he started going back to that same website over the next few months.

One day, his mom walked in on him, watching pornography. She exploded. She yelled at him and told him he had better shut that stuff off and never do it again. Brandon clearly didn't understand why she was so upset, until she said, "You are going to turn out just like your dad, aren't you? Are you going to cheat on your wife, too?" Confused by his mom's intensity and anger, he shut down. He apologized and told his mom that he would never do that again. It was at this point that he didn't know what to do or say. He was embarrassed, confused, and kind of angry that his mom accused him of being like his dad. He promised himself that he would never open up to his mom again.

In a later discussion with Brandon, he identified that key event as a significant turning point in his life. He pulled away from his mom and stopped seeing her as someone he could trust. As a result, their relationship became distant, and he interacted with her only when he had to.

This experience with his mom created a fracture in their relationship. I believe that the more fractures we have in our primary relationships, the fewer connections and trust we will have in people in general. After all, if we can't trust those closest to us, to whom can we trust? When individuals have one or more unresolved relationship fractures, trust in others is often low, and fears of being hurt are high. The consequence of unresolved relationship fractures is that human intimacy and meaningful connections become challenging to find.

When Brandon described his first experience with pornography while growing up, I found myself thinking about the many cases I have heard over the years. While each individual had his or her own unique story, the stories also have similarities. Usually, the first sexual experience was followed by confusion and curiosity. That was then followed by a return to pornography a few days or weeks later. If my client had available parents, they may or may not have told them. If they did tell them, usually their parents didn't know how to help. If they didn't have a close relationship with their parents, discussing their experience of viewing pornography or any other sexual activity certainly wasn't an option. The more I thought about my clients' first sexual experiences; I found myself thinking that they all needed to understand their own story in a deep and personal way.

I began thinking about the types of questions that I could ask to get them to explore their past and how their sexual behaviors evolved over the years. The more my clients shared their first sexual experiences, the more I realized how critical their self-awareness would be. Their understanding of their story was going to be an essential part of their healing and recovery process. Here's a list of questions that I have found to be helpful for my clients and me, as we discuss and explore their stories.

1. At what age did you have your first sexual experience?

2. How long after your first experience did you have your second experience?

3. Did your parents find out? If so, how did they respond? If no, what prevented you from telling them? How would they have reacted had they found out?

4. Did you talk with anybody about your sexual activities? If so, how did they respond? Was their response helpful or not?

5. If you could go back in time, what advice would you give yourself regarding your sexual behaviors?

There Is Always a Story

When individuals seek professional counseling, they share with their therapist the reason/s they are seeking help. Usually, when they describe their problem, their counselor hears about the primary issue that is most concerning to the client. For example, a client may say that he/she wants to stop engaging in a specific sexual behavior. In instances like this, I have found that, as we continue talking about what the client is going through, we often find that his/her presenting issue is the tip of the iceberg and that other problems may be contributing or driving the sexually acting-out behaviors. While the client's sexual behavior/s are essential to address, there are also underlying issues that have to be resolved for sustained recovery.

In the last chapter, we discussed two possible reasons some individuals sexually act out: 1) attachment/connection needs not being met; 2) adverse childhood experiences. While these are two of the most common drivers I have observed, there are additional reasons that sexual addiction can develop.

For example, some individuals experience high levels of anxiety; in an effort to fend off their anxiety, they sexually acting out to avoid their own emotions. Other individuals may have ADHD, and their sexual behaviors are just one of the many things they do to get their high. Still, others feel depressed and turn to their sexual practices because they don't want to feel down. They get a quick high from acting out but return to their depressive feelings afterward.

The point here is that, when individuals seek help for their unwanted sexual behaviors, there are additional factors that may be driving their actions. This is why, with each client, I strive to understand his/her story. Sometimes, it is unresolved issues from their past; sometimes, it is to cope with unwanted emotions (e.g., depression, anxiety), and still at other times it is to get the next rush (e.g., ADHD).

What's your story? Is there an "unmet need" or something else that is driving you to act out sexually? My experience has taught me that there is almost always something else driving people toward addictive behaviors.

Some of the things under the tip of the iceberg that you may want to consider as factors that add to you acting out could be

Mental Health

- Abuse (e.g., physical, emotional, sexual)
- Other addictions (e.g., drugs, alcohol); getting a high from multiple activities
- ADHD

- Anxiety
- Depression

Family Relationships

- Abandonment
- Arguing and fighting
- Divorce
- Loneliness
- Neglect

The challenge is to identify your personal story. How did you get to the point that you did sexually? Are there key drivers like those mentioned above that have contributed to you acting out?

Suggested Assignment

Take a few minutes and review the bullet points above. Then, write about the ones that you experienced and how they may have triggered you to act out sexually.

Example:

Abuse: I was emotionally abused. As a result, I felt like I wasn't enough. This, in turn, triggered me to seek approval from others. I think this is why I try to get others to approach me for sex. It is like a game. If I can get them to want me, somehow, that will mean I am enough.

Abandonment: I often felt inadequate because my dad left our family. He was never really around, and I always wanted his approval. When men started giving me their attention, I finally felt like I was enough. It didn't matter if they wanted sex as long as I felt like they wanted some part of me.

Authors note: When clients do this assignment, it is not uncommon for them to come to a belief about themselves. In the first example, this person felt like he was not enough. In the second example, this person felt both inadequate and that she was not worthy of attention from others. It has been my experience that addressing these negative self-beliefs is a critical part of my clients' healing journeys. As long as my clients believe that they are not enough, they will continue to act like they are not enough.

Looking at Your Family Tree

When my clients start looking at their family stories, one common theme is

51

their family. As we explore Dad, Mom, Grandma, and Grandpa's lives, we often see a story of addictive tendencies, relationship failures, avoiding problems, acting as if everything is going just fine, depression, anxiety, and many other challenges.

If you explore your family tree, you will likely discover parts of yourself that you have never considered before. Sometimes, family patterns are obvious. For example, Dad was an alcoholic, Grandpa was an alcoholic, and Great Grandpa was an alcoholic. This is a typical pattern.

While some patterns are apparent, others are more difficult to see. For example, Rick didn't drink because he hated his alcoholic father. Due to his dad's alcohol issues and anger that accompanied his drinking, Rick promised himself that he wouldn't ever drink. However, instead of drinking alcohol like his dad, Rick turned to being a playboy with women. In this case, while alcohol was avoided, addiction was not.

The critical point is this: Certain patterns are often passed on from one generation to the next. In his excellent book, It Didn't Start with You, author Mark Wolynn writes: "The latest scientific research, now making headlines, also tells us that the effects of trauma can pass from one generation to the next. This 'bequest' is what's known as inherited family trauma, and emerging evidence suggests that it is a very real phenomenon. Pain does not always dissolve on its own or diminish with time" (3,4).

Unfortunately, it is not always easy to look back at or even talk about the past. However, as Wolynn explains, certain life events don't go away with time. Therefore, if real change is going to occur in our lives, we cannot be afraid to look back and identify how family patterns from the past are influencing us now.

Over the years, I have had many clients question why I wanted them to look into their family history. My answer is that we can learn a lot from evaluating our family's physical and mental health across generations. By understanding these patterns, we can live more intentionally for our own benefit. For example, my family has a history of heart problems. This information has made me more aware of my blood pressure and cholesterol. I am using this information by choosing to exercise and watch my eating habits.

Let's now look at an example. A few years ago, I met with Justin, a man whose parents divorced when he was young. He reported that none of his family members had been married to just one person. His parents both cheated. His grandparents on both sides of his family had divorced, and all of his aunts and uncles had divorced. He ended up living with his dad after his parents' divorce.

While he was in high school, his dad encouraged him to go on dates and "get as much action as he could" from the girls. His dad wanted him to tell him about his experiences when he got home. Growing up in that environment, he learned that commitment didn't mean anything. He was taught that he should act out sexually any time he wanted to and with anyone who would be sexual with him.

When he came to see me for the first time, the tables had been turned on him. His wife was cheating on him. He was having a hard time with this. Upon further discussion, it was the same pattern as his parents' marriage. His mom had left his dad for another man. His dad hadn't been faithful, either, but it was his mom who left his dad. Now the pattern of being left for someone else was being repeated.

The more we discussed his family patterns, Justin realized that his dad was angry at women, and it wasn't just because of what his wife did to him. As he looked at his grandparents' relationship, he realized that his grandpa had treated his grandmother poorly. The way the men in his family treated women had ultimately triggered a cascade of divorces for at least three generations.

He realized that growing up, he didn't see couples who liked each other. Instead, he saw fighting and arguing. He saw women being degraded and treated like objects. However, he also observed that the women had silently fought back by ending the relationship. This awareness led him to evaluate how he had treated his wife. Humbly, he said, "I treated her just like I had seen my dad and grandpa treat my mom and grandma." In situations like this, I often say, "You can't do what you haven't been taught to do."

That didn't make Justin's sadness go away, but it did increase his desire to learn how to be better at relationships. "Somehow," Justin said, "I have to learn how to break these unhealthy patterns." He asked me where he should start. I suggested that he should identify as many of the unhealthy patterns as he could and then explore the outcome of those patterns. The purpose of this exercise is to increase awareness.

Here are a few family patterns and some of the outcomes from Justin's family that we identified:

Family Pattern	Outcome
Men treat women poorly by degrading them and talking down to them	• I treated the girls and women in my life the way I had observed

Fighting and contention in the family	• I thought it was normal to fight and be critical in relationships
Women didn't tolerate the way they were treated	• My mom and wife both cheated
Sex isn't for connection; get it as often as you can with whomever you want	• I grew up with the expectation that I could have sex anytime I wanted because that's what I was supposed to do

As we explored these family dynamics, Justin realized how his family patterns had set him up to fail in relationships. I told him, "When you grow up in a fishbowl with dirty water, you don't know that the water is dirty." He agreed.

While awareness is helpful, it doesn't change behavior. The next step is to take that information and intentionally plan on how you are going to change the pattern. For Justin, he had never seen a healthy couple who treated each other with respect. I gave him the challenge to start observing couples and, in particular, watch for couples who seemed to love each other genuinely.

A couple of months after giving him that assignment, I received a phone call from him. He wanted to report that, for the first time in his life, he had seen a couple who were happy. He told me, "I was at a professional conference and was watching an older couple holding hands and looking at each other with smiles. They loved each other. Part of me smiled for Justin, and part of me felt sad for him. Here was a 30-year-old man who had never seen a couple who genuinely loved one another.

When I first started working with Justin, he wanted help to get through his wife's sexual betrayal and her subsequently leaving him. However, as he developed a deeper trust in me, he opened up about his dad, his early sexual escapades, and how he was taught to treat women. As he opened up, he realized that he would need to change many parts of his life. In an effort to help my clients understand the importance of making lasting change, I share this quote by Dr. Joe Dispenza: "In order to change your life, you have to literally become someone else" (5).

Recovery: It's Not Just a Behavioral Change

Historically, in considering the change process when it comes to addiction, we have focused on behavioral changes. For example, we give chips to people in recovery so they can tell you how many days, months, or years they have been sober or clean. Fortunately, Dr. Patrick Carnes, the founder of the International Institute for Trauma and Addiction Professionals (IITAP), has suggested that professionals should also focus on the preoccupation (thought processes) individuals have with their addiction. In other words, addiction recovery is much more than just stopping a specific behavior; it also includes changing how a person thinks, feels, believes, and behaves.

As we have been focusing on your story throughout this chapter, it should be apparent by now that the goal is to help you begin altering patterns that may be generations old. In order to create lasting change, you will learn not only new behavioral patterns but also new thought patterns, new emotional patterns, and you will develop new beliefs about yourself.

Then, per Dr. Dispenza's suggestions: "If we repeat what we learn enough times, we strengthen communities of neurons to support us in remembering it the next time. If we don't, then the synaptic connections soon disappear and the memory is erased. This is why it's important for us to update continually, review, and remember our new thoughts, choices, behaviors, habits, beliefs, and experiences if we want them to solidify in our brains" (6).

In order to create the lasting change you desire, it is going to be essential to realize that your lasting change will produce a new you. If you are like Justin and have come to realize that you are trying to change generations of unhealthy habits and behaviors, you may initially feel overwhelmed. It will be important to remember that change is a gradual process that is going to take time. Eventually, you will realize that recovery is not a destination: It is a journey that continues over time. I have observed that clients who make the most progress do so because they continue to learn, grow, and develop into someone new.

For Justin, he realized that the way he saw women had to change. Instead of treating them like sex objects, he needed to learn about them. He had never considered what it was like for his mother to be married to his dad. He had been angry at her for cheating, but when he started thinking about how poorly his dad treated her, he began to see another side to her.

Then, in looking into his mother's family relationships, he realized she had suffered a lot at the hands of men. It began to make sense to him that she wouldn't know how to relate and connect to him, her son. This created a unique shift in how he thought about her and other women. No longer were they cold, heartless, and only good for sex, like his father had taught him. Instead, they were people who felt emotions, had concerns, and wanted happiness, too. This thinking didn't happen overnight, but, as he learned, he developed a better capacity for empathy.

You will notice in this example that Justin's change was much more than just stopping his sexual activities. His change included how he saw and treated women, how he interacted with his father, how he understood his family history, how it had influenced him up to that point in his life, and finally how he saw himself in relationships.

I would invite you to begin exploring your family patterns and identify some of the specific outcomes that resulted from those experiences (See Appendix A Family History/Genogram).

Chapter Summary

The best and most lasting change you make will be more than a behavioral change. Ultimate change happens when you change your thoughts, emotions, beliefs, and behaviors. When you seek to understand how your first sexual experiences have influenced your life, you will have gained valuable insight that can help you see why you do what you do, why you think what you think, and why you feel what you feel. By gaining this insight, you will hopefully be kind to yourself by having compassion for the younger you.

As you continue towards recovery, you will want to seek a deeper understanding of your personal story. This will help you see how that story has been written up to this point in your life. In this chapter, I also discussed the importance of discovering how your family history has influenced how you see yourself and others around you. Finally, I discussed that complete change not only includes a change in your behaviors, but you will also think, feel, and believe differently about yourself.

Support Resources:

Appendix A: Family History/Genogram (https://bit.ly/treating-sex-addiction)

Part Two

Developing the Foundational Skills for Long-Term Recovery

Chapter Four

Creating Your Recovery Plan

Plan your work and work your plan
(Napoleon Hill)

Are you ready to stop your unwanted sexual behaviors? This is the question I asked my client, who had been with more than 60 different partners over the last few years. He was married, but his wife had discovered his illicit sexual activities on at least two occasions, and she was done. Knowing that his marriage was over and that his entire family knew everything, the truth had finally hit him.

For more than 20 years, he had hidden the extent of his sexual behaviors from his wife. She was slowly gathering information about the many ways and times he had been cheating on her. He had created a completely separate world, and now the two worlds were colliding. When we first met, he reported that he really didn't understand how he got so deep into his behaviors, which is what Martin M. Broadwell refers to as unconscious incompetence in his writings "The Four Levels of Teaching" (1).

For purposes of this chapter and in my teaching, I have adapted Broadwell's teachings and apply them to the recovery process. In this particular client's case, he had been living in two worlds for so long; he thought he could manage them both. During the unconscious incompetence stage, individuals do not understand how their behaviors are influencing their own lives and the lives of others. In other words, they don't know what they don't know. Many of my clients have reported that, as they work on their recovery, they begin to see how many things they missed. During the early stage of recovery, they were not able to see how their addiction had blinded them. As their awareness grew, they began to see how their sexual activities had influenced their life. Broadwell suggests that, "The individual must recognize their own incompetence, and the value of the new skill, before moving on to the next stage" (2).

The next stage of Broadwell's model is the most difficult. He refers to it as conscious incompetence. During this stage, an individual's awareness increases, but his/her skills do not match his/her awareness. The individual feels completely exposed and does not know how to respond. This truly is painful. The individual doesn't know how to deal with his/her own emotions or a spouse's emotions.

I have observed that many clients get upset or angry during this stage because they are overwhelmed with feelings of shame. In this stage, individuals begin to see more clearly the consequences of their behaviors and do not yet have the skills to keep good on their promises. As a result, many people make promises in this stage that they cannot keep. For example, the client I referred to earlier in this chapter, after having been caught in an affair ten years before, told his spouse that he would never again have another affair. However, after promising he wouldn't act out, he found that, a couple of years later, he was back to his same behaviors.

The conscious incompetence stage is painful because most people do not know how to respond when their world starts to fall apart. My client was losing his wife and his children. He had been fired from his job because he was not performing. His lies had finally caught up with him, and there was nowhere else to turn. In addition, he still had to deal with his intense cravings and desires to act out. He had no "recovery capital" (a term from Chapter One of this book). Fortunately, for him and all others, once a person is given the necessary tools to start working toward healing and recovery, there is still hope.

In the next stage, the work of recovery begins. Broadwell suggests that, during this stage, "The individual understands or knows how to do something. However, demonstrating the skill or knowledge requires concentration. This is what Broadwell refers to as conscious competence. It may be broken down into steps, and there is heavy conscious involvement in executing the new skill" (3). This is when clients learn to respond to stress by reaching out instead of acting out. This requires more mental awareness and effort, but clients begin to see progress, and others observing them can see the changes.

I often tell my clients that the conscious competence stage can last a long time because new skills take time to develop. I tell them that, as they practice and implement the changes, they will see their progress. They begin to see how overcoming old habits is not easy, but with the right recovery plan, they begin to replace old habits with new ones. I also tell my clients that recovery is much more than being sober. When done right, we become a new being: one who has new knowledge, one who is excited to learn and grow, one whose quality of life has improved because he/she is thinking, feeling, and acting differently. This person is finally better at relationships and connecting with others.

A few examples of how individuals respond in this stage include:

- When individuals feel like acting out, they will quickly recognize what is happening in order to prevent a relapse. Instead of saying to themselves, "I can do this without reaching out, they will say, "I am going to reach out because I will relapse if I don't." This is often the difference between maintaining sobriety and relapsing.

- Instead of spending time alone, they will reach out to a friend for support.

- They plan in advance how to avoid places of vulnerability.

The fourth and final stage of Broadwell's model indicates that, "The individual has had so much practice with a skill that it has become 'second nature' and can be performed easily" (4). During this stage, individuals do many things without thinking about them. This is what is referred to as unconscious competence. In this stage, the individual has developed so many positive skills (recovery capital) that many things happen on autopilot. For example, at this stage, an individual will likely reach out to others when he/she feels stressed. Or the individual might naturally shift attention elsewhere when a fantasy thought arises. These things will happen almost naturally without having to give the response much thought. One client put it this way, "I just don't think about the things I used to think about."

It is during the unconscious competence stage that individuals reap the reward of their efforts. They have developed enough healthy habits that they feel confident in themselves and their ability to succeed. Others also sense their energy and feel a difference being around them. New knowledge with the right application creates a powerful and lasting change.

Here's a flow chart that demonstrates this process.

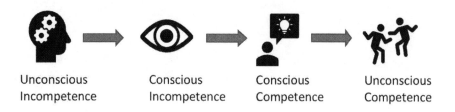

| Unconscious Incompetence | Conscious Incompetence | Conscious Competence | Unconscious Competence |

The Four Stages of Competence in Action

Steve was frustrated with himself. For the first time in years, he was confronting sexual activities that were creating so many problems for him and his family. As he sat down on my couch, he exclaimed, "For the longest time, I would tell myself that eventually I would stop meeting people for a random hook-up. I told myself it wouldn't hurt others because they didn't have to know. When my wife started asking if something was going on, I would lie. Then, she caught me in a lie about a year ago, and I promised her and myself that I was done for good. So, now a year later, I can't stop. Why do I tell myself over and over again that I am done acting out, and then, a few days later, I find myself doing that same behavior again? I wish I understood why I don't have more self-control."

This statement told me that my client was transitioning out of the unconscious incompetence stage and into the conscious incompetence stage. I have found that it is usually during the conscious incompetence stage that clients seek my help. If they come to therapy during the unconscious incompetence stage, they are not ready for the work that recovery takes. In Steve's case, something had happened: His wife caught him again, and he had been served an ultimatum, i.e., "Either you change and get help, or we are done."

Steve didn't want to lose his wife and family, so he was confused as to why he continued acting out. Over the years, I have observed many of my clients who have committed to themselves and others that they would stop their sexual behaviors, but, in moments of weakness, they find themselves engaging in the same unwanted behaviors.

Why does this happen?

While there are many potential answers to this question, I believe one explanation is that most people simply haven't prepared to succeed. Steve didn't have a recovery plan. He had been acting out for years, long before he met his wife. Also, he had many unresolved issues from his childhood. His parents had fought a lot, and, in his early adolescent years, he discovered that his father was having an affair. While he resented his dad, he also didn't like his mom, who was angry all of the time. Starting in his adolescent years, he formed a dual identity. He hid his porn use from his parents; further when he had a girlfriend, he was afraid to bring her home because of the tension between his parents.

When I meet with clients like Steve, I focus on understanding their whole story. In many cases, I am more concerned about their history than I am about the ways they have been sexually acting out. Usually, as we discuss their story together, we discover what is making it so hard to stop their behaviors. Many find that their patterns of acting out started long before their current relationship. It is at times like this that they realize how long they have been acting out sexually.

Once they clearly understand how their history is influencing their current behaviors, they also realize that they don't know how to stop on their own. It is at this point that many feel incompetent. Below I explain how I help clients like Steve develop a recovery plan. I also present the importance of gaining a better understanding of how their past may be influencing their recovery now.

I began by asking Steve about his current recovery plan. He looked at me a little confused and said, "That's why I'm coming to see you. I've tried a lot of things, and nothing has worked." I inquired about the things Steve had tried. He said that he had been attending a 12-step group, but that he had stopped going because it conflicted with his work schedule.

I asked, "Is there anything else you are doing to avoid relapsing?"

He said, "I have a filter on my home computer and my phone."

"Okay, how effective are the filters?"

"I can get around them if I want to."

Okay, I then inquired, "Is there anything else I should know about your recovery plan?" To this, he replied, "No, that's about it."

I reiterated to Steve what he had just told me to make sure I clearly understood. I said, "So, currently, you are coming to therapy, you have stopped attending groups because they didn't fit in with your work schedule, and you have a filter on your computers and phone, but you can get around them if you want to. Do I have this right?"

He replied, "Yeah, I think that's right."

I asked Steve a few more questions that I have found helpful as we develop a recovery plan. I invite you to consider these questions and what your response would be.

1. How many times have you engaged in unwanted sexual behaviors (e.g., pornography, random hook-ups, had an affair, visited a massage parlor, etc.)?

Response: I have viewed pornography hundreds, probably thousands of times in my life. I had a couple of random hook-ups before I met my wife. I have had a few random hook-ups since we were married, and I have had two affairs since we were married. I have never engaged in any other sexual behaviors.

2. How often do you find yourself fantasizing about the sexual behaviors you want to stop?

Response: It is hard to say precisely, but probably a few times each week. Some days it is much harder than others.

3. When are you most prone to engage in the behavior you want to stop?

Response: I usually view pornography while at work or late at night when my wife is asleep. I typically act out with pornography every few days. My two affairs have happened over the past couple of years. The first affair happened with a co-worker who is no longer at my company. The second affair happened over the past few months with someone who was working out at the same gym I use.

4. How many people know you are trying to stop these behaviors?

Response: The people who know what is happening are my wife, my boss, and you.

5. How many people know about the thoughts or fantasies that you are trying to overcome?

Response: I haven't talked about these thoughts with others.

6. What is your response plan when you are having a difficult time and wanting to give in?

Response: I don't have a plan for how to respond when I am having a hard time.

7. Do you have anyone you turn to for help or support if you want to act out?

Response: Currently, I don't have someone I can talk to if I'm having a difficult time, or I'm wanting to act out.

Once Steve answered these questions, I posed this question to him.

Suppose that you have a stressful week at work, with your boss pushing you hard to get a project done and you ended up staying a couple of hours later than you had initially planned. Then, worn out and tired, you return home much later than you anticipated, and you find that your wife is upset because you forgot she needed your help, and now it is too late to help her. Next, she starts yelling at you because you are unreliable, a cheater, and she isn't sure how much longer she can keep this up. Finally, she tells you that she is seriously considering divorce if you don't change your ways.

How would you respond to this scenario?

Steve, in a joking way, said, "Have you been watching us during our fights? Seriously, though, I would probably tune her out, go watch TV, or I might fight back and tell her she should have called to remind me."

"Okay," I replied. "How would you and your wife have resolved this issue?"

"We would have gone our separate ways and not talked about it again."

"If it's not resolved, do you have times when you do solve situations like this?"

"Rarely. We talked more in the beginning of our relationship, but right now, we hardly talk. We don't resolve problems like this. We normally just go back to living life and never really work through it."

"So, how would you deal with being disconnected from your wife?"

"I usually just avoid her until I feel like she isn't angry anymore."

"What do you feel inside at times like this?"

"I'm angry at her. I avoid her. I don't like being around her."

"Are you more vulnerable to act out at times like this?"

"Sure."

"So, how do you normally act out during these times?"

"Usually," he said, "it starts with me staying up late watching sports or a random movie. Then, as the night progresses, I might look at pornography. When I get really upset, I might start looking for someone to hook up with."

"How many times have you hooked up with someone in situations like this in the past?"

"A few times. I stopped doing that about a year ago."

"Why did you stop?"

"I knew it was wrong, and it would destroy my relationship. I don't want to do those things."

"Okay. How long do you and your wife ignore each other?"

"It might be for a few days."

"How does it resolve or end?"

"It doesn't resolve. We just brush over it. I might say, 'I'm sorry for being late.' And she will say, 'okay,' and that's the end of it."

"How long have you been in this type of pattern?"

"I think we have been in this kind of pattern for years. I don't even think she likes me anymore, and I'm not sure I care."

My response caught him off-guard. I said, "It's no wonder you're not able to stop acting out."

"What do you mean?"

"Listen to your story. You have stress at your job. When you get home, you and your wife are pretty much ignoring each other. When you fight, you stay disconnected for days at a time. You aren't enjoying each other or connecting. And instead of solving your issues, you have learned to turn to other things besides your wife. It sounds like you don't want to do those things, but you don't know how to connect with the person you care the most about. It sounds pretty lonely."

"It is!"

"Do you want it to be different?"

"Sure, but I'm not sure if she wants to be married anymore."

"I'm not sure whether your marriage will make it, but if you want to give yourself the best chance to make your relationship work, you will want to focus on your recovery. Up to this point, your attempts have been okay, but not great. They haven't prepared you to succeed in the long-term. We need to prepare you to succeed."

This was when I introduced Steve to the idea of recovery capital: "You have tried a few things as you have attempted to recover, but you have never developed a recovery plan that will help you succeed. The things you have tried are good, but we need to put them together so that you can make real and lasting changes."

I then suggested to Steve that he could learn more by reviewing the recovery capital model that we had covered in an early session. I also suggested that he take my free online class: Overcoming Sexual Addiction Through Recovery Capital. (Here's the link if you would like to review the recovery capital model: https://pathformen. com/course/sex-addiction-recovery-capital/.)

I hoped to help Steve develop skills so he could become consciously competent. After our discussion, I knew Steve had to spend time developing his recovery plan so he could see the benefit of developing recovery skills and ultimately see the process of his own changing behaviors. Then, he had to implement his plan successfully. We might refer to these as conscious competence skills.

I knew that Steve didn't have many deposits in his recovery capital bank. Sure, he had tried a couple of things, but they weren't working. He tried attending a group; then, he got too busy. He had a filter on his phone, but he knew a way around the filter. Even what he had tried, he wasn't committed to.

It has been my experience that lasting change requires a change of heart. This happens when the recovery effort is exceptional, and rarely have I seen just one thing (i.e., attending a group, therapy, or talking with a religious leader) on its own create lasting change. In most cases, the people I have observed who are succeeding are frequently learning new things, developing better habits, and making deposits into their recovery capital bank.

It was time for Steve to learn more and start practicing what he was learning. One of the reasons I gave him the assignment to start building his recovery plan was that he needed to realize that what he had tried was not enough by itself. The recovery capital model suggests that many activities lead to recovery (e.g., having a support team, feeling a part of your community, having a place where you feel safe), not just one or two behaviors.

There was something else that Steve needed but didn't feel he was ready for yet: He needed to learn how to interact more effectively with his wife. Usually, when my clients have recently relapsed, their level of shame is so high that they are not ready to communicate effectively with their spouses. I will explain more about why this happens in Chapters Nine and Thirteen. Finally, I told Steve that we would focus on helping him communicate more effectively with his wife soon, but he needed to identify a recovery plan first.

Let me explain why this matters. After discovery, many clients tell their partners that they are sorry and that they won't act out again. However, without a plan in place, apologies feel like empty words. Betrayed partners want to know why the behavior happened, how it's going to be stopped, and see a recovery plan carried out. In later chapters, in particular, Chapter Six, I will address strategies for communicating more effectively in relationships after discovery.

Building Your Recovery Plan (Conscious Competence)

If your story is similar to Steve's, you can relate to trying one or two things and then not succeeding. Unfortunately, in the recovery process, most people do not fully understand the effort it takes to stop unwanted thoughts and behaviors. It is difficult to stop actions that create intense feelings, trigger powerful emotions, and have happened hundreds if not thousands of times.

When I teach the importance of building a recovery plan, I invite participants to consider the following scenario. Imagine that you were a spy, and I was going to hire you to go into XYZ country to obtain documents that our country needs. I tell you that there will be enemy troops and others who will want to catch you, so you will need to be careful about who sees you, i.e., you need to be as discreet as possible.

Here are the two scenarios:

Scenario #1: We will fly you over XYZ country. You will skydive to a place close to where you need to pick up the documents. Once you have secured the materials, you will need to find your way to the border. We will pick you up there.

Scenario #2: We will fly you over XYZ country. You will skydive to a place that is about one mile from where the documents are located. Troops will likely be on the main roads. You will be best staying above the main road until you get to the location where the documents are located. I then tell you where potential enemies are and how to avoid them on your way to the border. I also review where potential hiding spots are located if you have to run.

If you were the spy in this case, which scenario would you prefer? While the answer is obvious, I tell my clients that having a more detailed plan during difficult times is critical. In many situations, when I ask my clients about their recovery plan, they haven't given one much thought.

So, now we are going to break your recovery plan into three specific stages.

The First Stage in Your Recovery Plan

Step #1: What and Why?

Every recovery plan needs a goal or a purpose. This is what we refer to as "the what you are wanting to change." Let's start by having you think about the specific thoughts and behaviors you are wanting to stop. Next, identify why you want to stop your behavior. It is essential to identify why you want to change (i.e., I want to be a better dad, I want to focus at work, I want to be known as a person who made the world a better place). I often say to my clients that, if they don't have a big enough why, they probably won't try when things get hard.

Step #2: The How of Change

How are you going to stop engaging in the behavior you want to stop? Your answer to this question should focus more on the details of how you are going to succeed in difficult or crucial moments. Below is a short example of how one client addressed the how of change.

Question: In what situation/s am I most likely to relapse?

Response: I usually relapse on weekends or late at night, so I am going to talk more with my sponsor on weekends. I am also going to avoid staying up late at night.

Step #3: Who can I enlist to help me in the following areas

1) To whom can I be accountable? 2) Who can I have on my support team? 3) Who could be my sponsor? 4) Who has the professional knowledge to help me through this problem?

In the literature on recovery capital, the people who were most likely to succeed had a support team (see Chapters One and Thirteen)(5). Therefore, in developing your recovery plan, I recommend that you think about the people who will be on your team, i.e., people you will turn to in your most difficult times. If you would like to understand how helpful others can be in your recovery, I have provided a link to a presentation I did at a large conference. The topic I was asked to speak on was the power of accountability in the recovery process (6).

Step #4: When am I going to start? And what actions can I start today?

The fourth step in your recovery plan focuses on "when" you are going to start implementing your plan. Each of the previous steps have brought us to this point. If you have adequately done steps one through three, step four will be like pushing on the gas pedal toward recovery.

Here's an example that combines all of the steps:

Step #1: What and why?

My what: I am going to stop viewing pornography and looking on Craig's list for someone to hook up with.

Why: I don't want to be like this. I want to be a person who is faithful and committed. I want to be involved in my kids' lives rather than being absent. I want a better relationship with my wife.

Step #2: The How of Change

I am going to avoid using my phone to view pornography. I will download a filter on my phone, so I can't readily access pornography. I am also going to delete my Craig's list app, so it is no longer a temptation. In order to make sure I do these things, I am going to tell my therapist and accountability team what I am committing to do.

Step #3: Who can I enlist to help me?

The following people can be on my team:

1. My friend Tom. He knows things have been hard. He would be supportive if I told him everything that has been going on.

2. I will attend a 12-step group and be accountable to the group.

3. I will find a sponsor and will be accountable to him/her. I will talk with a sponsor at least three times each week.

4. I will attend therapy to learn more about recovery and what may be driving my addictive behaviors.

Step #4: When will I get started on these activities?

Week Oct. 6th – Oct.13th

Sunday: My goal is to look up 12-step groups.

Monday: I am going to find a therapist

Tuesday: I am going to go to lunch with Tom and talk with him about what has been happening in my life and see if I can talk with him periodically about my progress.

Wednesday: I am going to focus on finding accountability software for my phone.

Thursday: I will get online and learn more about the recovery process.

Friday: I am going to take my wife out on a date.

Saturday: I will spend time with my children and do chores around the house. I will avoid staying up late.

Each week, I will create a plan of action. It will include new activities and events.

The Middle Stage of Your Recovery Plan

While the first phase focused on relapse prevention, the middle phase will help you to develop specific skills that will aid in your recovery. You will also gain more insight into what has been driving your behaviors. You will discover how honesty and vulnerability can accelerate your healing. Some of the key areas that I recommend my clients focus on during this stage are:

- Work through the roots that can drive the addiction (see Chapter Two)
- Deal with unresolved trauma (video: Treating Trauma)
- Prepare for and present a full disclosure (see Chapter Six)
- Resolve shame-based beliefs (see Chapter Nine)
- Learn to regulate difficult emotions (see Chapter Ten)

While the first stage is designed to help you establish sobriety and accountability, the goal of the middle stage is to increase your awareness, add to your support team, and address shame and loneliness. If you have experienced trauma in your life, I recommend that you seek professional therapy during this part. I have found that individuals who address trauma make better progress in recovery.

During this stage, you will also continue doing the things you did in the first stage. For example, continuous accountability by participating in recovery activities (e.g., attend a 12-step group, work with a sponsor, talk with a professional counselor) will be important. Next, you will begin developing new patterns that will replace unhealthy behaviors from your past. The middle stage of recovery is where I see my clients start to truly understand more about themselves and what improvement can be like. They discover that recovery requires work, but it is worth it.

Here are the action steps I encourage you to take while working on the middle stage of your recovery plan.

1. Review your recovery capital assessment and identify a specific area that you can improve upon. If it has been a few weeks since you last took this short assessment, I encourage you to retake it and to compare your score results.

2. Review your family history and complete the Genogram (see Appendix A as an example).

3. Take the ACE assessment and watch the video Strategies for Dealing with Adverse Childhood Experiences

4. Review the steps of preparing for a full disclosure and present it to your partner. (Note: A disclosure will likely be most effective if completed with a professional therapist present).

5. Read Chapter Nine on shame and complete the suggested assignments.

6. Acquire a greater awareness of your emotions and learn how to respond effectively when times are difficult.

While there are many other steps you can take, these will help you get started in your journey toward recovery. Remember, the more of these activities you do, the odds of you succeeding increase.

The Later Stage of Your Recovery Plan (Beginnings of Unconscious Competence)

What would you like your life to be like in one year from now? How about three years from now and five years from now? I'm inviting you to dream a little. Imagine what you will be doing at home, work, and with your family. Think about the dreams you had earlier in your life before you got caught up in your sexual behaviors. It is this life that you want to start working toward.

In my experience, by the time you start into the later stage of your recovery, you will have months of sobriety, and you will feel more confident in the steps you are taking. If you are reading this book and still in the early stages of recovery, what we discuss below may feel out of reach and may be difficult for you to imagine. How-ever, I believe it is especially essential for those in the beginning stages of recovery to understand and see some of the steps that successful people are making in their recovery journey. Dr. Joe Dispenza, in his book *Breaking the Habit of Being Yourself*, discussed the importance of seeing where we want to be. In other words, if you cannot see what you are trying to achieve, it will be much more difficult to obtain. Regarding this concept, he wrote, "To change is to think greater than how we feel. To change is to act greater than the familiar feelings of the memorized self"(7).

In the later stage of the recovery process, you will have formed new habits. For example, in most cases, you will have someone with whom you have talked to throughout your recovery process. This person has likely become a trusted confi-dant. You are likely to have a team of people that you can reach out to at any time. Also, when you recognize that you are experiencing stress, you will have learned to deal effectively with feelings that, in the past, would have triggered a relapse. These are just some of the skills you will have developed.

During this later stage, you will also become more creative, happier, and more confident. Your shame will be lower, too; as a result, you will feel significantly better about yourself. You will take appropriate measures to make amends for the pain you have created. You will have more compassion for yourself and others. Finally, you will be better at relationships. Does this sound like it will be impossible to do? I hope not—but, if it does, I invite you to engage in the work I have outlined in this chapter.

Here are some of the actions steps you can work toward in this stage of your recovery journey:

1. Develop a habit of learning. I often suggest to clients in the recovery process that they should be continuously learning, e.g., reading a book, listening to a pod-cast, or watching videos that support personal recovery and other great life habits.

2. Create healthy habits (see Chapter Eleven).

3. Create moments that will help sustain your recovery (see Chapter Twelve).

4. Learn to love deeper and enjoy the experience of being more kind and show-ing empathy for those who suffer (see Chapter Fourteen). Love is a choice and can be learned and developed. I invite you to set a goal to be more compassionate so you can be the best person you can be.

Recovery is a process and will likely come in stages. The steps you take in the early stage of recovery will likely be difficult and challenging (conscious incompe-tence). As you implement the steps, you will gain a better awareness of what it is going to take to recover. This stage can be overwhelming because you will begin to see the consequences of your behaviors. You will also have to respond to the emotional withdrawals of not being able to turn to your sexual acts when times get hard.

As you work on building your recovery capital and developing the skills for recovery, you will be more conscious: You will become consciously competent. You will discover the benefits of learning and growing, talking to others, and developing a team approach to your recovery.

Finally, you will discover that you think, feel, and act in ways that you haven't in years, perhaps most of your life. You will have renewed energy and will have entered the stage of unconscious competence. This can happen to you. There is power in developing a recovery plan and implementing it in your life.

Chapter Summary

An important step to take in your recovery process is to create a plan. In this chapter, I adapted Martin M. Broadwell's four levels of teaching (unconscious incompetence, conscious incompetence, conscious competence, and unconscious competence) to explain the process of change. During the early stage of recovery, some of the difficulties you will face are due to being unprepared for the challenges you experience. As you develop your recovery plan, you will naturally become more competent, and you will feel more confident. I finish the chapter by discussing how you can build your recovery plan and put it into action. The recovery process was broken down into three stages: early, middle, and later stage. Examples of activities you can implement into your recovery plan were given for each stage.

I hope that this chapter helped you see a map to your recovery. As you become consciously competent in your recovery efforts, you will feel more confident. Eventually, you will experience an increase in the quality of your life, and it will happen without you even realizing how much progress you have made because you will be living your life in the unconscious competence phase of recovery.

Support Resources (found at https://bit.ly/treating-sex-addiction—under Chapter 4)

- See Appendix B: Outlining Your Recovery Plan

- Strategies for Dealing with Adverse Childhood Experiences (video found at hhttps://bit.ly/treating-sex-addiction) under Chapter 4

- Take the Recovery Capital Scale at https://bit.ly/treating-sex-addiction

Chapter Five

Succeed in Crucial Moments

If you establish rules in advance of facing a challenge, you are far more likely to change your behavior when the crucial moment hits.
(Peter Gollwitzer and Paschal Sheeran)

As you work towards recovery, there will be moments that will determine whether or not you succeed. It is, therefore, essential that you prepare for these moments because they will inevitably arise. Often the difference between success and failure in these moments is having a plan in place so you do not have to think about how you will respond. In the last chapter, we discussed the importance of developing a recovery plan. The focus of the present chapter is to get into the details of that plan. When you prepare for the crucial moments, you will feel more confident when the battle comes.

As I was sitting in my chair listening to Sam describe his most recent relapse, I found myself thinking about what he was going through as he fought the cravings and then eventually gave in. He, like many of my clients, didn't act out on a single impulse. Instead, according to his report, he had been fighting the cravings for a few hours. Initially, he reported that being home alone was his first trigger. However, as we talked, he identified that, when his wife told him she was leaving for the afternoon, the initial thought to act out entered into his mind.

As we discussed Sam's initial thought to look at pornography when his wife left, he reported that he simply let that thought pass. However, when his wife left, and he knew that he had a few hours to himself, his triggers accelerated. He found himself trying to keep busy with chores he said he would be working on while she was gone. However, the more he attempted to push down the thoughts, the more powerful they became. According to Sam, when those powerful thoughts came up, he would almost always relapse. He said, "On days like that, I know that it is just a matter of time before I give in."

73

I asked Sam if he had ever created a plan for how to respond during those diffi-cult moments. He replied, "No, I haven't ever thought about that." Sam's response is common to most of my clients. He had developed parts of a recovery plan (i.e., talk with his sponsor, attend a 12-step group), but he wasn't prepared for the most challenging moments. I have found that some individuals think to themselves, "I have a sponsor or I am attending group, this will help me succeed." Unfortunately, while these two things can be useful, they won't help you win the battle if they are not activated in your most crucial moments.

In an effort to help Sam identify his crucial moments and how important it is to prepare for them, I said, "Okay, Sam, I am going to give you an assignment: I want you to go back and revisit your last relapse. I want you to break it down from the first moment that the thought to act out entered your mind up until you acted out. I asked him to focus on three parts: 1) identify as many of the thoughts he had to act out before he actually acted out; 2) how he responded to each of these thoughts; and 3) what an effective response would be when those thoughts and feelings arise. My hope in asking him to do this exercise was to help him identify specific mo-ments of vulnerability, how he usually responded at those times, and how he could have responded in a way that would have prevented his relapse. I let him know that, if he needed help with any of the moments, we could discuss them together. Below, you will see what he wrote and some of my suggestions as we worked together.

Here's what he came up with:

Critical Moment #1

Thought: My first thought to act out was when my wife told me she was leaving for the afternoon.

Response: My initial reaction was to ignore the thought and just move on.

Effective Response: I could have openly acknowledged the thought and commit-ted to reach out to a friend while my wife was gone.

Critical Moment #2

Thought: I recall the thought came again to my mind that I could get online and view pornography when she left. (Notice how he had not even thought about that when we first discussed what had happened. This is common. When individuals start reviewing their relapses, they begin to see the powerful pull of anticipation that they usually dismiss.)

Response: I think I am so used to these thoughts that I usually just dismiss them, but they are creating more and more buildup inside.

Effective Response: I'm not sure what to do. In the past, I just passed over these thoughts. I think I need some new ideas for this part.

Here are some of the ideas we discussed. I suggested to Sam that those moments are the building blocks that led up to his relapses. I suggested that, as he slowed down and paid closer attention to the thoughts, he could more effectively respond to them rather than react at a later time. This made sense to him. I suggested he listen to a short audio recording titled Cravings, I See You. You can find a link to that resource below.

Critical Moment #3

Thought: When my wife was getting ready to leave, I remember having the thought, "I could look up XYZ website." I also remember starting to feel some internal tension. I often get a little anxious before acting out.

Authors note: This is usually the time when the anticipation chemicals begin releasing into the body. You can tell this by Sam's awareness that he was starting to feel internal tension. That is a signal that the body is anticipating something exciting is going to happen.

Response: I didn't respond well to that thought. I now realize that, by that time, I was anticipating what I could be looking at really soon. I did start doing one of the jobs on my task list. That was simply a short distraction, though.

Effective Response: This is hard! I have tried a lot of things at times like this, but none of them have worked. I guess, at this point, I want to give in. What do you recommend?

Our Discussion: I pointed out to Sam that, by the time his wife was leaving, his mind and body were fully anticipating that he would act out. I guessed he would be disappointed if he didn't give in. We discussed how his body was physically preparing for a sexual experience. The sign of this was the internal feelings and tension he was feeling.

My suggestion to Sam was that he needed to respond earlier. The battle was nearly over by the time his wife left. He agreed and then asked me, "So what do you recommend?" I wanted him to think about some solutions first, so I invited him to go home and complete the assignment Five Things to Do Before I Relapse. You can find this assignment in Appendix C.

Critical Moment #4

Thought: While I was working on the household chore, the thought came to my mind, "You might as well get it over with; you know you are going to give in." This was the case in so many situations like this before. I didn't fight it.

Response: I acted on the thought and got onto the computer.

Effective Response: Even though the cravings were high, I still could have gotten up and left the house. That is something I have tried in the past, and it helped until I got back home. I could have also gone outside and not come back into the house until my wife got back home.

Authors note: There are many potential responses Sam could have used during this crucial moment. However, due to the intensity already present in his mind and body, for him to succeed at a time like this, he will likely need to rely on someone else (i.e., a sponsor or accountability team member). As individuals prepare to respond during critical moments, they must identify specific actions that they can commit to doing. I will share some of the ideas clients and group members have used below. Hopefully, these ideas will spark some ideas for you.

The Five Things List

Sometimes, while doing therapy, my clients and I gain insights or ideas into their challenge that really helps them. Often when this happens, I will try the same technique with other clients to see if it helps them, too. When the same strategy works over and over with clients, you realize that the approach is a winner. This was the case with Chris. He had just shared with me that he had relapsed a few days earlier. As we reviewed what had happened, he said, "I feel like I just need to be told exactly what to do when the cravings come up." That is when this idea came to my mind. I said, "Okay, I am not going to tell you what you need to do, but you are. In fact, let's do it right now."

I then introduced him to the Five Things List. Here's how it works. I explained that I wanted him to write down five things on a three-by-five card that he would commit to do before he relapsed. I then gave him a few minutes to make his list, which looked something like this:

1. Turn off the computer

2. Go for a walk

3. Play the piano

4. Call a friend

5. Do some push-ups

I thought this was a great start, so I then asked him how he would know when it was time to start doing his Five Things list. He thought for a bit and replied, "I think I need to be aware of the thought (craving) as soon as possible and identify it as a trigger before it grows." I then asked if that would be one of his steps. To which he said, "Yes. That has to be one of my steps because I need to recognize the craving as soon as it starts."

As we reviewed his list, I asked him about the time of day when most of his relapses occurred. He said, "Most of the time, I act out in the evenings after everyone has gone to bed." I asked, "How are you going to play the piano late at night?" He replied, "Hmm, I guess that one won't work when I am most vulnerable." So, he replaced playing the piano with "increase awareness and call my craving by name" (this is a simple technique we had discussed as a way to help him recognize his craving as quickly as possible). Next, I asked him about going for a walk late at night. Again, he realized that that probably wasn't the best option for him, given the fact that winter nights where he lived were cold and snowy. He replaced going for a walk by doing meditation, or he prayed and turned his desire over to his higher power.

He was not done making changes to his list. I asked him about calling a friend, and he quickly realized that calling a friend at 11:00 p.m. or later would not be something he would do. So, he again had to identify another strategy for late at night. He came up with reading a book. Ideally, he wanted to just go to bed, so we included that as a sixth thing to do before a relapse.

After our discussion, his new list looked like this:

1. Increase my awareness of the craving by calling it out and giving it a name

2. Turn off the computer

3. Leave the room and all electronic devices behind

4. Pray/meditate

5. Read a book

6. Sleep, if possible

Before Chris left, I asked him to do one more thing. I invited him to write down his Five Things list with his non-dominant hand each day at least once before our next appointment. There are many potential benefits of having him do this exercise. The first is that by using his non-dominant hand to write the five things list, he will slow down his mind. Slowing down the mind when dealing with a craving is always a good idea. Second, by writing down his list, he will use multiple senses (e.g., He will physically write down his list with his hand, he will see his list). Third, by writing it down each day, these ideas will begin to be etched into his mind, so, during the most challenging times, he will remember what he has committed to do.

In our next session, Chris was excited to report that he completed his assignment and had not relapsed. His list helped him to avoid a difficult trigger. Over the next few weeks, Chris reported success in avoiding relapses. Since that initial experience with Chris, I have used the Five Things list with many clients and in groups that I run at my center. I have found that those who utilize their list consistently make good progress in their recovery. This is my favorite crucial moment exercise.

Since I first started using the Five Things list, I have continued to adapt it based on feedback from my clients. Below are some of the things I have learned.

First, my clients seem to make the most progress when they start by acknowledging that they are in a vulnerable moment. This is the mental warning sign that it is time to pay closer attention. By directly identifying the trigger and giving it a name, I have found that many of my clients can carry out their Five Things list.

Second, when clients include as many of their senses in the Five Things list, it seems to help. For example, doing something physical is ideal (i.e., going for a walk, doing push-ups, leaving the room). Additional ways to include your senses are:

- Smell: Use a diffuser to get your favorite scent into the air

- See: Look at the pictures of some of your favorite people or places

- Touch: Pet an animal, cross your arms so your right hand is on your left shoulder and your left hand is on your right shoulder. Then, gently switch off tapping your shoulders while saying something kind to yourself (i.e., I am a kind and caring person).

- Listen: Create a playlist of music that calms your mind and gives you a sense of accomplishment.

Third, create a Five Things list for each situation in which you have relapsed. For example, if you relapse while on business trips, you will need a Five Things list for each time you leave town. Or, if you find that you are more prone to seek out someone for random hook-up during your lunch hour, you will need a Five Things list for that time.

Fourth, share your Five Things list with your sponsor, accountability team, religious leader, or someone who will ask you how it is going. In the book, Change Anything, author Kerry Patterson and his team found that individuals they studied who created significant change in their lives were willing to have a transformation conversation by asking others for help (2). Based on my observations, those who included reaching out to others as a part of their Five Things list were successful in avoiding a relapse.

Fifth, individuals who use this strategy most effectively change their list periodically to meet their individual needs. Some individuals have a list with more than five things. Still, others have created a list for the different seasons of the year. The critical part is that you identify the things you will do when the craving comes up and act upon those things. These meaningful strategies will go a long way in helping you succeed.

The Five Things List in Action

Business trips were especially difficult for Robert. As he became more aware about planning for success, he identified specific times and situations where he was the most vulnerable. Traveling for him was a challenge, as he would often start planning his sexual activities around his work schedule. His sexual ritual began long before he would arrive in the city he was visiting for work.

When he learned about the Five Things list, he began working on his list before he left. He created a specific plan for each time he traveled. He had a list of things that he did before he left and a list of things he did while he was on his trip. Here's his list:

Pre-Trip Five Things List

1. Talk with someone about my trip and ask for help. Tell them I will be traveling and ask if I could be accountable to them each day.

2. Plan vulnerable moments before leaving (e.g., evenings after dinner while out on the town). Strategy: Have a good book to read. Find the book before I go on the trip.

3. Avoid any pre-planning rituals (e.g., looking up massage parlors).

4. Plan my downtime and what I will do before I leave.

5. Find a productive activity to do in the city that will help me focus on succeeding.

During Trip Five Things List

1. Call home each morning and night to check-in.

2. Exercise each day (i.e., go for a jog, lift weights, do laps in the pool).

3. Use the computer for business only. Report if I keep that commitment to my sponsor/accountability person.

4. Pray or meditate each evening and morning. Make sure I am expressing gratitude.

5. Attend a 12-step meeting (online or in-person in the city).

Five Things List if It Gets Difficult

1. Call my sponsor and reach out before I act out/as soon as I sense a craving.

2. Go to the exercise room and lift weights or run for at least 15 minutes.

3. Write in my journal about what I am feeling and what I think is driving these cravings.

4. Review my relationships and how I can improve them.

5. Do some deep breathing.

In my experience, this type of planning is rare. However, researchers have discovered that planning before a crisis or crucial moment occurs provides the mind with a clear path to take during difficult times and reduces the stress in such moments (3, 4). In his book, Sources of Power, author Gary Klein explained this process. While studying how fire chief commanders made decisions, researchers discovered a concept called "recognition-primed decision making" (5). They found that commanders who had rehearsed their plan of action in multiple scenarios were quick to make decisions and skilled in making the right decisions.

Here's how Klein described their findings, "The commanders' secret was that their experience let them see a situation, even a non-routine one, as an example of a prototype, so they knew the typical course of action right away. Their experience let them identify a reasonable reaction as the first one they considered, so they did not bother thinking of others. They were not being perverse. They were being skillful. We now call this strategy recognition-primed decision making" (6).

What the researchers discovered next offers a valuable lesson that explains the difference between those who have prepared for difficult moments and those who haven't. Klein wrote, "Before we did this study, we believed that novices impulsively jumped at the first option they could think of, whereas experts carefully deliberated about the merits of different courses of action. Now it seemed that it was the experts who could generate a single course of action, while novices needed to compare different approaches" (7).

These findings are significant and can be applied to your recovery efforts. If you want to succeed in crucial moments, then putting yourself through the mental exercise of preparation will make it so you can make the best decisions when it matters the most.

Assignment

Go to Appendix C The Five Things List and create your five things list for each of the places or situations in which you find you are vulnerable. Then share your list of actions with someone else. Finally, write your list each day with your non-dominant hand for at least one week.

Chapter Summary

In the recovery process, you will face crucial moments. The question is whether or not you will be prepared for them. One way to prepare for your crucial moments is to review your last relapse and break down those moments one at a time. An example was given, so you could see how those moments could be broken down and evaluated. In the last part of this chapter, the Five Things list was introduced. Specific examples were given in how it could be used to prepare your mind for the difficult times. Finally, we discussed how researchers have discovered that having a plan makes it easier to follow a course of action during stressful times.

Chapter Six

The Power of Being Vulnerable

We cultivate love when we allow our most vulnerable and powerful selves to be deeply seen and known...
(Brene Brown)

"A year ago, if you would have told me that I was going to be attending group therapy, talking with a counselor, and daily sharing my progress with a sponsor, I would have told you that you were crazy," said Adam, as we discussed his progress. He continued, "It has been life-changing for me. I honestly thought I was going to go to my death bed with my sexual secrets. I felt that, if others knew about my affairs, porn use, and other sexual fantasies, they would reject me. Now, I am so grateful I got caught and have learned how to get out of the dark hole in which I was trapped."

Adam, as with many of the people I have talked to in their journey toward recovery, didn't believe he would ever tell others about his sexually acting-out behaviors. Yet, when he started sharing what he was really experiencing, things began to change. He found that he wasn't alone; that others also struggle to manage their sexual behaviors and fantasy thoughts. He had believed his struggles were unique to him.

Over my 25-year career, I have repeatedly found that, when my clients face their fears and share with others their internal battles (e.g., thoughts and fantasies) and outward behaviors (e.g., visiting massage parlors, hiring prostitutes), they make rapid progress in their recovery. As I was pondering on why opening up and being vulnerable with others helped in the recovery process, I decided to invite my clients and others to share with me some of the benefits they have found in opening up with others about their struggles. Here's a list of some of their responses:

- I no longer have anything to hide. It is amazing how freeing it is to no longer have to lie. I would make up a lie to cover up my other lies. Now I can just be honest and be myself. It is so nice.

- I discovered that I wasn't the only one who struggled to stop sexually acting out. It was nice to hear others share their struggles and how they were dealing with them.

- I wish I would have told someone earlier. I realized how destructive my thinking was and how critical I was of myself. I didn't see how mean I was being to myself until someone pointed it out. Having a peer tell me that they used to do that, too, and that they no longer talk to themselves that way was big for me. I respected him, and to have him tell me he used to think that way, too, was helpful.

- My religious leader responded with loving care. He offered me support in ways that I didn't think he would. I thought he would be upset and judgmental with me; instead, he gave me things to read and study and suggested I reach out for additional support. He also recommended me to your group. Now, I feel like I have the support I need to succeed.

In an effort to best illustrate the role of opening up to others in the recovery process, I sat down with a man working on his recovery to discuss how opening up to others changed his life. In the interview, we discussed how he used accountability to a support group and his sponsor to help in his recovery. You can see the interview and a presentation I did on the role of accountability in recovery by visiting the resources page (1)

Learning to be vulnerable in your recovery process may be the single most crucial skill you will develop as you heal. It will entail learning to be open and honest with yourself and others about the battle you have been fighting. It will also require deep self-exploration. For most people, the idea of opening up and being vulnerable in these ways is challenging.

I have observed over my years as a therapist that most of my clients long to stop the sexual behaviors that are hurting themselves and others. In many cases, they have hidden behaviors that they are terrified to share with others. They have resisted telling anyone about the tens of thousands of dollars that they have spent on prostitutes, the multiple affairs they have had throughout their marriage, or the countless hours they have spent viewing pornography.

Many will tell me that the reason they hide their behaviors was that they wanted to protect others from being hurt or that they were afraid of how others would respond. Sometimes, they have said something like, "I believed that if I let others know about my struggles, they would reject me like everyone else who has been in my life." Finally, others have said, "If others knew what I was like, they wouldn't want to be around me."

By the time most people come to see me, their sexual secrets are out of the bag. In most cases, they have been discovered or have voluntarily come forward. However, the discovery of hidden sexual behaviors or a single confession by itself usually does not change the underlying addictive behaviors and inherent cravings that often come after discovery. It is common for those who have been caught to initially downplay how involved they have been in their sexual activities. For example, in my personal research with more than 2000 individuals who have been betrayed, over 80% indicate that their partner only told them part of what was going on (2).

My goal in writing this chapter is to help you to discover the healing power of being rigorously honest. We will be discussing how to do a thorough self-evaluation, how you can prepare to share your story with others (this is called a disclosure), and how to utilize others to aid in your journey toward recovery. However, before we discuss these things, let me share why learning to open up and be vulnerable with others and honest with yourself matters.

Why Vulnerability Matters

As humans, we want to be accepted by others. We long to be a part of the group; we want to be enough. However, when we self-determine that our actions will be unacceptable to others, or if others have told us that what we are doing is wrong, we naturally pull back from them and others. Then, each time we engage in the same behaviors that we or others determine was wrong; we isolate ourselves even further because we know that what we have done doesn't fit into the norms. When this happens consistently, the most common outcome is shame, i.e., the feeling that I don't belong.

When we are shamed by others and/or ashamed as a result of our own behaviors, we want to hide so we can't be seen. This is how shame changes our life. We begin putting up walls, which prevent others from genuinely getting to know us. Over time, shame prevents others from connecting with us on a deeper level. The longer we stay in this mindset, the lonelier and more isolated we become. Note that issues of loneliness (Chapter Eight) and shame (Chapter Nine) are addressed later in this book.

In contrast with experiencing unresolved shame and suffering in silence, when individuals learn to open up and share their experiences, e.g., the examples given earlier in this chapter, individuals discover the power of being vulnerable, they learn that they belong, that others have similar challenges, and that they are not alone. When this happens, they begin to feel a connection with others. This is one of the reasons that attending a 12-step group or other educational group is a recommended treatment strategy for overcoming addictions (3).

Opening up to others may be difficult. Over the years, I have sat with many clients who struggled with the idea of sharing their sexual actions with others. Many have already been hurt by others responses or let down by those who they wish would have helped them. I know it will be hard opening up, but please consider that this is one of the most consistently effective actions people can take in their journey toward recovery (4). Simply said, those who are most likely to succeed in their recovery efforts are those who learn to reach out and share their struggles with others.

I recommend that you take the time to practice the exercises listed in each part below. These exercises have been designed to help you practice being vulnerable in ways that can change your life forever.

Be Vulnerable with Yourself

It is hard to admit to yourself and others that your sexual behaviors have escalated to the point that you have a problem. However, even though admitting you need help is hard, you are still reading this book. This tells me that you want help. I applaud you for being willing to learn and gain more knowledge. Even if you find that recovery is difficult, as you continue to learn and add to your recovery capital, each deposit will help in your long-term recovery efforts.

As I have watched individuals succeed in stopping their unwanted sexual behaviors, I have observed that those who do an honest self-evaluation have the most success. In the AA Big Book, the term used for this idea is "rigorous honesty" (5). "Rigorous honesty means telling the truth when it's easier to lie and sharing thoughts and feelings even when there may be consequences. In 12-step recovery, the requirement is taking a fearless personal inventory and promptly admitting to dishonesty. This means catching oneself in the middle of a lie and correcting it, even if it's embarrassing" (6). This type of honesty will require you to take inventory of your life and do a thorough evaluation. This process is not meant to make you feel ashamed; instead, it is designed to help you come clean, even with yourself.

"This self-confession can be understood as an emptying to make room for something better. That is, if we are willing to give up supposed innocence and self-defense, if we are willing to take stock of ourselves honestly and then (though this is neither easy nor quick) change how we live our lives" (7). This type of self-examination means that we need to slow down to think about where we are in life and what is happening to us.

I have observed that many of my clients have a hard time slowing down enough to listen to their inner voice. I have often heard clients say, "I cannot stand silence. I need something going on at all times." It is difficult to be honest with yourself when you don't take the time to listen to yourself. Even if you periodically slow down so that you can honestly look at your life, you will find that you can learn a lot about yourself and the life you are living on autopilot.

As you begin to listen to your voice, you will likely encounter a voice of shame (i.e., if people knew what I was really like, they wouldn't want to be with me). In Chapter Nine, I will discuss how to address shame, but for now, please know that your voice of shame will likely come up each time you attempt to evaluate your life. As you begin to recognize your internal voice of shame, you might consider giving it a name (e.g., there's dunderhead). By bringing out your truths, your shame will lose its power over you. Shame runs from the truth.

One of the most difficult tasks in the recovery journey is to identify as much of your sexual history as possible. This is what I refer to as a fact-finding mission. I am inviting you to just focus on the facts. You will want to start at your first sexual experience and then address all subsequent behaviors that you have engaged in. If you are familiar with the 12-step model, this may feel a lot like step four. In the AA Big Book, this step reads, "Make a searching and fearless moral inventory of ourselves." In the assignment below, you will be asked a few more specific questions about your sexual history.

Assignment

Take the time to answer each of these questions the best you can.

1. Make a sexual history timeline (see Appendix D for an example). Begin with your first sexual experience. Then, methodically move through your personal history. For example, if your first sexual experience was at age five playing doctor with a neighbor, start there. Then, ask yourself, "What happened next?" This will be followed by "Then what happened?"

2. As you identify each experience, list any resentments you've had about the experience. Are there people you are angry at because of those experiences? If so, how have those resentments continued to influence your life?

3. What are some of the ways that your sexual history has influenced your life?

4. How have my secrets influenced how I felt about myself and others?

5. What was it like for me to hold my secrets inside and not talk about them?

If you are in a 12-step program, you may have already done some of this assignment. I still encourage you to read each question, write your response, and then write down what you learned in doing this assignment.

As you do an honest search inside yourself, you will discover the thoughts and emotions that you haven't felt in a long time. There will be a persistent voice of shame, but if you listen carefully, you will also see the part of you that is finally recognizing the truth of what has been happening in your life. You are bringing the toxic darkness that has been in you out into the light. In the light, the darkness will fade, and you will find more peace and contentment. I often say that disclosing the truth is like throwing up. In most cases, after throwing up, people feel relieved to have what has made them sick out of their bodies.

Rigorous honesty will be hard, but, in not holding back, the truth of what your battle has really been like will be freeing. I have noticed that my clients report a significant sense of relief when they finally unload the burden of their secrets. Many also report that they have been longing to be open because the emotional toll has been so heavy.

Deep within every human heart is the desire to be good (8). As you seek a deeper understanding of yourself, you will be looking into the mirror. This is how you will be vulnerable with yourself. This is how you will see the real you—not the self you have been running from but the self that has been suffering in silence. When this happens, and you have compassion on yourself (self-compassion), you will eventually be able to look in the mirror without judgment and say, "I see you."

Now that we have discussed ideas for how you can be vulnerable with yourself, it is important to also look outside yourself. It has been said, "It isn't enough to be honest with oneself (Step 1), but addicts must also be honest with their higher power and other people (Steps 4 and 5), including family, health care providers, therapists, peers in a 12-step group, and so on" (9). Let's now turn our attention to the next courageous step to take.

Be Vulnerable with Others

There was no way that John wanted to attend a group. When I first introduced the idea to him, he said, "I will do just about anything else you ask me, but I don't want to go to a group." When I asked him why, he gave me the usual concerns I hear when I encourage my clients to consider attending group. His concerns were that he would see someone he knew there and that he didn't have time.

Other concerns I hear include:

- I will feel out of place

- I can't possibly talk about what I have done with strangers

- I'm too anxious

These are all valid concerns. My typical response to clients in this situation is this: "The recovery process will be filled with many things that you don't want to do." The question I then pose to my clients is this: "What price are you willing to pay to heal and recover?" Learning to be vulnerable with others is not easy, learning to admit that you have a problem is not easy; dealing with your addiction is not easy. In other words, there is no easy path. What we do know is that those who succeed have chosen to open up and pay the price. If you, too, follow the path of doing an honest self-evaluation and then learn to open up to others, you will soon reap the rewards.

In this section on being vulnerable with others, we are going to discuss three possible options you can use when it comes to being vulnerable. These options include: 1) attend a group (educational or 12-step group or both); 2) find a sponsor; and 3) reach out to a friend, family member, and/or religious leader.

Attend and Participate in a Group

In one of my online surveys, I asked individuals about their group attendance during the past year. I was surprised to learn that only 10% had participated in a group, and only 8% had enlisted a sponsor to aid in their recovery. These numbers surprised me because the research on effective outcomes from drug and alcohol rehab found that 12-step involvement was one of the primary indicators of what people who had sustained recovery were doing (10). It was also interesting to note that it wasn't just attending a 12-step group that led to a positive outcome. It was participation in the 12-step activities, which include:

- Having a sponsor

- Considering oneself a member of AA, NA, or CA

- Having a home group

- Working the steps

- Doing service

- Having contact with 12-step members outside of meetings; reading 12-step or recovery literature outside of meetings, and

- Socializing with 12-step members outside of meetings (11)

One of the most consistent findings in the literature on how individuals can increase their chances of succeeding in recovery points back to each of the bullet points above. In an effort to understanding the value of group attendance, for example, I interviewed someone who is close to my family. He is a recovering alcoholic, and his story illustrates the power of group participation.

In our discussion, I asked him what made him decide to get involved in a group. He told me that his wife had left him for another man. Over the next few months, he found himself inebriated nearly every day. One morning, his adult daughter, who was living with him, came into the front room, where he had passed out from the night before, and opened the curtains. He said, "What are you doing?" She replied, "Dad, today, I am going to take you to a 30-day treatment program to get you sober."

He agreed to go. Over the next 30 days, he started attending his first 12-step group. They became his support and helped him remain sober, essentially saving his life. Today, over 30 years later, he still visits his home group periodically and talks with his sponsor, who he has maintained throughout his 30 years of recovery. This might make it seem simple, but it hasn't been. During the past 30 years, he has had many setbacks. He lost two wives who died from health complications. In both cases, he'd been a primary caregiver. Taking care of them took a toll on him, as he felt a tremendous loss with their passing. I asked him how he dealt with their losses. He reported that his group, his sponsor, and his family helped him through the difficult times.

Find a Sponsor

In my discussion with my family friend, I asked him about the role his sponsor had in his recovery process. I asked him how often they talked. He said, "Over the years, it has varied. In the beginning, it was almost daily." As he has maintained sobriety, it has tailed off to about two times a month, sometimes longer. Imagine the power of having someone to talk to who understands what you are going through and knowing that that person will be there when you need him/her the most. This is the role of a sponsor.

Many have asked me what they should talk to their sponsor about. My answer will usually vary, depending on where the individual is in the recovery process. I have found that there are some things are always important to report, i.e. any slips or relapses. Ideally, the sponsor is someone you could call before a relapse for additional support. Sponsors can also hold you accountable for dailies that you are working on (e.g., working your steps, attending a meeting, reading a book on recovery, being productive at work, etc.). A sponsor can be many things (e.g., someone who holds your feet to the fire when you are struggling, someone to lift you up when you feel down or hopeless, someone who you report to daily). A good sponsor can save you from yourself when your mind can't fight the battle alone.

An Accountability Team (Building Your "A" Team)

After discussing the importance of having a team of people to support their recovery, one of my groups decided that it was going to hold one another accountable and support one another when times were difficult. The members shared contact information, and one of the group members created a private group using an app. They affectionately called themselves the "A" Team. As I watched the group throughout our time together, I observed an increase in their bonding. They had started to develop trust in one another. They supported each other when times were hard. Often, if one was struggling, another offered support. After observing them for a few months, I discovered the power of group in a way that I had never seen before, i.e., they were developing meaningful connections one with another.

If you currently do not have a team of people to support you, that is okay for now. I am going to invite you to consider how you can build up your team. Here are a few ideas that I have found to be most effective for my clients and others I have watched through their journey to recovery.

1. Attend a group and reach out to one another during the week (e.g., go to lunch together)

2. Make a list of friends, religious leaders, or family members you can reach out to when you are having a difficult time with cravings or during other stressful times. Identify which people you will call first, second, and so on. You can give them a list of questions to ask you. Let them know that, periodically, you may be reaching out for support and have them ask you specific questions (e.g., Can you identify your trigger? Do you have a plan to avoid relapsing that you can use right now? Can you talk me through what you are feeling and thinking? Can you commit right now that you will not relapse?).

3. Share your struggles with a co-worker who can help you be accountable (e.g., if you go on business trips together, ask that co-worker to help you be strong by asking you how you are doing).

Building your "A" team may take time, but as it grows and you have extra support, you will find that these people become much more than a team to be accountable to: they become some of your best friends.

Being Vulnerable with Your Spouse (Preparing for a Full Disclosure)

There may be nothing more difficult than sharing your sexual misdeeds with your spouse. In the therapy world, revealing an affair or other sexual activity out-side of the relationship is referred to as "disclosure." Regarding this, Drs. Deborah Corley and Jennifer Schneider wrote in their book Disclosing Secrets: "It is safe to say that all revelations are painful for everyone, often initially traumatic for the partner, and hard for the couple" (12).

So, what is the value of being vulnerable if it is painful for everyone? The answer to this question is important to understand, as per Drs. Corley and Schneider: "... most partners and addicts (over 90% in our study) report they are glad the dis-closure happened" (13). The authors suggest to begin this disclosure process with preparation (in fact, the book includes a chapter that discusses how to do a former disclosure). Here, I include some of the ideas for the disclosure process, along with additional ideas that are taught to therapists who train to become certified sexual addiction therapists (CSATs); these ideas are designed to help you learn about this process. I have also included additional steps that couples can take to aid in the recovery process. These steps go beyond the initial formal disclosure by including an impact letter (read by the betrayed spouse after a disclosure) and an emotional restitution letter (a response to the impact letter read by the betraying partner). My friend and colleague, Dr. Stefanie Carnes, has published a book called, Courageous Love: A Couples Guide to Conquering Betrayal, that discusses this process in great detail.

Here are suggestions on how to prepare for a formal disclosure, impact letter, and emotional restitution letter.

1. Get honest with yourself: Doing a partial disclosure (meaning that you are leaving information out) can do more harm than good. A full disclosure can take a few weeks or more to prepare for. During this time, you are seeking to identify the ways that you have mislead your spouse, ways you have been upset or angry at her/him or the kids, and how your behaviors have not shown respect toward her/him.

2. Write a letter of amends: The purpose of this letter is to let your spouse know what you did and what you are going to do to stop the behavior. It can also include how you desire to repair your relationship. You can include information about how the behavior has stopped (i.e., all contact with the affair partner has ended), ways that you lied or deceived your spouse, and how you will be accountable moving forward.

3. Read the letter to a friend/therapist/religious leader: This will provide you feedback in case that something you wrote could be taken wrong or be hurt-ful to your spouse (e.g., minimizing your behavior, justifying your actions,

or shifting the responsibility onto your spouse).

4.   Write a letter as if you are going to read it to your spouse: This letter will consider the ways you have betrayed your partner. It can also include how you tricked, lied to, or manipulated your spouse while you were acting out. Corley and Schneider offer this suggestion: "My goal in this letter is to be accountable for what I have done that has hurt you and the children/ family/ business" (14).

5.   Invite your spouse to write down questions s/he has and give them to your therapist to review: This will allow your spouse to have questions answered that you may not have thought about. Also, if they are asking for too much detail, your therapist can counsel you on how to respond. In a best-case scenario, your spouse will also have a therapist to help negotiate which questions may be appropriate and which ones may be asking for too much detail.

6.   Arrange a time with your therapist, religious leader, or sponsor to read the letter: Usually, this process should not be rushed. When I schedule a disclosure with a couple, I plan for the session to run at least 90 minutes.

7.   Mentally prepare for a difficult conversation: A formal disclosure will be one of the most challenging and yet helpful parts of the healing and recovery process for you and your spouse. Therefore, you will need to be prepared for a wide range of emotions, additional questions, perhaps anger, and yelling. This is why it is essential to prepare with a therapist or someone else who can help you remain calm. One way to prepare is to increase the empathy you feel for your spouse. Remember he/she is hurting deeply; further, at this time, you will be telling your spouse about things that you have done to betray the trust in your relationship.

8.   Make sure your spouse has support available to him/her: Usually, it is best if the betrayed partner has support during a formal disclosure. If your therapist, sponsor, or religious leader is there for support, it will be important that your spouse has support, too. The process of doing a formal disclosure can be traumatizing; therefore, it is essential that this suggestion not be overlooked. (Note: if there is elevated trauma in your spouse, then having a professional therapist available may be essential to help her/him negotiate the painful emotions.)

9.   Read the letter to your spouse: This is the moment that you have been working toward. It is your opportunity to come completely clean. You no longer have to hide behaviors from your past. You have prepared, done a thorough self-evaluation, and are seeking to make amends for the hurt and pain you

have created through your actions.

10. Allow your spouse to ask questions: Often, spouses will ask questions to clarify something you have said. They will be trying to make sense of what you have just told them. I have found that some partners have lots of questions, while others do not. Some are completely surprised and in shock and as a result they do not know what questions to ask. Others begin trying to put timelines together; often, they are asking about who and where these things happened. It is usually this time of the disclosure that it is best to have professional guidance, as emotions can get tense between the two of you. Be careful not to avoid your spouse's questions. Instead, listen carefully and respond honestly. If you don't remember the answer to his/her question, let your spouse know that you will think about his/her questions and will get back to them.

11. Prepare for post-disclosure time apart: After doing a disclosure, it is usually best to have separate cars, so you will avoid continuing the conversation while driving. You and your spouse may agree to sleep in different locations or a different bed that night and perhaps longer. Usually, it is best to let the betrayed spouse make these decisions. Sometimes he/she will want to sleep in the same home; other times, he/she will want time to think.

12. Invite your spouse to write an impact letter: An impact letter is designed to allow your spouse to share with you how your actions have influenced her/him over the years. It gives them the opportunity to respond to your formal disclosure letter. This is an invitation for you to listen to your spouse and genuinely understand their pain. This, too, should be done with professional support or with the support of someone who can help you negotiate the difficult emotions that often come up.

13. Prepare and write an emotional restitution letter: This letter is a response to the impact letter and is to continue your effort to make amends. It may include acknowledgment of the betrayal and how it has impacted your partner. When done properly, in this letter, you can acknowledge to your spouse the ways that you "gaslighted" them, which refers to the ways that you lied, deceived, and manipulated your spouse while you were acting out. I often tell my clients that they are giving the playbook to their partner for how they used deception and lies to cover up their behavior. This step may be one of the most critical steps you can take as you attempt to repair your relationship. (For a full explanation on why this is so important, you can watch my free video Gaslighting No More at Treating Sexual Addiction Support Class: Chapter Six. The website link is: https://bit.ly/treating-sex-addiction.

Authors note: If you have already done a disclosure without support, or if it was a partial disclosure, meaning you withheld information, I would recommend that you seek professional help from a Certified Sexual Addiction Therapist who is qualified and do a formal disclosure.

The process outlined above has been proven to be one of the most effective things you can do to begin the healing process after sexual betrayal. Multiple researchers have revealed the power in disclosure — for example, Drs. Corley and Schneider found that "most couples did not split up after disclosure," which led them to think that the couples who had acknowledged the secrets had a better chance of saving the relationship than those who had not (15). Dr. Peggy Vaughn, in her research with more than 1000 couples where infidelity had occurred, discovered that couples who discussed the details of the affair were much more likely to stay together than couples who did not talk about the details. In her study, 86% of couples who discussed the details were still together after an affair. In contrast, only 55% of the couples who didn't discuss the details of the affair were still together (16).

As I have discussed the process of doing a disclosure with my clients, some have asked me if there are times when I do not recommend doing a disclosure. There are times when a formal disclosure is not recommended. The first is when there is a pending divorce. The second is when the trauma in the betrayed partner is significantly elevated, and he/she does not have support. The third is when the betraying partner is not prepared to do a full disclosure and/or is still engaging in the sexual behavior. Other than these three situations, I have found that, with adequate preparation, a formal disclosure can be one of the most effective ways that couples begin repairing their relationship.

Chapter Summary

By learning to be vulnerable with yourself, others, and your spouse, you can make significant progress in your recovery. As you do a thorough self-examination, you are learning the skill of being rigorously honest. This is a foundational step in personal healing and recovery. Next, as you learn to reach out to others by participating in a group, you are doing what successful people do. Also, by finding a sponsor, you are taking an important step to help you succeed. Then, as you develop an accountability team, you will find that you are not alone. Finally, as you open up to your spouse and do a formal disclosure, you will be taking a step that has helped many other couples stay together to work through their challenges.

Chapter Seven

Compassion: The Secret of Successful Recovery

Self-compassion is the foundation of compassion for others
(Dr. Christopher Germer)

If you want to have the best opportunity to succeed in your recovery, you will need to develop self-compassion. I don't believe recovery comes without increasing your level of compassion for self and others. Regarding this idea, Dr. Christopher Germer wrote, "Change comes naturally when we open ourselves to emotional pain with uncommon kindness. Instead of blaming, criticizing, and trying to fix ourselves (or someone else or the whole world) when things go wrong and we feel bad, we can begin with self-acceptance. Compassion first! This simple shift can make a tremendous difference in your life" (1).

As I sat with a group of eight men, most of whom had struggled with sexual compulsivity since they were young, I felt their fears and anxieties. This was our first week together, and they didn't know what to expect. They were beginning an 18-month journey together. As I often do in situations like this, I had them introduce themselves, share where they were from, and then share with the group one or two things that they were hoping to achieve by attending this group. In their responses, I could hear and sense their concerns. Most of them had been trying to stop their unwanted sexual behaviors for years but hadn't been able to succeed. One man said, "I want to stop my sexual behaviors. I need to get this under control or I am going to lose my wife." Another indicated that he had been attending a 12-step group and had been going to therapy, none of which had worked for him. A third group member said, "I need more tools and ideas so I can respond more effectively when I'm feeling stressed." Each participant made it clear they wanted help.

In a group like this, I have three primary goals for the first session: 1) Help each group member feel safe; I want them to feel like they belong; 2) Help them to understand their own suffering. Many have been fighting their unwanted sexual behaviors for years and long to feel more in control of their lives. Still, because they haven't been able to stop their unwanted sexual behaviors, during that whole time, most of them have been mentally berating themselves. Their internal dialogue, in other words, the way they speak to themselves, has become so negative towards self- that they have struggled to find sustained happiness.

My third goal is to give them direction and hope that healing and recovery are possible. I have watched many of my clients overcome their challenges and reclaim their lives. It doesn't mean that they have been perfect in their journey to recovery, but they have built the skills and have the necessary resources in the event of slipping back toward out-of-control sexual behaviors.

In an effort to start addressing their shame, I will usually say something like this in the first session: "I know that you have likely been suffering from significant shame. I know this because I have been doing therapy for 25 years, and I have never met someone whose life feels like it is out of control tell me that genuinely love themself." As we discuss this idea, I ask them that, if I could be in their head for 24 hours and listen to their every thought and feel their every emotion, what would I hear? What would I feel? Often, they say something like, "You wouldn't want to be inside my head." When I ask why, they share some of the ways that they speak to themselves, e.g., "You are so stupid," or "Nobody is going to want you," or "You are never going to get over this." This is when I tell them that that is the voice of shame. I continue by telling them that we are going to deal directly with this voice; as long as that voice is playing in their mind, their journey to recovery will be nearly impossible. In other words, you can't mentally beat yourself up and expect to succeed.

This is what I call a compassionate approach to addiction recovery. This approach is gaining momentum because addiction recovery is not just about stopping your behaviors. It includes developing a mindset that includes self-compassion. According to Dr. Germer: "Compassion-focused therapy was designed for people who suffer from high levels of shame and self-criticism because developing compassion for ourselves and for others is one of the biggest antidotes to shame" (2). If you are like most of the clients I have worked with, increasing your self-compassion will significantly help you to address toxic levels of shame.

The Process of Developing Self-Compassion

In the early stages of recovery, most of my clients have exhibited little self-compassion. They have become so accustomed to negative self-talk that they hardly recognize it. I let them know that in our work together, one of the most important things we will need to work on is the development of self-compassion. In my research, I have found that many of them struggle to like themselves. For example, in a survey, I asked participants (n = 1420) to respond to this item: I feel like I am a bad person when I view pornography. Over 75% reported that sometimes, frequently, or almost always, they felt like they were bad after viewing pornography (3).

In the beginning stage of recovery, many of my clients feel so much shame that it is difficult for them to do a thorough self-evaluation. It is hard for them to slow down because, when things are quiet in their mind, they can't sit with their own thoughts and feelings. One man told me, "I hate it when I don't have anything to do because then I have to be with myself." For him, like many others, his shame was so profound that, if he paused to reflect on his behavior, he wouldn't know how to deal with his own emotions or the hurt and pain he had created in others. This is one of the reasons that many people say that the first steps toward recovery are so difficult. When you can't be with your thoughts and emotions, it is easy to numb out or return to unhealthy habits.

Because I understand that many of the people who come to see me struggle to pause and reflect upon their life and their actions in the beginning phase of recovery, I will share with them a story I read by Rory Vaden. Rory grew up on the plains of Colorado, where he observed that cows and buffalos share the same land. He noted that, when storms come over the mountains, it was always interesting to see how these two animals responded. He wrote, "When storms come, they almost always brew from the west and roll out toward the east. What cows do is very natural. Cows sense the storm coming from the west, and so they start to try to run toward the east. The only problem with that is that if you know anything about cows you know they aren't very fast. So, the storm catches up with the cows rather quickly. And without knowing any better the cows continue to try to outrun the storm. But, instead of outrunning the storm, they actually run right along with the storm. Maximizing the amount of pain and time and frustration they experience from that storm!" (4)

In contrast, he observed that the buffaloes respond quite differently when the storm comes. Regarding the buffaloes' response, he wrote, "What buffalo do on the other hand is very unique for the animal kingdom. Buffalo wait for the storm to cross right over the crest of the peak of the mountaintop, and, as the storm rolls over the ridge, the buffalo turn and charge directly into the storm. Instead of running east away from the storm, they run west directly at the storm. By running at the storm, they run straight through it. Minimizing the amount of pain and time and frustration they experience from that storm" (5).

My hope in sharing this story with my clients is that they will learn that, by running from their challenges, they will only expose themselves to the storms of life for a more extended time. As we discuss, and as they evaluate how they have been running, they begin to see the many ways they have been avoiding their own emotions (e.g., turning to sex when stressed, after a fight with their wife justifying their sexual chats with others online or viewing pornography rather than dealing with a financial problem).

As we discuss the cow and buffalo story, some clients will ask me how they can learn to be like the buffalo. First, I let them know that giving up a primary coping mechanism (e.g., their unwanted sexual behaviors), while simultaneously looking at how their behaviors have altered their life and the lives of others, will not be easy. In looking and observing, however, they are "buffaloing up." Second, I let them know that successful people are those who learn from their past and intentionally learn to move forward without shame. They replace shame with compassion for self and for others.

This is when I usually emphasize that increasing self-compassion is more of a process. I have found that individuals often start the recovery process with elevated shame and gradually shift toward a more compassionate approach as they recover from addiction. Rarely do individuals just change to a completely self-compassionate approach. In most cases, my clients gradually begin to let go of their shame and turn toward a self-compassionate approach.

One way to look at this experience is to see self-compassion as if it were on a continuum. In the beginning, many of my clients' self-compassion scores are low. As they learn more about their own story, they see how their interaction with their family has played into their behaviors; they also often discover that addictions have run for generations of time in their family; further, they discover when they bought into the idea that there was something wrong with them. After increasing their awareness, learning, and applying the skills outlined in this chapter, they develop a deeper sense of loving-kindness for themselves and then for others.

Chart #1

Early Recovery   Later Recovery

No Self-Compassion   Self-Compassion

|—————————————————————————————————|

Buffaloing Up

Are you ready to buffalo up? Maybe you already are and have been. Either way, the journey to sustained recovery is to turn and face the storms that life is presenting. I have watched many individuals who have felt helpless face the storm instead of turning away from it and attempting to outrun it.

Here's a story of a client who learned how to buffalo up.

Jonathan had a lot going for him. He had a wonderful wife and three children. He had a good-paying job, although it was stressful. His boss gave him nearly impossible deadlines, expecting him to finish them at all costs. Initially, he felt like his boss trusted him, but those feelings changed when he was being asked to do more and more with little compensation or appreciation for what he was doing.

Jonathan didn't have good coping skills for high stress. He had started staying at work to finish his projects and coming home later. His wife asked that he try to come home at least a couple of nights a week to spend time with her and the kids. When he didn't do this, they began arguing and fighting more frequently.

He started coming home later; instead of working on the projects that were due, he viewed pornography and began visiting Craig's list to look for ads of women looking for a companion. He sent a few messages to women, but never actually met up with them.

One day, about a year before I met him, he got home later than usual and stayed up late. The next morning, he and his wife got into a big argument. Then his boss gave him another project, with another impossible deadline. That evening, he went onto Craig's list and sent a message to a woman. He met her and ended up crossing his self-imposed sexual boundaries, i.e., he had sex with a random person. Shocked by his behavior, he attempted to push away what he had done and ignore it.

Over the next few months, even though he knew he didn't want to do that again, when times were stressful, he would stay at work, watch pornography, and look on Craig's List. Eventually, he gave in and met with two other women. On his third hookup, he found himself having sex with someone to whom he wasn't attracted. It was then that he realized he needed to get help. It became a turning point for him.

Over the next few months, he battled with the idea of telling his wife. She had asked him multiple times if something was wrong. Each time, he would say to her that work was stressful and that she needed just to support him. Finally, one evening when she was upset that he had come home late, he told her he had been cheating. In a state of shock, she yelled at him, called him all kinds of names, and told him to get out.

He spent the next few weeks at his sister's house. This was when Jonathan contacted my office and set up his initial appointment. During our first session, it was clear Jonathan was still in shock by what was happening. He said, "How could I have done something so stupid? I have risked everything that matters to me—and for what?" He was feeling lost and helpless. He didn't know if his wife was going to give him a chance or if they were going to divorce. I could feel his despair.

As a therapist, this is one of the more difficult times I have with a client. He/she may be losing everything that matters. The client feels shame because his/her actions have created relationship problems. Usually, in situations like this, I simply ask my clients to hold on and do what others do to reclaim their life. I let Jonathan know that it would be important to trust the process. I explained that I would ask him to take difficult steps, but that he could succeed if he took them.

He agreed but also openly questioned if he really could stop his sexually acting-out behaviors. He opened up that he had secretly viewed pornography for years without his wife knowing. As we explored his whole sexual history timeline, he opened up about a long history of porn use, a few sexual encounters with girls in high school, and a few random hookups in college. For some people, these behaviors may seem normal, but for Jonathan, he reported that he felt out of control. He indicated that, some days, especially when he was stressed that he would escape into pornography or fantasizing about some of the sexual things he had done. He felt a lot of shame about his behaviors. He wanted to stop. He wanted to be better. He wanted to save his family. He was torn between feeling a sense of hope and tremendous shame.

He was ready to wake up.

I let him know that if he engaged in the work of recovery, he could change. I told him what I tell all of my clients: Change is not optional. At this point, your life is going to change whether you want it to or not. If you work toward recovery, you will change for the better. You will begin to think better thoughts, learn how to deal with difficult emotions, and act in ways that you haven't in the past. He wanted to change, as evident by the questions he asked about the recovery process. He wanted to know what others have done to succeed. He was reading books on his own and watching videos from my website, Path for Men, which provides support to individuals dealing with sex addiction.

We talked about his level of cravings in our first few sessions. He soon reported that he had had none since he told his wife what he had done, i.e., he had a lot to lose if he acted out again. I often say that the initial disclosure is like having a cold bucket of ice water thrown on you. For many, this is a wake-up call that they need.

Over the next few sessions, we developed a treatment plan that included many of the elements outlined in this book. He began transitioning out of high levels of shame as he began working on the items in his treatment plan. Here are some of the highlights and insights he gained as he took the necessary steps that helped him shift out of shame and toward more self-compassion:

1. A family relationship timeline

Jonathan asked his mom about addictions in their family. She indicated that, on both sides of their family, addictions were common. His dad's dad was an alcoholic. His mom's grandpa had had multiple affairs. She also told him that his dad, who died when he was in junior high, had also cheated on her. He hadn't known that before. He began seeing how he had a family history of addiction. For the first time, he realized that his family members had similar issues. This also helped him feel less shame. Unfortunately, his family had not talked about these things. He wanted to change all of that and make things better for his children and grandchildren.

2. Personal sexual history timeline

As Jonathan worked through his sexual timeline, he realized how early exposure to pornography had influenced him from middle school on into his adulthood. He had hidden his pornography use from his parents and had viewed three to five times a week, sometimes more during high school. He realized that this influenced his subsequent sexual encounters and what he wanted to do with the girls he watched in the porn videos. One sexual experience stood out to him. When he was 15 years old, an older high school girl showed interest in him. For a few months, they were very sexual, and he thought he was special because an older girl took an interest in him. After a few months, she broke up with him. He was heartbroken, and she didn't seem to care. He believed that that experience triggered him into fantasy about meeting someone who would want him. This helped him to understand his Craig's List encounters better. Even though he was married, when he and his wife were emotionally distant from each other, he was looking for others' validation. As he began to understand his own story, his awareness helped him to identify the roots of his sexual behaviors. This knowledge enabled him to understand himself better as well as reduce some of his shame. His self-awareness helped him to develop more compassion for himself and others.

3. Return to his original belief system

I often tell my clients that our beliefs are like a computer's operating system, i.e., they control how we function. When we have negative self-beliefs (e.g., I am unlovable, if people knew what I was really like, they wouldn't want to be around me), we have a virus in our operating system. Jonathan needed to change this system. He hadn't realized how much negative self-talk had been running through his mind. By learning how to alter negative beliefs and return to his original belief system, he made significant progress. So, what exactly was his original belief system? I believe that each of us are born with high self-worth, and, early in our life, we know we are good. It is only through life's experiences that we begin to question our worth and value. This idea made a lot of sense to Jonathan; I hope that you, too, understand it. Healing happens when you know your worth. This is the compassionate approach to healing.

Below, you will find that each of the skills Jonathan developed helped him to increase his recovery capital, and simultaneously they helped increase his sense of confidence and self-compassion.

4. Adding to his recovery capital

One awareness that Jonathan gained from completing the Sexual Addiction Recovery Capital Scale (SARCS) was in an area he needed to improve upon. He needed to add support to his recovery plan. He also needed to improve his personal habits (e.g., eating better, improve sleeping patterns, which would also help his relationship with his wife), and he wanted to get more involved in his community. (See Chapter Two for a review of the SARCS.) As Jonathan added to his recovery capital, his confidence and self-compassion continued to grow.

5. Emotional Regulation

Jonathan also needed to develop the ability to deal with difficult emotions. He often found, when he was feeling disconnected from his wife or when his boss pressured him to meet a deadline, he would find himself seeking sexual comfort. He learned to apply the skills taught in Chapter 10, which provides ideas and exercises that will help regulate difficult emotions. In particular, Jonathan learned to observe his emotions and thoughts rather than ignore them. As he learned, he developed better awareness of when he was vulnerable. At those times, he learned to reach out to his sponsor or accountability for support. He also learned to attend to his own emotions, so that when he was stressed, he could do something to help himself (i.e., breathing exercises, use the COAL approach as outlined in Chapter 10). I have found that, as clients develop their skills in emotional regulation, they simultaneously increase their level of self-compassion.

6. Letting go of shame

Some of the best work that Jonathan did was related to his work with shame. He realized that he had been carrying shame with him since he had his first sexual experiences. Eventually, he developed compassion for the younger version of himself.

He saw the boy not understanding what was happening. He saw how that boy grew up without fully understanding what those sexual experiences had done to him. He practiced doing mindful meditations, and he created his own self-compassion mantra (i.e., I am good, I am kind, I can do hard things). We also did some EMDR around some of his early sexual experiences (see Chapter Nine to learn more about how to let go of shame).

7. Attend a group

Jonathan was initially hesitant to go to a group, but, after his first session, he felt hope. He realized that others were struggling just like him. He discovered that he wasn't alone; that others were struggling with similar fantasies and unwanted sexual behaviors. More importantly, he saw the power of opening up to others. As he heard their stories, he realized he had been suffering for so long by himself. He was no longer alone. As he attended the group, he began making friends. His shame again was going down by bringing his battle into the light, and his compassion for self was increasing. One particular moment was powerful. One guy asked him, "How do you feel about others in the group as they share their stories?" Jonathan replied, "I feel bad for them. They have had a really hard time." His friend in the group said, "You should treat yourself the same way." That was a game-changing experience for him. He realized he had been so negative and critical of himself.

8. Healthy habits

Jonathan struggled with eating. Because he spent long hours at work, he developed a habit of eating fast food for lunch and sometimes for dinner. He committed to eating healthier by going home earlier at least two nights a week. He also decided to bring healthier food with him to work. This simple idea helped improve his relationship with his wife and children. It also helped him to remember how important it was to spend time around the dinner table with his family. He was so lost in his addictive behaviors that he'd forgotten how important even the basic things were to him. He also started going to bed earlier. This improved his relationship with his wife, as she had been asking him for years to come to bed earlier. It also improved his overall sleep and energy so he could complete tasks at work. Jonathan also decided to exercise at least three days a week (see Chapter 11 to learn more about building better habits). Finally, Jonathan chose to work the 12-step program and read a couple of books that I had recommended, including *Self-Compassion* by Kristen Neff. I have found that when individuals engage in healthier habits, they naturally develop more self-compassion.

9. Develop more meaningful relationships

In Jonathans recovery, he realized that he needed to improve in all of his relationships. He had distanced himself from his wife and children for too long. His wife, especially, had felt alone in their relationship. He also wanted to be more involved in his children's lives. He decided to focus on spending time with each of them individually at least once a week. Sometimes, it would be watching a television show, playing a video game, or playing a sport with them (e.g., shooting baskets). He'd been putting off friends as well, as he felt guilty being around them. He began reaching out to them or to his new friends from the group for bike riding and other activities. As his relationships improved, so did his confidence in the recovery process (see Chapter 13).

10. Increase vulnerability

One of the most challenging things I asked Jonathan to do at the beginning of recovery was to share his sexual story with someone besides me. He ended up sharing his formal disclosure with me, his sponsor, and his wife. He also talked with his religious leader to begin his spiritual healing (see Chapter 6 for more on this topic).

11. Develop a plan for responding in crucial moments

One of the questions Jonathan asked early in the recovery experience was whether he could ever stop turning to sexual behaviors to cope with stress. As we discussed the content as found in Chapter Five on responding during crucial moments, Jonathan realized he needed a game plan. He liked this idea, as it gave him something to focus on during challenging moments. He responded well to having a plan.

By now, I hope you can see that developing self-compassion isn't some magical activity or event. Instead, it is a journey. If you could see Jonathan today, you would see a man who is very different than the man who sat in my office a couple of years ago. He has energy, confidence, and he knows what it takes to stay on the path to recovery. Ask him about self-compassion, and he will tell you that you won't heal without it.

There is a final point to make regarding self-compassion: As your levels increase, you will almost naturally come to see the suffering of others. This will especially be true of the ones you have hurt. This could trigger your shame, but, because you have increased your self-compassion, you will withstand the storm. You will turn and face the storm, and, as it passes, you will be grateful you learned how. The people around you will see that you are different. You are more capable of being with them in their suffering. This is the definition of compassion, i.e., the ability to be with people in their suffering. First, you learn to be with your suffering; then, you will turn to help others who are suffering because you genuinely care about them. My last chapter on loving your way to recovery will further address this process.

Chapter Summary

Self-compassion is the antidote to shame. When individuals learn to identify their voice of shame and address it, they will face the storms of life. Learning to be like a buffalo in a storm means you will face the thoughts and emotions that you haven't been willing to address. Finally, Jonathan's story demonstrates how he developed self-compassion by engaging in acts of recovery. Some of which are 1) doing a personal family inventory; 2) exploring his sexual history; 3) addressing his negative self-beliefs; 4) learning to deal with difficult emotions; and 5) implementing actions to improve on his recovery capital. Finally, as you become more self-compassionate, you will be more likely to feel compassion for others.

Part 3

How to Address the Barriers that Prevent Recovery

Chapter Eight

Addressing Loneliness: A Silent Driver of Addiction

Loneliness developed as a stimulus to get humans to pay more attention to their social connections, and to reach out toward others, to renew frayed or broken bonds.
(Dr's. John Cacioppo and William Patrick)

Early in my career, I began to observe that many of my clients spent a lot of time alone. During our conversations, in fact, I learned that many of those who were single spoke about spending weekends alone viewing pornography. At the same time, many married clients reported a different kind of loneliness. Even in their relationships, they reported feeling alone; this was especially true if they'd been caught acting out sexually by their spouse. The relationship conflict from a disclosure or being caught acting out triggered discord that they didn't know how to repair. Based on these observations, I began wondering about the role that loneliness played on my clients' sexually compulsive behaviors.

These thoughts led me to start asking more questions about the relationship between pornography usage and levels of loneliness, depression, anxiety, and stress. The results were not surprising. Individuals, regardless of being single or married, who viewed pornography three to five times a week, reported elevated levels of loneliness. They also reported higher levels of depression, anxiety, and stress than the general population. Finally, they reported lower levels of life satisfaction (1). This is when I discovered that my clients who were seeking help for sexual compulsivity also needed help dealing with other challenges like loneliness.

I realized the need for attachment and connection as discussed back in Chapter Two was once again playing a critical role in my clients who were struggling to stop sexually acting out. In many cases, their loneliness triggered a need for something soothing so that when they were feeling disconnected or alone, they would act out. However, the basic need for healthy touch, meaningful conversations, and overall connection wasn't just going to disappear. What was needed in childhood, was also needed during the adult years.

This is when it dawned on me that helping my clients address their loneliness was essential to the healing and recovery process. I began asking myself, "How can I help my clients overcome loneliness?" I believe that, as a mental health professional, I should provide the best answers and solutions to this question as I can.

In an effort to deepen my understanding on the influence of loneliness on my clients, I read Dr. John Cacioppo and William Patrick's book, *Loneliness*. In their book, they wrote, "Loneliness arises from having a deficiency in meaningful relationships, particularly attachment relationships (2). When we do not have close relationships, we naturally feel isolated and alone. Loneliness, they concluded, becomes an issue of serious concern only when it settles in long enough to create a persistent, self-reinforcing loop of negative thoughts, sensations, and behaviors (3).

Drs. Cacioppo and Patrick suggest that "Physical pain protects the individual from physical dangers. Social pain, also known as loneliness, evolved for a similar reason: because it protected the individual from the danger of remaining isolated." These authors also believe that "Loneliness developed as a stimulus to get humans to pay more attention to their social connections, and to reach out toward others, to renew frayed or broken bonds" (4).

The more I read and studied loneliness, the more I realized that I had to help address the isolation that many of my clients were experiencing. It simply isn't optional if recovery is going to happen. However, I still had questions: "What is the lasting influence of loneliness on my clients?" "What is the best way to help clients realize that addressing their loneliness is critical to their long-term success?"

As I studied the consequences of loneliness, in general, I was surprised that, as a society, we don't talk more about how unhealthy it is for us. Some of my key discoveries are as follows:

1. Loneliness is "an emotion that signals unsatisfied needs for proximity, love, and security due to the unavailability of attachment" relationships (5).

2. Loneliness is a form of separation distress that results from failure to have one's basic attachment needs fulfilled (6).

3. One study suggests that loneliness has the power to alter DNA transcription in our immune systems (7).

4. Loneliness makes us less capable of screening out distracting cultural "noise" and focusing on what is truly important. Further, these behavioral trends have a snowball effect in depriving us of self-regulation and executive control. Loneliness assaults both our self-restraint and our persistence (8).

5. It distorts cognition as well as empathy, in turn disrupting other perceptions that contribute to social regulation. These include our perceptions of the give-and-take of social synchronization, appropriately measured acts of deference and dominance, peacemaking, social sanctioning, and alliance formation (9).

In summary, as loneliness increases, it weakens one's ability to see people correctly. They begin to feel like others don't care or don't want to be around them. In worst-case-scenario thinking, they may even consider others as an enemy because they cannot accurately see or understand them.

As loneliness progresses, individuals become more vulnerable to unhealthy habits. Drs. Cacioppo and Patrick suggest that the impact of loneliness can be seen in three distinct parts.

1. Level of vulnerability to social disconnection.

Each of us has our own need for connection. Some of us have more needs due to parental influence and genetics. When our emotional needs are being met, we are typically happy and content. When our need for connection is not being met, loneliness settles in, along with unhealthy coping mechanisms.

2. Ability to self-regulate emotions associated with feeling isolated.

One of the more interesting findings on loneliness is that those who experience a higher level of it will likely have a harder time regulating his/her stress responses, which means we become more vulnerable to stress when we are feeling lonely. Drs. Cacioppo and Patrick wrote this about the role of loneliness and our ability to regulate our own emotions: "As loneliness increases and persists; it begins to disrupt some of this ability, a 'dysregulation' that, at the cellular level, leaves us more vulnerable to various stressors, and also less efficient in carrying out soothing and healing functions such as sleep" (10).

3. Mental representations and expectations of, as well as reasoning about, others.

Finally, loneliness has a dramatic impact on how we see ourselves in relationship to others. Often, in my work, I find that lonely people feel like they don't belong or that there is something wrong with them. Their mental model of relationships has been warped by their innate sense of not belonging. Unfortunately, if they had parents who were disconnected or if they experienced relationship trauma (i.e., being bullied in school), their sense of not belonging or not fitting in can be overwhelming.

How Loneliness Can Trigger Addictive and Other Unhealthy Behaviors

We learn how to approach human intimacy in our childhood. If it is not developed early, weak attachment bonds are likely to form. When healthy connections are not established in childhood, loneliness increases, and social skills are not developed. If loneliness increases and is not addressed, additional relationship problems increase, which, in turn, adds to social isolation. Over time, isolation plus unhealthy relationship patterns will trigger a person into using coping mechanisms that are often destructive. Once destructive patterns, e.g., addiction, settle in, it is common for individuals to isolate themselves from others further because they feel like others would not accept them. This isolation creates a perpetual pattern that, if not interrupted, can last for years.

I have observed that many of my clients who are starving for connection will seek out sexual experiences with anyone who will give them attention. Their loneliness is driving them into sexual experiences that are empty and meaningless. The temporary comfort doesn't solve the long-term desire for connection, but instead leaves them hungrier for a bonding relationship. Unfortunately, the longer they experience short-lived bonding without connection, their loneliness increases rather than decreases. As a result, they are being sexual, but their loneliness is still off the charts high. They discover that meaningless sexual experiences do not solve their deeper needs for bonding and connection.

Loneliness is painful for everyone. People faced with loneliness often turn to a variety of coping mechanisms because they don't feel connected. The more isolated and alone they feel, the easier it is to drink, spend, gamble, eat, turn to drugs, or act out sexually. Generally speaking, none of us respond well when we feel chronic loneliness.

I've also noted that, when individuals feel alone, they are more prone to anger or being critical of others. I believe some of this anger stems from observing others who have connections. Seeing others who are in relationships can serve as a reminder that "I'm not like others"; it can also remind them of what they don't have. In such situations, their anger is masking underlying feelings of loneliness. Thus, some individuals may experience intense anger or rage because they do not have a pack with whom to connect.

Helping individuals address their loneliness isn't easy, and there are no easy answers. I have observed that many of my clients experience tremendous amounts of shame due to their sexual behaviors. As a result, they have isolated themselves away from others. Still others grew up in an environment where they didn't see a good relationship modeled; as a result; they didn't develop the necessary relationship skills. Finally, there are many potential reasons for loneliness, e.g., being bullied, feeling rejected, witnessing abuse, and being excluded from participating in social events. When both family and social life produces pain and isolation from others, the outcome of coping in unhealthy ways makes more sense.

In many cases, the loneliness that my clients experienced stemmed from not having the knowledge and skills for how to create meaningful friendships. In other situations, my clients did not know how to solve their relationship problems. As a result, their feelings would often be hurt, or they would hurt the feelings of others.

So, what are the solutions to combating loneliness? What I have learned is described in each of the strategies listed below.

Six Strategies to Help Combat Loneliness

I have identified six strategies that have helped my clients address their feelings of loneliness. The strategies are based on principles that, if applied, will help you develop better relationship skills, which will, in turn, will help reduce loneliness.

Here are six strategies you can use to address loneliness:

Strategy #1: Unlearn unhealthy attachment patterns

As I encountered more and more clients dealing with loneliness I often asked myself, "Where is the best place to start in reducing loneliness?" In nearly every case, it began by understanding early attachment patterns. What I discovered was that when my clients resolved some of their early life traumas, then worked to improve their relationship skills, and they then began to make a significant improvement in their recovery efforts.

Regardless of how old you are, you can learn to form healthy relationships. Over my 25-year career, I have observed that some people genuinely do not know how to interact with others in a positive way. Usually, our relationship patterns are formed by what we observed in relationships growing up. Therefore, if you saw bad patterns, it will be critical for you to intentionally learn better habits and then incorporate healthy interactions into your relationships.

It is not easy to acknowledge that some of the patterns and behaviors we observed growing up were not good for us. However, some experiences hurt us in deep and profound ways, even if we don't think about them much after they happen. An example of this is the young boy in a convenience store noting a magazine with a woman on the cover. He opened up the magazine and saw naked women. His dad noticed, quickly slammed the magazine shut, and hauled him to the family car—then he proceeded to shame the boy in front of his family. While the boy later understood that his dad simply did not want him to view pornography, at that moment, the shame and embarrassment the boy felt in front of his family made him feel like he didn't belong.

Unhealthy attachment patterns typically start with these types of experiences. In recalling this memory, it brought up some painful emotions for my client (i.e., the boy), primarily about not belonging. Together, along with supportive group members, we were able to help him create a new memory of that experience.

Here's an example of how that happened. He shared the experience in a group where we were discussing first sexual experiences. After telling his story, I asked him what he wished his dad would have said and done. He said, "I wish my dad would have asked me to put the magazine away and then walked me outside the convenience store and talked with me about what it was I was viewing and how it could make me feel. I wish he would have, in a loving way, warned me what influence it could have on my life if I wasn't careful."

After that, I asked a group member to role-play that same experience with him. The purpose of this was to help the client create a new memory to replace the old one. As the group member role-played a caring dad, he saw the experience with fresh eyes. He wasn't a bad boy, after all. He was a young boy who didn't understand what he was doing. His dad wasn't bad, either. He simply didn't know how to respond to his son's behavior in a healthy way. Unfortunately, that memory with his dad made him feel like he was terrible, and he carried that belief for more than 25 years.

Usually, when individuals realize the patterns they experienced growing up were not good, they begin to ask more questions. They see what didn't work for them, but they still don't know what to do about it. The answer I give them is to learn what does work: for example, when they grew up in a home where behaviors such as being critical, negative, or pessimistic were common. Learning to see others and treat them with dignity and respect is a good starting point. Also, listening to others more intently and caring about them helps as well.

Strategy #2: Deep Listening

Thich Nhat Hahn shared a story in his book *True Love*, which I have thought a lot about. He said, "In Plum Village, our practice place, deep listening is a very important practice. Every week we get together once or twice to practice listening deeply to each other. As we listen, we do not say anything; we breathe deeply, and we open our hearts to listen to one another. One hour of this kind of listening is very effective, and it is something very precious that can be offered to the person you love." (11) Mindful listening may be one of the most valuable skills we can bring to our relationships. In many of my cases, the suffering I have observed in my clients' relationships is related to not having anyone who listened to them. In some cases, I became the first person to hear their life story for the first time.

We can all practice deep listening. It is a skill that, as you develop, you will begin seeing people in a new and improved way. One powerful way to combat loneliness is to discover who others really are. I often give my clients assignments to work on between our sessions. In situations where my clients are lonely, I invite them to set a goal to meet somebody new, have a conversation with someone they don't know, or reach out to an old friend or acquaintance. I am always pleasantly surprised when they come to a session and report their experience.

As you read about deep listening, how does the idea of it sound to you? Does it sound like something you would want in your life? Or, are you feeling like, "I don't need that?" Your answer to my question will likely determine how you approach loneliness. In the first case, if you long for a relationship where you experience someone who is listening deeply to you, you are someone who will experience deeper pangs of loneliness when you don't have someone around you.

On the other hand, if deep listening sounds like psycho-babel, you may have built walls around yourself because of the hurt and pain you have experienced in the past. Most likely, you don't care a lot about connecting with others. This often happens because of the hurt and pain of not having those experiences earlier in your life.

Regardless of whether you long for someone to simply hear you, learning how to listen deeply to others is a skill that can improve your relationship skills and reduce your level of loneliness. Here's why deep listening matters: We all need someone; we need to feel that people care about us. When we do this for others, we elevate them. We make them feel important, like they matter. This, in turn, makes us feel better because we are genuinely helping someone else.

Here's a short assignment that may help you see the power of deep listening.

Assignment

Think of a time in your life when someone made you feel special, that you mattered. It may have been a surprise birthday party or a simple compliment, when a grandparent put you on his/her lap and read you a story, or when a teacher said you did an excellent job.

Once you have the memory in your mind, think about how you felt about yourself when you were with that person. Next, imagine that you could have a conversation with that person now. What would you want to say? Imagine that conversation and how you would feel once it was over.

I invite you to practice deep listening this week. Whether you start with a friend, a coworker, your child, or your spouse, ask that person how their life is going. They may be surprised and a bit uncomfortable in the beginning, but, as you genuinely seek understanding, you will experience a deeper awareness of who they really are and what their life is like. This is one of the more important activities that help my clients to combat their loneliness.

Strategy #3: Develop Empathy for Others

In the book, *The Art of Empathy,* author Karla McLaren wrote, "We all long to be seen and understood, to be valued and honored, and to be loved for exactly who we are" (12). In working with individuals dealing with sexual addiction, or any addiction, I have observed that many of them have not felt understood. In one case, a couple had come to see me from another state. After being with them for three days, the husband said, "This is the first time I feel like someone has taken the time to get to know me." I have found that, when my clients feel understood, they open up and share more of their deeper thoughts and emotions with me. I hear about their life challenges. When they can be vulnerable with me and share some of their most painful experiences, I know they are making progress.

Unfortunately, we live in a culture that has lost the art of seeing others. This may be one of the reasons that you have felt lonely. Our society is filled with individuals who are not seen nor understood. What is the solution? I found that Thich Nhat Hahn's writings helped me to understand one thing that our society can learn to be better at: "The most precious gift you can give to the one you love is your true presence" (13). Our presence suggests that we are aware of others' needs and concerns, their joys, and their sorrows. This is one way that we can develop empathy for others.

What is the outcome of developing empathy?

According to Karla McLaren, "Empathy helps you connect with others, feel alongside them, understand them, work with them, meet their needs, love them, and be loved by them. Empathy is essential for the health of your relationships, and empathy is fundamental to your social and emotional skills" (14). If you want to combat feelings of loneliness directly, you can do so by developing empathy.

So, what exactly is empathy, or how would we define it?

Here are a couple of definitions of empathy: "Empathy is the art of stepping imaginatively into the shoes of another person, understanding their feelings and perspectives, and using that understanding to guide your actions" (15). Karla Mc-Laren wrote, "Empathy is a social and emotional skill that helps us feel and understand the emotions, circumstances, intentions, thoughts, and needs of others, such that we can offer sensitive, perceptive, and appropriate communication and support" (16). I have observed that, when an individual has someone who cares enough about him/her to have genuine empathy for them, they heal from their wounds, their sufferings, and their addictions. Empathy is at the heart of healthy relationships.

One of the best ways you can overcome your feelings of loneliness is to develop empathy for others (I will provide additional strategies for how you can do this in Chapter Fourteen). Perhaps you may be thinking, "Why would I care how others feel when others don't care about me?" My answer is simple: If you want to be good in your relationships, the skill of empathy is critical even if others haven't given it to you.

If you weren't shown empathy growing up, it might be especially difficult for you to feel for others who are suffering because you were never given such a gift. However, you can break the chain of unhealthy patterns. You can learn to see others and help them feel understood. This is what Dr. Daniel Siegel refers to as "feeling felt." When we feel felt, we experience the gift of that person's presence.

Assignment

I invite you to think of someone close to you who is having a difficult or hard time. Then, I want you to write the answers to the following questions. Even if you don't know exactly how this person is feeling, try your best to guess what he/she is experiencing.

Think of the event or events that this person is struggling with. How do you think this person is feeling? What are some of the thoughts he/she is having? Try to feel how this person's body is responding to this experience.

What might this person believe about him or herself as a result of this experience?

Now that you have identified this person's thoughts, emotions, and beliefs, what would you want to say to them?

Now, take a minute to write about what you learned from doing this assignment.

Strategy #4: Learn to Play Again

It might seem odd to include play as a strategy to combat loneliness. However, when you were young and the most innocent, your primary task for growth was to play. Somehow, the curious and playful mind we once had gets lost in the world of responsibilities and day to day stressors. As we get older, we forget that play is good for us. By allowing yourself to play you will find that it is a powerful way to change your emotional state; it also might boost your overall health and well-being. One example of learning to play can be found in merely learning to laugh. I know this may sound crazy but hang with me here. Researchers have found that laughing can boost the immune system in cancer patients (17). Yes. Laughing can boost your immune system. This is not all. Here are some of the additional benefits of regular laughter (note the third bullet point):

- promote relaxation

- improve sleep

- strengthen social bonds

- improve overall attitude

- produce a general sense of well-being (18)

When individuals get stuck in certain emotions, e.g., depression, anxiety, and loneliness, activities that are enjoyable and playful can shift them out of an un-wanted emotional state. Daniel Hughes wrote, "Playfulness enables you to step back from the primary effect associated with an event and to experience it from a somewhat different perspective and different affective state" (19).

If you are like some of my clients, you may be thinking when I mention play that I don't understand what you are going through. You may be right: I don't know what you are feeling or what you are going through, but I do know that, by improving your thoughts through play, you will create new hormones that can begin the change process of healing that you are striving toward.

"One study found that humor led to increased pain tolerance, believed to be caused by the release of endorphins, the body's natural pain relievers. Laughter therapy even works if patients can't find anything to genuinely laugh about, as forced or fake laughter still releases endorphins. Another study found that neuro-endocrine and stress-related hormones decreased during laughter (20). A little bit of laughter can begin the rewiring process and push the pangs of loneliness away.

In addition to laughter, here are additional ways you can play (again). When most of us were young, we played all kinds of games. We played with dolls or fire trucks; we played with balls; we rode tricycles and bicycles. We also played imaginary games. At that point in our lives, play was our job. Unfortunately, as we get older, we forget how to play and focus on the harder things of life.

So, one way to play is to rewind the clock and find something that you used to love doing and do it again. Play catch with your son or daughter. Go for a bike ride. Even better, join a biking club, so you have more social interaction.

I often tell my clients that it is easy to see the cow pie (addiction). However, if we don't stop once in a while, we may think the cow pie is the only place in the pasture. It's time to turn your attention to playful activities that increase your joy and bring you more satisfaction. This is one way to push out the feelings of loneliness.

Assignment

Below is a list of ideas that can help you learn to play in healthy ways. I would encourage you to choose one of the ideas below and do it each week until you get into the habit of playing again.

- Take a class (there are many offered through community outreach programs--everything from computer skills to landscaping to woodworking to painting to ukulele--anything you may want to learn)

- Join a club (hiking, sports, book clubs, music -- these are often advertised at the library, there are also game stores that have RPG or game nights)

- Organize your own regular thing (go out to eat with your brother once a month, start a game night with old friends that you haven't seen because you're all so busy--be in charge of the gathering once a month).

Strategy #5: Learn to Let Others Help

A few years ago, one of my dear friends shared a valuable lesson with me. Her grandson was visiting her, and she could tell something was bothering him. She said, "What's wrong? He said, "I don't want to talk about it, Grandma." To this, she said, "That's okay, but know that, whenever you need to talk, I will be here. I don't even have to know what you are going through; I will be here no matter what. Call me anytime."

He said, "Okay."

A few days later came this call, "Grandma, I need your help."

"With what?" she asked.

"You know the other day, you said I could call at any time, and you wouldn't ask me what it was about?"

"Yes."

"Well, today, I just need to talk with you."

"It's tough today, huh? Do you know I am here and that I love you?"

"Yes, Grandma. Why is temptation so hard, Grandma?"

"Good question. It comes to all of us. Today, you had a lot of courage to call me. I am so proud of you."

"Thanks, Grandma. I already feel better."

This exchange between a grandma and her grandson is beautiful. The grandmother was attuned enough to him to realize something was wrong. She created the right environment, a loving environment, that welcomed his call. As such, the grandson was willing to be vulnerable with his grandma and avoid giving in to temptation.

Learning to open up and be vulnerable with others is a skill that requires effort. However, when appropriately understood, opening up to others and sharing your difficulties with them can be a critical step in the healing process.

Additional ways you can be vulnerable and allow others to help you include:

- Attending a 12-step meeting and sharing in the group
- Preparing and reading a letter of disclosure to your spouse, therapist, or religious leader
- Meeting new people who support your recovery
- Inviting someone to be your sponsor

At the beginning of your recovery journey, I don't expect that this strategy will be easy for you. However, as you progress, you will find that learning to be vulnerable with the right people will pay significant dividends. It will be vital for you to learn with whom you can be vulnerable. When you find the right people, you will find that your loneliness will melt away.

Assignment

Think of someone with whom you could share your sexual history and behaviors. Once you identify this person, write a letter to him/her outlining the challenges you've had with your sexuality. Write about how hard it has been for you. Tell this person the things you have done that you are not proud of.

Now, imagine their response. Did they reject you? Get angry at you? Or did they support you and show they cared? Most people are afraid of the adverse outcomes and rarely see that there are people who genuinely care about them. If you have someone with whom you could share this letter, you are fortunate. If you currently don't have someone, that is okay. Eventually, this is something that you could share with your sponsor, a therapist, your religious leader, or someone else who could offer support.

Strategy #6: Seek Healthy Touch

In Chapter Two, I emphasized the importance of our basic needs being met while we were young. Researchers have found that touch is an essential part of healthy human development. Whether we are a young child or a mature adult, our need for physical touch never goes away. If we experience touch deprivation at any age, we will likely experience feelings of loneliness. In fact, the longer we go without touch, the more mental health problems we will face (22, 23).

On the other hand, some of the benefits of healthy touch include:

1. Positive thinking and expanded trust

2. Reduced social anxiety and stress (24)

3. Alleviated depressive symptoms

4. Reduced pain

5. Reduced stress hormones

6. Improved immune function (25)

The key point here is this: One powerful way to address loneliness is to incorporate healthy touch into your life. If you believe you're sexually acting out behaviors were due to touch deprivation, it will be vital for you to develop new strategies to address your need for touch. The need is not bad; the method of getting touch is what has been getting you into trouble.

It is important to emphasize here that it is common to seek out others to meet the basic need for physical touch. In most cultures, people give hugs to one another, hold hands, and cuddle with each other. The problem that many of my clients face is that their basic need for touch has turned into unhealthy sexual pursuits. In cases where sexual activities are not bond-building, and instead are solely sexual exchanges, my clients end up feeling more lonely, not less.

In situations where sexual behaviors (i.,e., getting a sexual massage, hiring an escort, or viewing pornography) are used to escape feelings of loneliness, new methods of connection can be developed. Here is a shortlist of possible solutions:

- Get an animal that likes to cuddle

- Get a massage that is not sexual

- Get a hug from 12-step group members, if appropriate

- Wrestle with your child/ren, just be careful not to be too rough and be sensitive to their comfort level of touch

- Get involved in a sport that includes physical contact (teammates often give each other high fives and in some cases pile on to celebrate a victory)

We humans need to be touched. When we are touched both our mental and physical health improves. A key contributor to feelings of loneliness may be touch deprivation. One way to solve this problem is to create experiences where healthy touch is the norm.

Chapter Summary

One of the core components of recovery capital is related to relationships. For example, if my clients could overcome their fears and worries about relationships, their loneliness scores would decrease, they would find more happiness, and their overall well-being would increase. This idea is supported by Berschied, who found that "When people are asked what pleasures contribute most to happiness, the overwhelming majority rate love, intimacy, and social affiliation above wealth or fame, even above physical health" (22). This chapter is my response to help you deal with your feelings of loneliness. Recovery is much more likely to occur if you can reduce or eliminate the loneliness you are experiencing.

In summary, loneliness can destroy your attempts at recovery. When you are feeling lonely, implementing specific strategies can help you to combat these feelings, which will increase your social skills and decrease your loneliness.

The six strategies to combat loneliness included in this chapter are: 1) unlearn unhealthy attachment patterns; we need to unlearn what didn't work and learn new relationship skills and implement what does work; 2) develop the skill of deep listening; when we sit with others and genuinely seek to understand them, we begin to see them differently; 3) develop empathy for others; one of the most powerful ways to combat your loneliness is to feel what others feel, think what they are thinking, and give them the gift of your loving presence; 4) learn to play (again); when we laugh, we boost our immune system and give our bodies a break from stress; 5) learn to be vulnerable; when you let others in by opening up and being vulnerable, you don't have to carry the burden you have been carrying by yourself. By becoming vulnerable, you will discover that your loneliness will go away; and 6) seek healthy touch. When we experience connection with others through healthy touch, our physical and mental health increases.

If you are looking for more ideas on how to combat loneliness, here are a few more ideas you might consider:

- Join a religious congregation

- Join a service organization like Kiwanis or Rotary

- Invite a friend to go dancing once a month (also a great way to get touch)

- Volunteer (work at a museum, help at a school, research at www.justserve.org for lots of service opportunities, or your local government).

Support Resources (found at https://www.discoverandchange.com/TSA —under Chapter 8)

Video: Confront your relationship demons

Video: Resolve negative internal voices

Chapter Nine

Letting Go of Your Shame

Many of us have a dark corner where a secret lurks, a secret that has power over us, that we will do anything to avoid looking at squarely. It has far more power, we rationalize, than we could ever deal with. Why fight the unfightable? So we give in.
(Paul Wilkes)

"I just can't get over what I have done. I have told myself over and over again that I will stop acting out sexually, but I always revert to my old behaviors. There is no way I am going to ever get over this." This is one of the most common statements I hear from my clients after they relapse. Usually, these feelings are associated with hopelessness and a low sense of confidence. Many individuals carry an excessive amount of shame, which remains with them, regardless if they've been clean for a few days, a few months, or even a few years. One of the damaging elements of sexual compulsivity is what it does to one's sense of self. Sexual addiction usually carries a significant amount of shame that seldom resolves itself by sobriety alone.

Let me explain why.

In many cases, individuals trapped in their acting-out behaviors have lived with secrets for a long time. Consider the case of Tommy, who was first exposed to sexual behaviors by an older neighborhood girl. He was just seven years old when she introduced him to various sexual acts. She also told him that he shouldn't tell anybody, or they would get in trouble, especially him. He was confused by what he was feeling. He felt bad and guilty, but he also remembered liking the feeling at that time. After that experience, he found himself masturbating to the fantasy of that memory.

On one occasion, when he was nine years old, his mom walked in on him masturbating. It was the look of disgust on her face that he remembered. "I honestly felt like I was the 'scum' of the earth at that time," he recounted to me. Even before his mom caught him, he felt like his behaviors were wrong, but his mother's look and subsequent line, "You need to talk with you dad," made him feel like he had done something wrong. He reported that his dad didn't have much to say to him. He did ask him what he was doing when his mom walked in on him. Tommy had no idea what to say. At the time, he didn't even know what the term "masturbation" meant. His dad said, "Your mom told me what you were doing; just try not to do it again." That was the last conversation that he had with his dad about anything sexual.

Over the next few years, Tommy continued masturbating, making sure not to get caught. At age 11, he looked at pornography for the first time. He heard other boys talking about it at school, so he began exploring the Internet. Soon he was looking at pornography as often as he could. He found himself gravitating to it so much that he would tell his parents he was going to sleep, then wait for them to go to bed, and then excitedly get up to view pornography.

While he was developing a sexual addiction, nobody would have known it. In all other areas of his life, he seemed to be doing well. He was doing well at school; he had friends and was getting good grades. He also seemed to be getting along well with his family. Yet, in the background of his mind, he knew something was wrong. He couldn't talk to anyone about it; it would be too embarrassing. He kept telling himself over and over again that he was going to stop, but his commitment to himself only lasted for a few days before he was back viewing it again.

By the time he was a sophomore, he had a problem, but he had nowhere to turn. He began to show signs of depression, but his parents chalked it up to the pressures of school and the pressure of the sports teams he played on. He started spending more time alone in his room when he was home; his parents were so busy, they didn't notice. It was during this school year that pornography and masturbation shifted to other sexual behaviors. About halfway through his sophomore year, he started liking a girl from school. Within a few short weeks together, they started a sexual relationship, which excited Tommy. His parents observed that he was happier since he was in the relationship, but they were concerned about how much time he was spending with his girlfriend. He reassured them that things would be "okay," but knowing in his mind that they would be upset if they knew what he was doing.

What was surprising to Tommy was that, even though he was sexual with his girlfriend, he was still looking at pornography and masturbating on the days they were not messing around. He couldn't seem to string together more than a day or two without some form of sexual stimulation. His sexual desires had escalated to the point that he felt that he had to have something sexual almost every day. He was afraid to tell anyone. He was hiding his behaviors from his girlfriend and his parents. His parents had no idea he was having sex and viewing pornography; neither did his girlfriend.

He often thought to himself, "If anybody knew what I was doing, they would think I was disgusting." He internalized his shame, and he felt out of control. Soon he found himself arguing with his girlfriend, usually about the fact that she wanted to spend more time with her friends than she did him. She began pulling away because she wanted to attend other school activities and be with her other friends. At this time, he developed another self-belief: "I am not good enough for others. Even those who are close to me don't want to spend time with me."

At this point, his shame began to influence multiple areas of his life. It was guiding the way he thought about others, the way he felt about himself, and his day-to-day activities (e.g., social isolation). Eventually, his girlfriend broke up with him, saying he was too needy. He got upset and accused her of only caring about herself. Some of their mutual friends from school got word of their fighting and turned on him. He began feeling like he didn't fit in and that he wasn't liked. He turned inward and felt ashamed of his behaviors.

Tommy had developed many negative self-beliefs that triggered depression. He didn't know who to turn to, so he began isolating himself even more from others. He escaped into pornography and masturbation. It was a dark time in his life. Eventually, he did find support from friends on the school football team, i.e., friendships that sustained him through high school, but his use of pornography was still a regular habit. When I asked him about the extent of his involvement with pornography, he reported that, by the time he was 18, he had viewed pornography more than 750 times.

What is the aftermath of Tommy's experience? And how can he start the healing process? Let's look.

A Long History of Shame

At some point, individuals like Tommy go to college, get a job, and get involved in a committed relationship. On the outside, they appear to be functioning well; yet, inside, they are filled with shame-based thoughts (e.g., others wouldn't like me, I'm not as good as others, I'm unlovable). These toxic thoughts then influence their emotions (depression, anxiety, loneliness) and behaviors (anger, irritability). Sexual secrets almost always lead to toxic shame.

Here's an example from holy writ that shows how attempting to cover your sins leads to shame.

In the book of Genesis, the story of Adam and Eve teaches us about shame and covering up our sins. We read, "And they (Adam and Eve) were both naked, the man and his wife, and were not ashamed" (2). However, after partaking of the forbidden fruit that God had told them not to eat, we read, "And the eyes of them both were opened, and they knew that they were naked; and they sewed fig leaves together, and made themselves aprons. And they heard the voice of the Lord God walking in the garden in the cool of the day: and Adam and his wife hid themselves from the presence of the Lord God amongst the trees of the garden" (3).

This example illustrates the pattern that has been followed for generations. When we have nothing to hide, we are not ashamed. We know who we are and experience a sense of self-confidence. Simply said, we have "no thing" to hide. On the other hand, much like Adam and Eve, when we have secrets, it is natural to want to cover our mistakes and hide (isolate ourselves). In our efforts to cover up our unwanted thoughts, emotions, and behaviors, we suffer. We typically pull back from others because we do not want to be seen.

In contrast, one of our deepest desires is to find and experience human intimacy. To achieve the most intimate relationship possible, we have to be seen. We have to be willing to be naked in front of others. This meaning of "nakedness" offers much more depth into what it means to be naked, mind you. In essence, what we are saying is, "look into me and see who I am." When this type of relationship happens, intimacy might be spelled this way (in-to-me-see). This is an invitation for others to look "in-to-me-(and)see." If our most natural and best desire is to find and create human intimacy, one of the most destructive feelings is shame because it causes us to hide from others.

In a fascinating book titled, *Power vs. Force: The Hidden Determinants of Human Behavior*, author David R. Hawkins suggests that, of all our energy fields, shame is at the lowest level. He writes, "All (energy) levels below 200 are destructive of life in both the individual and society at large; in contrast, all levels above 200 are constructive expressions of power. The decisive level of 200 is the fulcrum that divides the general areas of force (or falsehood) from power (or truth)." So what is the energy level of shame on his scale? It is the lowest of all energy levels we produce, i.e., a 20. Other common energy levels are as follows: guilt (30), apathy (50), grief (75), fear (100), anger (150), and pride (175). The energy levels of constructive emotions are courage (200), neutrality (250), willingness (310), acceptance (350), reason (400), love (500), joy (540), peace (600), and enlightenment (700–1000). (4)

These measurable energy levels make it clear that shame is the most destructive of all emotions. For this reason, I find it interesting that shame is the first identified emotion of Adam and Eve. If indeed we have an enemy, it would only make sense that shame, which creates the lowest expression of energy, would be one of the first emotions in recorded history to be felt. In our battle for healthy living and healing, shame is among the most significant detriments to our well-being. Thus, it is imperative that shame-based thinking be resolved as a part of your journey to healing.

Development of a Shame-Based Identity

The process of healing shame may feel overwhelming to you because you have likely have felt it for many years. It may be so familiar to you that you do not even realize you are experiencing shame. In his book, *Breaking the Habit of Being Yourself*, Dr. Joe Dispenza wrote: "The body becomes addicted to guilt or any emotion in the same way that it would get addicted to drugs. Every time you think a guilty thought, you've signaled your body to produce the specific chemicals that make up the feeling of guilt. You've done this so often that your cells are swimming in a sea of guilt chemicals (5). As we mature, if left unchecked, the emotions associated with guilt become automatic; in other words, we have memorized the feelings of guilt without thinking about them.

About 95% of who we are by midlife is made up of a series of subconscious programs that have become automatic, e.g., driving a car, brushing our teeth, overeating when we're stressed, worrying about our future, judging our friends, complaining about our lives, blaming our parents, not believing in ourselves, and insisting on being chronically unhappy, to name a few (6,7). If indeed, 95% of our thoughts, emotions, and behaviors are automatic, then learning to turn off the patterns and create new ones is essential to our healing.

Let's review Tommy's case and how his shame developed, along with the steps he began taking to move toward the healing process.

One of the most powerful ways to help heal shame is to understand how it developed in the first place. A quick review of Tommy's case provides valuable insight into how his shame grew over time. In our work together, we outlined certain key events that triggered his shame. In working with clients like Tommy, I like to have them complete a key life event inventory (see Appendix E). As they work through the inventory, we begin to see the picture of how their shame-based thinking developed.

In Tommy's case, he initially thought it was the look his mother gave him when she caught him masturbating that started his shame. However, after further review, he identified shame from his sexual experiences when he was seven. He reported that, for many years, he thought about the experience he had with his neighbor girl at age seven as common child play. However, as he explored how the experience changed him, he realized that it had triggered a cascade of sexual feelings and experiences that he had never considered. What seemed to him to be child's play had altered him sexually. For example, he noticed that, soon after their first sexual exploration, he started touching himself more often, i.e., masturbating. The more he thought about it; he realized that he had began thinking more about sexual behaviors. He had a growing interest in finding someone else with whom he could act out. When he discovered how easy pornography was to access through the Internet, his life again changed. He had gone from masturbating to fantasy thoughts to exploring sexual acts online. The more he reviewed his sexual history, the more insight he had into how his shame developed. Together, we looked at these critical sexual experiences and the shame-based thoughts that came from those events. You can see these below.

Key Event	TimeLine
Age and Experience	Outcome (Focus on specific thoughts, emotions, beliefs, and subsequent behaviors associated with your experience)
Seven years old, I played doctor with a neighbor girl. Sexually acted out multiple times over a few months. It ended when she moved.	Initially, I was excited and liked playing doctor. However, she told me that I shouldn't tell anyone. I felt it was wrong, but I didn't dare talk about it. I now see how that was when I pulled back from being close to my parents. I thought they would be mad at me.
Age nine, mom caught me masturbating.	The look she gave me of "disgust" changed me a lot. I knew I was disgusting to my mom. That day, I formed a belief that *I was a disgusting* person. Someone that others wouldn't like.

Age eleven, I viewed pornography for the first time.	I was drawn to pornography. From the first time I saw it, I got such a high. I knew I had to hide it from my parents and others. I began seeking it out as much as I could. Pornography changed what I thought about and felt. I no longer was just fantasizing: I was looking at real people doing sexual things. I couldn't stop. I lost control over myself and didn't know what to do. I distanced myself from my parents even more. Sure, we went through the motions of being a family, but they had no idea what was happening to me. I felt like *I was a bad person.*
Age 16, began doing sexual things with my girlfriend.	By the time I was 16, I had already viewed pornography and masturbated hundreds of times. By the time I met _____, I had fantasized hundreds of times about actually being sexual and now being able to have the real thing. I thought I was in heaven. I couldn't get enough of what we were doing together. I always wanted it more than she did. Eventually, I was pushing her for more and more, and she began pulling away. When she broke up with me, that was the worst time of my life. I felt like *nobody would ever love me.* I also felt *ashamed of myself* because all I could think about was sex. If she didn't want to, I would view pornography and blame her in my mind. I began hating the way I was. I felt like, if others knew what I was really like, they would think *I was disgusting.* Nobody really knew me. It was a good thing because if they did, they, too, would think *I was bad.*
Age 16 to current, still viewing pornography and masturbating.	After my girlfriend broke up with me, I didn't date much after that. I was viewing porn and masturbating daily. Some days when I was alone, I would view porn multiple times throughout the day, and then after my parents came home and went to bed, I would look again.

Age 18–19. After leaving home for college, I met a girl that changed me. She had strong values and was super cool. I didn't want to push sexual things with her because I knew it would ruin our relationship. She made me want to be better.	*I never felt like I was good enough for her.* For the first time in my life, I wanted to be better. I tried my best to stop viewing pornography and masturbating but still gave in at times. When I did act out, I found myself pulling away because I knew it would upset her. Although I *never felt good enough* for her, I wanted to be a better person because of her. When I couldn't stop viewing pornography, I was afraid it would end our relationship. I knew that if she knew about my past, she would end the relationship. Eventually, I think my negative self-talk and behaviors ended our relationship. She broke up with me because she felt like something wasn't quite right with our relationship. I knew it was coming because *I didn't believe I was good enough for her.* I had sabotaged the relationship because I wasn't good enough for her. Even though I had sworn off pornography and other sexual behaviors because I was tired of how it was ruining my life, I wasn't able to stop.

In the above example of Tommy's key event timeline, I have italicized the key phrases I look for as a therapist. These are thoughts that help me understand the level of shame Tommy was feeling. As a therapist, I look at shame-based thoughts as points of intervention. Because Tommy had been feeling and thinking these thoughts for so long, he didn't anticipate or realize the profound impact that they were having on him. One of my goals in therapy is not only to bring these shame-based thoughts to his attention but to also help him interrupt these patterns, so he can begin establishing new ones.

In order to get started we began by writing down the thoughts from his list above that indicated shame. Each of the statements below is what is referred to as the language of shame. Here's what we came up with:

- Mad at me

- I was disgusting

- I couldn't stop myself (indicates a sense of powerless; it is stronger than I am)

- I was a bad person

- Nobody would ever love me

- Ashamed of myself

- If others knew what I was like they would think I was disgusting

- Never felt like I was good enough for her

By identifying the language of Tommy's shame, he was able to see how frequently he was using the phrases listed above in his day-to-day thinking and how these thoughts influenced how he felt. While it took time, he began seeing how frequently he was putting himself down. His negative self-thoughts had become so automatic; he hadn't realized that they were always playing in the background of his mind.

I explained to him that while awareness of the language of his shame could be helpful to him, they wouldn't stop on their own. To change thoughts, it is also beneficial to alter the interpretations of the images associated with shame as well.

In order to do this, we began identifying the images associated with his shame. Often these images are experiences that have a visual representation that is related to the shame.

Images of Shame

As we talked about specific memories, Tommy held in his mind particular phrases like "I am disgusting" and "nobody would ever love me." I asked him to think of specific memories or experiences that stood out to him that represented these statements. The first memory that came to his mind was the one associated with "the look" his mother gave him. That memory was seared into his mind, and each time he thought about the experience, he had a deep visceral response. He felt such profound rejection from his mother that he could hardly talk about it without becoming emotional. He felt ashamed of his behavior and the pain of her look. He had let her down. That moment had altered how he saw himself and his mom. As his therapy progressed, he identified that experience as one that had not been resolved. It had influenced his relationship with his mother from that time to the present.

Additional images stuck out in Tommy's mind as well. He remembered the day his girlfriend broke up with him, and he felt like their mutual friends had turned on him. The rejection he felt was profound, and the only way he knew to cope with his rejection was to escape into pornography. As he went home that day, he was upset by his behaviors, angry at his girlfriend for the way she had told others what had happened between them. That evening, he viewed pornography and masturbated. The image that came to Tommy's mind was being home viewing pornography and imagining what she was telling others. He had created a memory of what he thought she was telling others and had developed a shame-based belief that he was a bad person.

As I talk with clients like Tommy, I begin to see the moments that they are stuck in. These are the memories that are indelibly imprinted upon their minds. As we worked together, I talked with Tommy about various strategies we could use to help him work through and resolve those painful experiences. He was curious about how to address such painful memories that he had carried with him for years.

Before we move on to what happened next with Tommy, it is important to pause here and understand that, when clients seek help to stop acting out, they seldom realize that beneath their addictive behaviors are a myriad of unresolved underlying issues. There is always a reason for addiction; unless we stop and explore the story; however, we may attempt to treat the symptoms and completely miss resolving the root of the problem.

The Emotions of Shame

What does it feel like when I ask you to say, "I am a bad person"? Tommy thought for a moment and said, "I have felt that way for so long I don't know any different." I then asked him to think more about how it made him feel. He hesitated and said, "It makes me angry. For years, I have been upset at others. I don't know why, but it seems like I am so used to feeling upset or angry, that I don't know any different. What I do know is that being angry makes me feel like I'm doing something wrong. I think that is why I often feel like I am a bad person. There are days or moments in days where I think I'm a pretty good guy, but more often than not, when I am by myself, which is often, I don't like who I am. I find that I have to distract myself because I don't like the thoughts racing through my head. When I am by myself, I usually have the television on, or I am on my phone playing a game or checking the score of a game."

I asked him again to reflect on what made him feel like he was a bad person. He said, "It's bad to be angry, it's bad to look at pornography, and most women I know don't want someone who is looking at pornography." At this point, I stopped our conversation and shared with him some of the things that I have learned about pornography and feeling bad about oneself. I asked him why he thought about 70% of individuals who completed my online survey, Assessing Pornography Addiction, felt like they were bad persons when they viewed pornography. He gave me a surprised look and said, "Really? 70% of the people who view pornography feel the way I do?" I said, "Yes, that's what I have found in my research." I then repeated my question, "Why do you think that nearly 70% of those individuals viewing pornography indicated that at least some of the time, they felt like they were a bad person when they viewed pornography?" (chart available at https://bit.ly/treating-sex-addiction).

He was curious now as well. He thought for a few seconds and replied, "I think it is bad because society tells me it is, and when I view it, even though I want to stop, I end up feeling like I am bad." I then asked him more about his view of pornography and not what society is saying about it. He thought for a few seconds and said, "I know it's not good for me." I asked him why he felt it wasn't good for him. He replied, "It doesn't make me happy, and I feel better about myself when I am not viewing it. When I am viewing it, I distance myself from others and feel like I am in a corner all by myself. This is when I get angry at myself and others. I don't' believe anyone would want me." He concluded by saying, "I don't have a lot of friends, and I think viewing it prevents me from trying to get close to others." The more I talked with Tommy, the more his story made sense. Statements like, "I'm bad" and "I don't have a lot of friends" and "I'm angry" have a lot more meaning when we understand the story behind them.

After hearing thousands of stories like Tommy's, I began to wonder why emotions like anger and sadness were common to my clients. Why do people like Tommy become angry at themselves or others? Why do they become sad and depressed? Many of my clients are like Tommy and prone to turn inward on themselves and develop self-hatred or turn outward and become critical of the people around them. In Tommy's case, he was doing both.

I learned a valuable lesson about these emotions from a colleague, Thomas Tullos. He said, "Anger, even rage, is almost always shame-based." To illustrate his point, he shared a story that happened to him just after boarding a plane. He found his seat and was waiting for others to finish boarding. As he was observing others, a man not paying attention bumped the stewardess, who then bumped into someone else. She said excuse me to both of them, even though it wasn't her fault. The man who bumped into her looked at her and, in an angry tone, said, "Watch what you are doing next time." The man who was bumped by the stewardess said: "Excuse me, but that was not her fault." Embarrassed, the man said, "Well, she needs to just get out of the way." As Thomas told us the story, he said, "His anger was a way for him to deflect the shame he was feeling." As I have observed others who are living in anger, I, too, have found that, underneath their rage, is unresolved shame.

As we explore internalized and externalized anger, we often discover self-incriminating thoughts like, "I am bad." We also think critically about others like, "People are just stupid." Such statements are rarely looked at as thoughts associated with shame; more often than not, as we explore the deeper emotions, we find that shame is the underlying emotion.

Additional emotions that may be linked to shame include:

- Sadness (e.g., I don't deserve to be happy)

- Hopelessness (e.g., It doesn't matter what I do, nothing works out, so why try?)

- Disgust for self or others (e.g., I am disgusting, people are disgusting)

- Loneliness (e.g., I don't fit in)

It took a few sessions for Tommy to identify the depth of his shame, but the more he looked, the more he found. It was such a big part of his life, and he had hardly realized it. We began a series of mental exercises to help him rewrite new pathways in his mind.

Four Steps to Healing the Shame-Filled Mind

When individuals like Tommy realize how much of their life has been lived in shame, they usually want to know how to resolve it or let it go. I have found that lasting change occurs when each of the three areas: a) language, b) emotions, and c) memories, as seen in Chart #1, are identified, understood, and changed. For the remainder of this chapter, I will offer specific strategies on how this can be done.

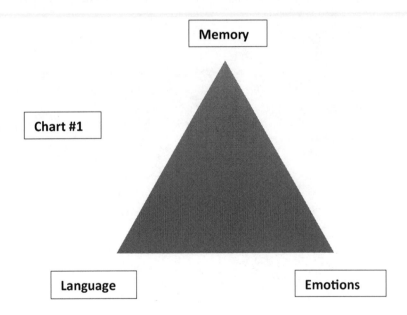

As outlined above, in my work with Tommy, we had already identified the language, emotions, and memories associated with his shame. Through our discussions and his work, he was beginning to understand how they were influencing his life. Now our challenge was to help him change the thought patterns and underlying emotions that were associated with his shame.

Here are four steps that I have found helpful in altering the core shame.

Step #1: Identify the stories (memories) associated with the shame

In Tommy's case, he identified four core events that triggered his most profound shame:

1. His first sexual experiences with his neighbor girl. Initially, he didn't think this event was a part of his shame, as he explored it more in-depth; however, he realized that it was the beginning of his shame. He had hidden what happened from his parents. He was able to see how her words, "Don't tell anyone about this because we will get into trouble, especially you," had triggered shame in him. He learned to hide his behaviors from others at that time. This awareness helped him to identify where his feelings of shame began. He saw how his silence and embarrassment kept him trapped in those sexual acts. It had also hurt his relationship with his parents. Shame held in silence grows like weeds in fertile ground.

2. The second core event was when his mother caught him masturbating. As we talked, he told me that it was the most painful for him. Her look of disgust had been so painful that he could hardly talk about it. The nine-year-old Tommy felt much shame from that memory.

3. The third core event was when his girlfriend broke up with him, and he felt shunned by their group of friends. That evening, going home by himself with no one to talk to, he created a story in his mind about what was being said about him. That memory was painful to him. What made it more painful was that he turned to pornography for comfort that evening and was disgusted with his behavior. His shame solidified that evening as he reviewed how awful he felt about himself.

4. The fourth key event that triggered his shame was when his girlfriend in college broke up with him because she "felt" like something wasn't quite right. After years of feeling inadequate, as if he were disgusting and that others wouldn't like him, this experience reinforced his beliefs. He internalized the belief that "nobody would ever want to be with him." She was so good and kind that his belief was even more deep-seated. It was "nobody good would want to be with me."

These experiences were at the core of Tommy's shame. Now that we had outlined the memories, we turned to the language associated with his shame.

Step #2: Look for and review the language of shame

As we reviewed Tommy's key life event inventory, we were able to see the language he had used to describe what had happened. He was also able to see how that language had become a part of his day-to-day thinking. Statements such as, "I am disgusting," "I'm a bad person," and "Nobody will ever love me" frequently ran through his mind.

Linking the memories with the language was an important step in raising awareness of the internal voices running through his mind. Understanding the voice of shame is one thing, but changing it is entirely different altogether.

The voice of shame is sneaky. It creeps into our minds while we aren't looking, and suddenly we find ourselves saying things like "I'm so stupid" or "Who would ever want me?" When this happens, I tell my client's that we have to increase awareness; that the purpose of building self-awareness is to prevent the thoughts from running wild. As clients slow down and pay attention to their thoughts, they will gain a deeper understanding of their thought patterns. Ironically, just sitting with our thoughts can help us alter them.

Yes. I am asking you to sit with the thought, "I am disgusting." Tommy looked at me like, "Are you crazy?" While we had joked about various things in the past, this time, I said, "I am serious." When you identify a negative thought, I invite you to pause and explore it. Seek to understand it. Ask yourself questions like, "Why am I having this thought now?" "What does it even mean?" "What is the truth, really?" By slowing down the thought process, the thoughts that have run wild in your mind no longer have free reign. In other words, we are corralling them in and harnessing them.

Once the thoughts have been identified and corralled, it is time to let them go. This is where I incorporate a mindfulness technique with my clients.

Here's how it works.

Exercise: Once you have the thought in mind that you are trying to understand and you have sat with it, it is now time to let it go. Imagine placing the thought in a river and watching as it flows away from you, then continue to imagine it is getting farther and farther away. Feel your body relax, as the thought turns the corner out of your mind. Now pause and reflect on the experience. Ask yourself, "What just happened to me?" You can also replace the thought with a feeling of gratitude. It might sound like this: "I am grateful that I now have an awareness of the thoughts that have been running through my mind. I am now going to shift my attention to other things I am grateful for." In your mind, list one thing that you are grateful for and why.

You are now on your way to creating new neural pathways in your mind that are not shame-based. The new pathways are filled with self-awareness and gratitude. By practicing this daily, you are intentionally rewiring your brain. Lasting change often comes from regular practice and the development of new habits.

Step #3: Observe and work to resolve the emotions of the shame

The third step to resolving shame is to discover the emotions associated with it. Up to this point, we have found the memories associated with shame and the thoughts as well. Now, our attention shifts to the specific emotions of shame. For Tommy, the two top emotions were sadness and anger. As we learned with the other two areas, it was through raising his awareness and paying attention to what he felt that his change began. The general rule of change is that you can't change what you don't understand. For Tommy, learning to pay attention to his emotions was going to be imperative.

In the beginning, as he attempted to understand his emotions, he often said, "I don't know." This is a typical response of clients whose expression of emotions were shut down when they were younger (e.g., boys don't cry or buck up and be tough). Learning to overcome the fear of expressing emotions begins by identifying and understanding emotions as we feel them. Learning to pay attention to our feelings is an essential part of the healing and recovery process; yet, some clients have never been taught how.

For this reason, I often tell clients that our emotions can teach us so much, but we have to learn to listen to what they are trying to teach us. As an example, Tommy didn't like to be sad, and he didn't like the feelings he felt when he was angry; to him, however, they were just normal emotions. He wanted to stop being angry and sad, but he did not know what to do to stop them. I let him know that the goal was not to stop them; instead, it is to learn from them.

My friends Ken and Sharon Patey taught me how to do this. They call it "unlayering the onion."

Let's start by saying that anger is the core emotion, i.e., the unwanted emotion.

Question: What is it that makes you angry?

Level 1: I think people are just stupid.

Question: What makes you think that?

Level 2: They don't care about others.

Question: What experiences have you had that makes you think people don't care?

Level 3: Lots. My high school girlfriend breaking up with me; how my supposed friends talked about me afterward.

Question: When she broke up with you, what did that make you feel or think about yourself? (Notice, we are moving away from something external his girlfriend and turning inward to himself).

Level 4: Nobody would want me. That I'm a nobody. I'm insignificant.

As we unlayer the onion, we gain a greater appreciation of what was driving the anger. There is always a story beneath intense emotions like anger; unfortunately, we can get lost in the anger and ignore what is driving it. To create lasting change, we have to identify the root of the problem. By doing this, true healing can begin.

Let's see how getting to the root of the problem helped Tommy.

As we unlayered the onion, Tommy began to see his anger differently. No longer was his anger confusing to him. As we talked, he began to realize that anger was his way of covering up his shame (nobody would want me...I'm insignificant). In the end, shame-based beliefs are at the root of the problem; when we resolve them, real and lasting healing can begin.

Let's now turn our attention to how to heal the painful memories from the past.

Step #4: Desensitize and reprocess the memories associated with the shame

For nearly 20 years of my career, I have helped my clients understand their core beliefs and the influence those beliefs have had on their lives. In many instances, assisting clients in getting to the root of their pain proved both helpful and healing. However, in some cases, especially when there was significant trauma and unresolved memories, I felt limitations in my effectiveness as a therapist. Today, that has all changed. I have seen firsthand that painful experiences can be healed and resolved through a powerful therapeutic approach, which is based in research and is now one of the most effective treatment approaches for treating trauma (8).

Here's the story of how I discovered the power of EMDR.

A few years ago, while I was learning to become a certified sexual addiction therapist (CSAT), I was asked to complete a trauma egg. This is a writing exercise in which you are instructed to identify difficult or painful memories from your past with your key caregivers and explore your role (e.g., caregiver, scapegoat, fixer, etc.)

in the family. During this exercise, we identified various experiences from our life that were painful or difficult. The instructions read, "Usually these are events that were there as profound disappointment, betrayal, or abuse. Think of times when you were embarrassed or let down or when there was some upset or crisis that involved you" (CSAT Manual Mod 3, pg. 70). I had a difficult time working on my egg, as I enjoyed my childhood immensely. I had friends and loved playing sports. Even though my parents had divorced, I still felt loved and appreciated by them. I had grandparents, great-grandparents, cousins, and aunts and uncles who were loving and supportive. Trauma and me? Not possible.

As instructed, I responded to the questions about my mom and dad. While I was doing this exercise, a memory came to mind that I hadn't thought about for 35 years. I was with my mom and older brother in my mother's car heading south; my father was in another vehicle heading north. We came to an intersection at the same time. He had another woman in the car with him. My mother and father both got out of their cars (mind you, we were in the country, not a busy intersection) and talked for a short period of time. Mom came back to the car, crying. We turned around and headed to my grandparents' home. My brother and I sat in the car for what seemed like forever. When my mother came out, we didn't talk about what had happened. It had been 35 years since that incident, and I had not thought about it since then. Suddenly, I felt emotions welling up inside of me that I had not explored. I was uneasy and didn't know what to do with those feelings. The awareness of what had happened to the little boy me made me sad. However, the recognition of what had happened didn't make the sadness and pain go away. I talked with my wife about what I had experienced at the training, but the memory sat with me for almost another year and a half. It wasn't overwhelming or debilitating, but it was there.

While I was evaluating newly released books in the fall of 2014, I found an excellent book, *The Body Keeps the Score*. In this masterfully written book, Dr. Bessel van der Kolk discusses the most powerful ways to treat trauma and traumatic memories. I wasn't thinking about the memory I had had from my past; I was reading the book to see if I could learn how to better help my clients who were suffering from various types of traumatic experiences.

In Chapter 15, Dr. van der Kolk described the effectiveness of using eye movement and desensitization reprocessing (EMDR) in therapy (9). The research outcomes made me question why I hadn't paid attention to this treatment approach before. Then, he shared some profound case studies in which he had personally witnessed incredible changes in clients. I thought to myself, "I want to help my clients that way." I wanted to learn how to use this life-changing approach. I knew

I was not as effective in treating trauma as I could be, so I was excited. I quickly enrolled in an upcoming class.

It was everything that I had thought and more. The method was clear, and the case studies were game-changing for the clients we observed. I watched video cases of individuals they tracked for months and years afterward have profound healing experiences from painful life traumas. As the training progressed, they asked us to identify an issue that we would like to address. Now it was my turn. I was eager to see how doing EMDR with my childhood memory would influence me.

As a part of the EMDR protocol, the participant is asked to identify a difficult memory from his/her past. They then focus on what they came to believe about themselves as a result of the experience. My memory was of that intersection when we saw my dad with another woman. I had identified my belief related to that experience as, "I didn't matter." The person working with me asked me to go back to the details of this experience. As I brought it to my mind, I saw myself in an intersection. Our car was heading south; my dad's truck was heading north. I was in the backseat of the car that my mom was driving when my dad stopped at the same intersection with another woman in his passenger seat.

I followed the index finger of the person I was practicing with, as she moved rapidly from side to side about 12 inches from my eyes. EMDR therapists call this bilateral stimulation (BLS). As my eyes tracked her fingers, I found myself triggered with the most profound rage I had ever felt. I felt my head burning and the vivid sensation of wanting to scream. I saw myself getting out of the car and stomping out to the middle of that intersection enraged. I was yelling at my dad and saying, "What are you doing? You are ruining our family!"

That is when my colleague's finger stopped. I was crying, tears running down my cheek. By this time, the supervising therapist was there. "Just stay with those moments and let me know what are you are noticing," he said. I reported what I had just seen, thinking to myself, "Didn't you see it, too?" After reporting what I experienced and felt in my body, we continued.

During the next set of eye movements, I saw the little boy (me) being loved by his family. I saw my grandparents, aunts, and uncles. Then, the boy saw his dad at his baseball game supporting him. Here, my colleague stopped again and asked me to take a deep breath and let it out. She asked, "What are you noticing now?" I related what I had experienced.

We went through one more series, where I felt this tremendous weight on my shoulders. As we moved on to the next BLS, I found myself thinking, "My dad is a good man who had a problem." At this, the weight lifted, and I felt free. My original belief, "I didn't matter," no longer felt true. I knew I was loved. Within a few short minutes, I had processed a painful and disturbing memory from my past and had changed my belief. When I started the processing, I had ranked the memory as a six or seven in terms of how disturbing it felt to me (on a scale of 0–10, in which zero is completely calm, and 10 is very disturbing). After processing the memory using EMDR, the emotional pain and level of disturbance were gone. The memory felt like a zero.

This is a treasured experience. I can still see the little boy in the car at the intersection, but he is no longer filled with any kind of emotional pain. His hurt has been healed. I am a therapist who has worked with thousands of individuals over the past 25 years, and I could have never shared that experience with others had I not experienced EMDR.

Since that time, I have used EMDR with clients struggling with addiction, anxiety, depression, and significant trauma. Watching them experience life-altering healing has been very rewarding and a significant blessing for me.

How Healing the Memories Resolves the Shame

Perhaps at this point, you may be thinking, "How can changing a memory reduce my shame?" The answer is that shame often resides in unresolved memories. The best way to address how desensitizing and reprocessing painful memories alters the shame is through sharing Tommy's story with EMDR.

As we already outlined above, there were four key memories that Tommy identified. When we do EMDR, we invite our clients to focus on their first or worst memory. The reason we do this is that these memories are usually the most disturbing ones; when we can address and heal those memories, other subsequent painful memories can often be resolved at the same time. Tommy chose to focus on the experience of his mother's look. The belief that he held was, "I'm disgusting."

Once we have the belief that clients feel are associated with the memory, we ask them this question: "When you think of that memory, what would you like to think (believe) about yourself instead?" He thought for a bit and said, "I'm a good guy." I asked him to think of the disturbing memory and then think about the statement, "I'm a good guy." I then asked him how true that felt to him between a 1 (not true at all) and 7 (it is true, meaning I am a good guy). He quickly said, "Maybe a 2"; in other words, he didn't believe he was a good guy.

In the EMDR process, the clients identify the emotions associated with the belief and where they feel them in their body. Tommy identified sadness as his core emotion, and reported that he felt it in his neck and shoulders. As we prepare to do the bilateral stimulation, we ask clients how disturbing the identified memory is between a score of 0 (not disturbing) and 10 (very disturbing). Tommy identified the memory with his mother's look as an 8 or 9 out of 10.

As we begin the EMDR process, we invite clients to think of the memory, their belief, and where they feel these in their body. I asked Tommy to do these three things, and we began. One set of bilateral stimulation (BLS) can take between 30 seconds and a few minutes, depending on what the client is experiencing. As we worked through a few sets of BLS, Tommy recounted seeing that look his mother gave him. He was visibly upset. I have found that the more emotion is expressed in these experiences, the better. Tommy began showing more emotion; after one set of BLS, he said, "My mom was going through a lot at that time. She and my dad were frequently fighting, and I wonder if he was hurting her in the same way." I asked him to notice that, and we kept going. After the next set, he seemed almost relieved. He said, "I was so young. She didn't know about my experiences with my neighbor. All she saw was her boy doing something hurtful like his dad. She was scared for her son."

Usually, after a couple of sets, where insight is gained, and change in perception is manifesting, we stop and reassess the level of disturbance that the original memory holds. I asked Tommy, "How disturbing does the memory feel to you know on a scale between 0 and 10? He thought for a few seconds and said, "Maybe a 2 or 3." I said, "Okay, let's go with a 2 or 3 and see what else comes up. We do this because a 2 or 3 indicates that there is still something that is disturbing about the experience. As we moved on, his mind shifted to a memory of his first sexual experience with the neighbor girl. After one set, he noticed the following, "She looked at me and said, 'Don't tell anyone or we will get in trouble, especially you.' That was the moment I started feeling bad about myself. I had done something wrong. I was bad." After the next BLS set, Tommy showed compassion for the little boy. He said, "He was just a boy. He didn't know any better." At this insight, he seemed relieved. When I asked him to think of the memory and how disturbing it was, he said, "0." We finished the rest of the EMDR protocol, and he looked at me and said, "What just happened to me? The pain of those memories is gone."

Tommy then asked me, "Will the memories come back?" I said what I have experienced with other clients and my own experience: "The memory will come back, but the pain associated with the experience is gone." He was excited.

Note to the reader: It has been more than one year since I did that EMDR session with Tommy. He recently told me that, as he thinks of those early life memories with his mom and with his neighbor girl, they are no longer disturbing. More importantly, he does not feel like he is a disgusting person. I've had many experiences like this with clients since being trained in EMDR. Not all experiences are like the ones I had with Tommy, however. Sometimes, it takes a few sessions to see this type of progress; further, with some clients, the EMDR process feels uncomfortable to them and is not as effective. However, a majority of my clients respond well to this process and make great strides in their healing from the shame that has bound them.

So, what happened to Tommy?

Memories from our past create shame-filled beliefs (I am disgusting). Through the EMDR process, the level of disturbance associated with the memory is reprocessed. The painful memories that had influenced the way he thought and felt about himself for all those years was gone. After that, his shame decreased dramatically. He began making great strides in his recovery process. He still had to deal with cravings and some setbacks. However, even after a relapse, he didn't beat himself up as he had in the past. He was no longer a disgusting person. He was beginning to see that recovery was possible. The next part of Tommy's healing was in relationships. We will discuss the strategies I used with Tommy's in Chapters 13 and 14.

Chapter Summary

In this chapter, we addressed how shame develops over time, as illustrated through Tommy's story, and how it manifests itself in the lives of those who are experiencing it. By understanding the language, emotions, and memories associated with shame, we deconstructed the process of how shame develops. By looking at these three key areas, we then implemented a four-step treatment strategy for helping to resolve the toxic shame: 1) identify the stories (memories) associated with the shame; 2) look for and review the language of shame; 3) observe and work to resolve the emotions of shame; 4) desensitize and reprocess the memories associated with shame.

Support Resources (found at https://bit.ly/treating-sex-addiction — under Chapter 9)

Questions and Answers

- If shame is a destructive emotion after a relapse, what should I feel about myself after a relapse? (Video)

- Charts and results related to shame

Chapter Ten

The Healing Power of
Emotional Regulation

Emotional resiliency and tolerance are hallmarks of mental health.
(Daniel Hill)

Researchers have discovered that, in a crisis, people generally fall into one of three categories: 1) the 80% who freeze under high pressure; 2) the 10% who make matters worse; 3) the 10% who have discovered the art of effectively analyzing a situation and acting in a manner that leads to resolve (1). If only 10% respond effectively in difficult or stressful circumstances, then the other 90% need help during difficult times. Fortunately, researchers suggest that those who freeze up or make matters worse during a crisis can change their behaviors and learn how to navigate through difficult circumstances effectively.

Why does this matter? The 10% who know how to respond during a crisis didn't just accidentally find this skill. They have developed techniques through training that prevent their "emotional brain" from being hijacked and becoming unusable. Through their practice, they know how to respond quickly and effectively under pressure; in fact, they become so adept that they can remain emotionally calm, quickly assess a situation, and act accordingly.

Learning how to do this by regulating your own emotions in a crisis may be one of the most valuable skills you can learn in this life. If you are reading this book, I am going to assume that your ability to regulate emotions in stressful times is not natural for you, especially when it comes to dealing with cravings. By learning how to regulate your emotions like the experts, you will gain confidence in your recovery, and you will acquire skills to help you face difficult situations in a healthy way. Aristotle understood that this is not an easy process when he said, "Anyone can become angry—that is easy. But to be angry with the right person, to the right degree, at the right time, for the right purpose, and in the right way—that is not easy" (2).

Emotional regulation generally occurs when we discover how to effectively identify thoughts, feelings, and physical reactions to stressors and respond, as Aristotle described, "in the right way." When we are regulating our emotions, we are able to cope with everyday stresses. However, when we are unable to regulate our emotions, we act compulsively, take risks, hurt ourselves and others, and lose control of our emotions. When this occurs, we feel disjointed, and everything feels chaotic.

In this chapter, we will explore what emotions are, discuss why emotions aren't good or bad, reveal how your brain can easily be hijacked, and then conclude by offering a step-by-step approach designed by professional counselors to help regulate your emotions. Learning how to regulate your emotions is so important that researchers who study addiction believe it may be one of the most essential skills to learn in the recovery process. As you gain insight into your emotions and practice the methods found in this chapter, your awareness will increase, and you will naturally develop better strategies for regulating your emotions.

Understanding Emotions

Emotions, according to emotional intelligence expert Daniel Goleman, refer to feelings and their distinctive thoughts, psychological and biological states, and range of propensities to act. Most researchers who study emotions refer to core emotions, which include anger, sadness, fear, enjoyment, love, surprise, disgust, and shame (i.e., primary emotions). There are also secondary emotions, e.g., embarrassment, jealousy, guilt, pride, and background emotions, e.g., well-being, malaise, calm, tense (3).

In most instances, our emotions run in the background and are not brought into the conscious mind. As a result, you may feel many of the primary or secondary emotions but pay little attention to them. One of the reasons that we don't pay much attention to our emotions is that they change so frequently. Rarely are feelings constant. They vary from hour to hour and from moment to moment. If we experience a feeling for an extended period of time, like a few hours, we would typically refer to this as a mood (e.g., he seems irritated this evening). An extension of our mood is our general temperament, and, according to Dr. Goleman, beyond our emotional temperament are emotional disorders such as depression and anxiety (4).

Throughout this book, we have discussed the relationship between sexually acting out and your emotions (i.e., stress, anxiety). For example, the more frequently individuals use pornography, the higher their rates of depression, anxiety, and stress. Due to the strong relationship between sexually acting out and your emotions, it is essential to include a deeper understanding of emotions and how to regulate them effectively in the recovery process.

Our emotions often guide our thinking and lead to certain behaviors (e.g., "I was feeling anxious and found myself worrying about all of the things I had to get done, but, instead of getting my work done, I wasted time on the computer"). While our emotional states frequently change, our coping mechanisms for certain emotions can become predictable. For example, if you turn on the computer and view pornography each time you feel anxious, you will quickly develop an unhealthy coping mechanism to deal with your emotions. If this pattern is repeated frequently enough, an anxious feeling will trigger a craving to escape and act out sexually.

This process was first described by Donald Hebb, who proposed that when two neurons fire at the same time repeatedly (or when one fires, causing another to fire), chemical changes occur in both so that the two tend to connect more strongly (5). Another way to describe this process is "neurons that fire together wire together." In essence, what happens inside your brain is that, when you begin to feel anxiety, your mind evaluates how you should deal with the stress. If your typical response is to sexually act out, once the anxious neurons fire, the urge to act out will also be ignited. Over time, you train your mind to link these two things, i.e., anxiety and pursuing a sexual release, together.

Fortunately, our minds can unlink these neural connections. One way to begin the unwiring process of these two powerful feelings is to develop a curiosity about your emotional state of mind and learn from your emotions. By paying close attention to your feelings, you can see them as a warning sign, indicating that something is amiss. As in the situation above, you can use it as a reminder that you are uncomfortable with the task you are being asked to perform. So, instead of avoiding a task that needs to be completed and escaping into an unwanted sexual behavior, you would step back and assess your emotions. It might sound something like this in your mind:

> *I find it interesting that I am feeling anxious about the things I need to get done. I wonder why I feel like running away and escaping. I certainly am used to dealing with my problems this way. Is there something specific about this assignment that makes me want to run away? It could be that I don't understand what needs to be done, and I fear that I will make a fool of myself. I sure don't like looking bad. As I think about this, I wonder what it is that makes me worry so much.*

Notice the amount of interest paid to the anxiety and the awareness of what this person is feeling. You will see that there is no judgment of the thoughts and emotions. Being non-judgmental is a critical component of emotional regulation.

By avoiding judgment of emotions, you allow yourself to explore what is going on inside your mind. This opens the door to emotional awareness. Conversely, when you judge your emotions (e.g., I shouldn't be feeling this way), you shut down the learning process by thinking that what you are feeling is unacceptable. The danger of shutting ourselves off from our emotions is that we become self-critical and emotionally stuck.

Later in this chapter, a step-by-step approach to help you better understand and deal with your emotions using the strategies mentioned above will be discussed. We will also discuss how simple concepts like curiosity, being open to what you are feeling, accepting difficult emotions, avoiding judgment, and developing self-compassion will help you to understand your emotions. This process will aid you in rewiring neural habits that aren't working.

Emotions Aren't Good or Bad

One of the solutions to remaining open to our emotions is to realize that they aren't good or bad. Instead, when we attend to our feelings, we discover that they can help us respond to our environment so that we can act appropriately. For example, if I feel anxious about getting a work assignment done, my worry may help me stay focused and attentive to the task until it is completed. However, if I focus on the anxiety and judge it by saying something like, "I just don't respond well to all of this stress," I am less prone to get the task done. Note the judgment on the initial emotion.

The problem of placing judgment on emotion is that most emotions first occur in the unconscious mind. So, this statement, "I don't respond well to stress," is self-criticism regarding something that is already happening in your mind. In other words, you are telling yourself that you shouldn't be feeling what you are already feeling.

So how can this problem be solved? Let's go back to the example above. The statement, "I find it interesting that I am feeling anxious about the things I need to get done," does not place judgment. Instead, it is an expression that shows interest in the feeling. Next, "I certainly am used to dealing with my problems this way," is a clear acknowledgment that this is typical behavior but again avoids judgment.

Both of these examples demonstrate how a nonjudgmental thinking process eliminates labeling what you are feeling, either good or bad. By accepting these emotions, it becomes easier to regulate your emotions. After all, it isn't wrong to feel like running away or escaping. At times, we all want to do that. These are just feelings.

Also, by acknowledging the anxious feeling rather than mindlessly accepting it, the autopilot response of avoiding the task and turning to sexual behavior can be averted. When you implement this type of thinking, you will have the same ability and insight that individuals, who effectively respond during a crisis, have. Armed with this strategy, you will be able to evaluate a situation and make critical decisions that can help you to be more productive. An audio example of this process can be found in the resources section in this chapter (see The Power of Observing Your Emotions).

Hijacked Emotions

Have you ever felt out of control? Have you had a strong emotion overcome you to the point that it felt like it was taking over your life? If you've had these types of experiences, you then know what it is like to have your emotions hijack your mind. Dr. Joseph LeDoux, a leading neuroscientist, found that the amygdala, a part of the limbic system, is the emotional center of the brain, which responds to sensory input (e.g., smell, touch, sight); he also found that the amygdala receives feedback from our senses first before the thinking part of our brain, i.e., the neocortex (6). This means that you experience an emotional response to a trigger before you process the meaning of what is happening.

Let's put this into perspective. Suppose you return home and find that everyone is gone. In the past, this has been a time when you have given in and viewed pornography. Once you are triggered, your mind begins to anticipate giving in before you think about the consequences. It is at times like this that your emotions surge, and the emotional brain runs rampant (7). When the brain begins to anticipate viewing pornography, the mind becomes flooded with powerful chemicals, e.g., dopamine, which increases the chance of an emotional hijacking. Not surprisingly, all rational thought is lost. It is at times like this that emotional regulation becomes a critical tool for success.

If we were watching a movie of what happens in your brain as you returned home, we would likely see a tremendous surge of dopamine, i.e., the anticipatory chemical. Dr. Wolfram Schultz, who studied this process, found that the brain begins firing dopamine neurons before it receives the reward. He called these "prediction neurons" (8). When your mind begins to anticipate an outcome like viewing pornography, the dopamine neurons begin firing rapidly. This happens primarily because the mind knows the reward, due to past experiences with pornography, and it begins to anticipate that you are going to give in and view porn again. This sudden surge of chemicals due to anticipation is very much a part of the hijacking process.

Unless you have trained your mind to analyze a situation, your brain is ill-prepared for the emotional intensity that the mind associates with sexual activities, e.g., meeting someone online, or having an affair. This is similar to individuals who freeze up or make matters worse during a crisis. The emotionally hijacked brain, in most instances, is given free will to act as it wants—and it wants to shove out any logical reasoning.

When I teach clients about how emotional surges hijack the mind, they quickly identify with this and acknowledge that this has happened to them many times. Then, they ask this question: "So what can I do to stop it?" My answer begins with awareness building. In other words, before you can make changes, you need to understand what is happening inside your brain.

The first strategy for reducing the chances of your brain being hijacked is to increase your awareness. Everyone knows the warning signs of their mind being hijacked, but few slow down to realize what is happening inside of them. They feel a strong desire to give in. Then, they begin to feel sexually aroused. Next, they become tense or on edge. This is followed by a struggle with fantasy thoughts and images that they have seen in the past. These are all indicators that the brain is being hijacked.

Once you are aware and have identified that you have been triggered, you have begun the process of "slowing down" your mind. This critical first step allows the rest of the brain to at least join in the decision-making process. Ultimately, you want to learn to slow down, analyze your emotions, and allow the thinking part of your brain to catch up with the emotional brain. Dr. Daniel Goleman described the benefit of slowing down and letting the rest of the brain catch up in his book, Emotional Intelligence: "This neocortical area of the brain brings a more analytic or appropriate response to our emotional impulses, modulating the amygdala and other limbic areas" (9).

As a part of building your awareness, it is important to understand that slowing down your mind won't make your cravings go away. Dr. Schultz found that, with monkeys, once the prediction dopamine neurons were activated, it was common for them to become upset if the outcome they expected was wrong (8). In other words, once your mind and body begin to anticipate that you are going to give in, and then you avoid relapsing, you could become irritated.

Here's a short analogy that may help you to understand better why it is so hard not to give in once your mind starts anticipating a relapse. Imagine that you are at your favorite restaurant, and you have just ordered your favorite dish. You anxiously await its delivery. Soon you see the waiter headed in your direction with the food you ordered, but instead of giving it to you, she gives it to the table next to you. While you are disappointed, you think your order must be next. However, she then turns to you and says, "I'm sorry, we just ran out of what you ordered, and unfortunately, the chef just took a 15-minute break." Not only are you disappointed, but you don't have time to wait because you have to get back to work.

Much like Dr. Schultz's monkeys, when our minds begin to anticipate a specific outcome, they become disappointed when the expected action does not take place. Fortunately, as we increase our awareness and develop strategies to deal with these difficult moments, we can cope better with the initial disappointment. In the remainder of this chapter, we will discuss a step-by-step process you can use to aid you in regulating your emotions.

A Strategy for Regulating Emotions and Improving Your Well-Being

The strategy that I am about to introduce you to can significantly change your life for the better. For many, it will be a new way of being and thinking; it has also become a powerful tool for my clients who learn to use it in their battles to stop their unwanted sexual behaviors. In addition to seeing my clients use this tool, researchers have discovered that individuals who practice this way of being, develop skills to help them better regulate emotions, combat emotional dysfunction, improve patterns of thinking, and reduce negative mindsets (10). This approach is called "mindfulness."

According to one of the leading mindfulness experts, Jon Kabat-Zinn, "Mindfulness is the awareness that emerges through paying attention on purpose, in the present moment, and non-judgmentally to the unfolding of experience moment by moment" (11). Another way to describe mindfulness is deliberately paying attention, being fully aware of what is happening both inside yourself—in your body, heart, and mind—and outside yourself in your environment (12). As mindfulness traits develop, we enhance our capacity for awareness and for self-knowing. This skill is instrumental in helping to regulate emotions and aids in the development of building a more meaningful life.

Imagine what it would be like to be alone for weeks at a time. You have no one to talk to, no electronic devices, and no access to the outside world. What would you think about? What would you feel? Now suppose I gave you a piece of paper and asked you to pay close attention to every thought and feeling and to write them down. Most likely, your self-awareness would increase. You would learn more about yourself and the things that you think about. After a few days of being completely alone, you would likely have a deeper understanding of yourself and why you do the things you do.

Because you likely don't have days or weeks to take off from life, I am going to invite you to slow down daily to evaluate your thoughts and emotions. As you attend to your feelings, you will gain a higher capacity to be aware of what is happening inside your mind and body. You will also pay more attention to your outside environment.

One strategy for learning how to be more mindful is taught by Dr. Daniel Siegel. It is called the curiosity, openness, acceptance, and loving (COAL) approach. He writes, "COAL is the essence of what it means to be in a mindful state" (13). We will look at each of these elements and how you can use them to be mindful.

Curiosity

During times of vulnerability, most of my clients report that their minds are on autopilot and that they just give in to their sexual cravings. This makes sense because, when we engage in any action repeatedly, eventually, our mind stops paying close attention to the details of what we are doing and why we are doing it. For example, if you have viewed pornography hundreds of times, or met multiple people for a random hook-up, you likely have stopped thinking about why you are acting out. Initially, you may have liked the feelings these behaviors produced or how they helped you deal with stress. However, as time passes by, if you engage in these behaviors each time you feel stress, soon you will turn to these behaviors without thinking about what you are doing. As a result, these activities become automatic responses when your stress increases. This is referred to as "mindlessness" or "mindless living."

One way to break out of mindlessness living is to be curious. Curiosity is a valuable first step to help wake up the mind as it helps us return to the "what we are doing" and "why we are doing what we are." The following story illustrates how curiosity can pull you out of mindless thinking.

When Abe was a few weeks away from his final exams, he found that his stress levels increased. He felt pressure to maintain good grades so he could keep his scholarship. As the end of the semester approached, he felt so overwhelmed that he would frequently give in and view pornography or he would reach out to women with whom he had been sexual with in the past. After a few semesters of this behavior, he understood that his stress was causing his relapses, but he didn't know any other way to deal with this pressure other than turning to his sexual behaviors.

After describing to him the process of being mindful, I invited him to search deeper into his mind and ask a couple of questions:

- Why am I turning to pornography and unwanted sexual activities during finals?

- What do these sexual behaviors do for me?

I intended to help him be more curious about his thoughts, feelings, and behaviors. He had long ago stopped thinking about why he was sexually acting out because it had become a habit. He had a difficult time answering the questions. In the end, he said, "I turn to porn and random hookups during finals because I don't know what else to do when I feel that much stress." My question back to him was, "Why pornography? And why sex? Why not something else?" Again, I hoped to increase his awareness and to get him to think more about his behavior. As he thought about my question, he said, "I guess viewing pornography and sex are easy, and they help me escape."

Next, he said, "I don't know why it couldn't be something else."

His thought, "Why it couldn't be something else?" is a good beginning that invites more curiosity. This type of thinking often leads to more questions, which I refer to as curiosity questions. When clients begin asking their curiosity questions, I know that we are heading in the right direction.

Once I knew that he understood the idea of how to implement curious thinking, I explained that this was the first step toward increasing his self-awareness and how he could use questions to better understand and deal with his stress.

Openness

While curiosity can increase our awareness, being open to what we are feeling and thinking is a critical next step. Over the years, many of my clients have shared their experience of trying to ignore, avoid, and push away their cravings. They report having thoughts like, "Don't think about this, it is wrong. What is wrong with me? You shouldn't be thinking about doing these sexual behaviors." Researchers have found that these types of thoughts make matters worse.

In a study conducted on thought suppression, researcher Daniel Wegner and his colleagues discovered that individuals who were asked to avoid thinking about a white bear, couldn't do it. During a five-minute period, the average person rang the bell, indicating that they were thinking about a white bear six times and mentioned a white bear out loud several times (14). In other words, trying to suppress thoughts about your sexual desires does not work.

On the other hand, learning to be open to what you are feeling and thinking is helpful. Openness doesn't mean that you will act out. Instead, openness allows you to acknowledge, without judgment, what you are experiencing. The critical element here is to avoid judgment. Here's how Abe learned to do this as he approached finals:

"I am beginning to feel the stress of getting everything done before finals. I am open to this stress. It is normal during this time of the semester to feel extra pressure. I am sure I am not the only one who feels overwhelmed and anxious. I find it interesting that my desire to escape and sexually act out has gone up. What else could I do besides view pornography or meet up with someone when I am feeling stressed?"

The final question Abe asks himself here is a step in the right direction. It shows that he has allowed his thinking brain to catch up with the emotional brain. It also demonstrates a desire to find a solution. Another thing to pay attention to here is how Abe is talking to himself. Let's contrast this approach with a more common approach.

Common Thoughts and Feelings	Mindful Approach
I hate all of the pressure I feel at work/school. I never respond well under this kind of pressure	I am beginning to feel stress (awareness)
What is wrong with me?	It is normal to feel extra pressure when there are deadlines
Not only am I stressed about work/school, my cravings to act out are off the charts. These feelings are just stupid. This battle is never going to end.	I find it interesting that my desire to escape and act out has gone up. What could I do besides give in?

The difference in these thoughts and feelings are significant and demonstrate the power of utilizing the first two steps of the COAL approach.

Acceptance

For most of our lives, we have been taught that we can control our own destiny. This idea is ingrained in us from an early age. We have heard statements like, "Be the master of your own destiny" and "Take charge." While these motivational statements can be encouraging, they can be discouraging and daunting when you are stuck in an addiction. These mantras inherently imply that all things are or should be in your control. This is an illusion. No one can continuously predict what is going to happen to them, their family, their business, or their finances.

Significant problems arise when the idea of being in control creep into our lives and dominate how we behave and think. When this happens, we begin to think things like, "I should be able to control my thoughts" or "I just don't have enough willpower."

Both of these statements imply that you should always be in control of your thoughts and your willpower. This is not realistic. Instead, it is healthy to realize that we have little control over our initial thoughts and emotions, as described earlier in this chapter. When we understand this concept, instead of engaging in self-critical thinking or reckless optimism, we learn to accept that we will experience challenging cravings, painful emotions, and other challenges. In other words, we will give up the illusion that we are "in control" and can avoid common pitfalls and difficulties in life.

When we learn to do this, we become more likely to accept and accurately describe our thoughts and emotions without feeling guilt or shame. By accepting our sensations and remaining with them, even when they are unpleasant or painful, we give up the idea of always being in control; ironically, we gain more control in the process.

Here's how this works. When you are feeling overly stressed and the craving to give in and sexually act out increases, you accept that desires are typical in situations like this and will not be avoidable. You learn to accept that cravings and withdrawal symptoms are expected as you go through the recovery process. By accepting cravings as normal, you avoid self-judgment and criticism and allow your mind and body to feel the difficult and sometimes ongoing cravings. You will no longer be afraid of difficult emotions, and you will openly acknowledge that you are stressed. The idea of acceptance is that you allow all emotions and feelings to be felt: hurt, pain, cravings, excitement, fear, anticipation, etc.; in the end, by learning to accept these emotions, you are teaching yourself how to regulate them. Instead of trying to control your emotions, you acknowledge that you have them, you accept them for what they are, and, by doing this, in the end, you gain more influence over your own life and your emotions.

The concept of acceptance of feelings and emotions proved valuable for Abe as he approached his finals. Instead of automatically giving in and sexually acting out when his stress levels were high, his curiosity led him to identify the source of his stress. His openness enabled him to feel his feelings, understand his thoughts, and accept what was going through his mind without judgment. By being open and allowing his thoughts and emotions to come, he was able to move through the cravings and focus on his school work.

Loving Kindness

The last and final element of the COAL approach is loving-kindness. Loving-kindness is the essential component that makes being mindful so effective. Dr. Daniel Siegel described it this way: "When we have a COAL state within ourselves, we can call this self-compassion, which certainly is a form of non-narcissistic self-love" (15). Clients who have been involved with pornography and other hidden sexual behaviors often struggle with the idea of self-compassion and loving-kindness. Many people report that their behaviors have made them feel less likable, and they become less tolerant of their thoughts and emotions.

They are critical of their own behaviors.

Fortunately, individuals who feel trapped by their sexual behaviors can reclaim their sense of worth by learning to have more self-compassion. An effective way to do this is to shift from a critical self-evaluation to self-compassion. This can be accomplished by implementing and practicing loving-kindness meditations. This entails applying the first three elements of the COAL approach, i.e., curiosity, openness, and acceptance with your thoughts, feelings, and behaviors. It involves less judgment and more self-awareness, acceptance, and understanding.

When I describe this process to my clients, many of them say something like this, "But if I ignore or minimize what I am doing wrong, I won't change." I readily agree with them that they shouldn't ignore or make light of their sexual behaviors. However, I quickly point out how their negative self-talk and self-loathing will never solve their problem; in fact, it only makes matters worse.

So what is the solution?

Researchers who study self-compassion and mindfulness now have substantial evidence suggesting that self-compassion is a powerful antidote to negative self-talk and an effective form of emotional regulation. Dr. Neff, in her work on self-compassion, reports the following:

- People with higher levels of self-compassion are significantly less likely to suppress unwanted thoughts and emotions than those who lack self-compassion.

- People who are more self-compassionate have more emotional intelligence, meaning they are better able to maintain emotional balance when flustered.

- Self-compassionate people experience less anxiety and self-consciousness when thinking about their problems.

- Self-compassionate people can deal with the challenges life throws their way with greater emotional equanimity (16).

The long-term benefits of developing self-compassion are clear. However, becoming self-compassionate is not always an easy task. An excellent first step toward developing compassion for the self is to increase awareness in your thinking patterns. One way that I have found to raise awareness is to invite clients to consider their self-talk. How much of their internal dialogue is positive, and how much of it is negative? By tracking their thoughts, many realize that they are critical and demeaning of themselves. Literally, over the years, they have accepted negative thinking about themselves and internalized it. However, even when they understand the value of self-compassion, it is difficult to let these old thinking patterns go. They have been building a case against themselves for so long. Nevertheless, as they learn to be more self-compassionate, having loving-kindness toward themselves, they find significantly more peace of mind. The result is that they are more capable of regulating their emotions.

One young man came to my office with his head hung low, feeling a sense of worthlessness. He felt as if he was flawed because of his long history of involvement in pornography and in participating in random hookups with women. "I'm broken," he told me as he sobbed. I realized that, if he were going to heal, he needed to face his belief that he was broken. I introduced him to the COAL approach and encouraged him to consider applying more self-compassion when negative self-talk tapes began running in his mind or when he was feeling painful emotions. I also invited him to pay closer attention to his self-talk. Soon he realized how often he was criticizing himself with statements like "You can't do that" and "Nobody will ever want to be with you." In other words, he had built a case against himself.

As his awareness increased, and he began implementing the COAL approach, he learned to accept his emotions and pay closer attention to his desire to run away from them. Instead of running, he began to be curious about each negative emotion and wanted to learn from his emotions. He also started to accept what he was feeling. Finally, as he began to see progress, feelings of compassion for self increased. He found that, by applying self-compassion, he felt more capable of dealing with his stress and was less likely to turn to pornography when he identified anxious or other unpleasant feelings.

His experience validates Dr. Neff's words: "Self-compassion gives us the calm courage needed to face our unwanted emotions head-on. Because escape from painful feelings is not possible, our best option is to clearly but compassionately experience our difficult emotions just as they are in the present moment" (17). While there are many benefits to applying loving kindness to self, one of the most powerful is that we discover that we don't have to run from our emotions. We can lovingly look at them and seek a more in-depth understanding from them. In approaching all thoughts and emotions we experience this way, we no longer run from stress or difficult situations; instead, we embrace the opportunity to learn what we can from them.

Chapter Summary

The COAL approach is one of many methods that can be used to help you regulate your emotions. In this chapter, we have discussed specific ways that you can deal with your emotions, especially when you are feeling vulnerable to cravings. I have watched as clients implement the methods in this chapter, and they begin to act like experts do when they are dealing with a crisis. I invite you to review this chapter often, especially when you are dealing with difficult emotions.

Finally, if you would like to understand your level of self-compassion better, take the short assessment written by Dr. Kristin Neff, i.e., The Self-Compassion Scale, which is a valuable instrument that you can take for free. When you complete the evaluation, you will receive quick feedback regarding your level of self-compassion. A few of the statements she asks you to evaluate in the survey include:

- I try to be loving toward myself when I'm feeling emotional pain.

- I'm tolerant of my flaws and inadequacies.

- When I see aspects of myself that I don't like, I get down on myself.

- When things are going badly for me, I see the difficulties as part of life that everyone goes through.

- When I fail at something important to me, I become consumed by feelings of inadequacy.

Note: You can take this assessment and obtain your score results at http://www.self-compassion.org/.

Support Resources (found at https://bit.ly/treating-sex-addiction — under Chapter 10)

Audio: The Power of Observing Your Emotions

Part Four

Improve the Quality of Your Life

Chapter Eleven

Building Healthy Habits

Healthy Habits are formed the same way as unhealthy ones - through practice
(Wayne Dyer)

By now, it should be clear that recovery should focus on much more than achieving abstinence or sobriety. I hope that your priority has shifted to improving the overall quality of your life. I want you to be more creative, filled with new energy, and feel more hope for life. I want you to dream again. Often when I talk with clients about making progress in their recovery, I see them looking to the future with more hope and optimism. One client said, "I can see things in color again." When your focus shifts to improving your overall well-being, you will naturally have an improved quality of life. Based on the findings of the researchers who identified the key recovery capital traits, you should naturally experience an increase in the quality of your life (1, 2). Mind you, I don't believe that recovery is complete if your life has not improved, which brings us to the focus of this chapter. If the quality of your life is going to improve, you will need to establish healthy habits.

Before we dive into the strategies for creating better habits, I invite you to keep an open mind about how important this topic is to your recovery. Sometimes, I think it is easy to overlook the critical role our habits play in our day-to-day living. Often it is our subconscious habits that are guiding how we live; because they are in the background of our minds; however, we rarely give them much attention. In his book, *Breaking the Habit of Being Yourself,* Dr. Joe Dispenza discussed an article from the U.S. News and World Report from Feb. 2005, which said, "About 95 percent of who we are by midlife is a series of subconscious programs that have become automatic—driving a car, brushing our teeth, overeating when we're stressed, worrying about our future, judging our friends, complaining about our lives, blaming our parents, not believing in ourselves, and insisting on being chronically unhappy, just to name a few" (3). To think that almost all we do is done on autopilot is kind of scary. Yet it makes sense: If we had to think about everything we did all day long, we wouldn't get anything done.

Imagine what it would be like if you had to think about how to get out of bed in the morning, go to the bathroom, shower, get dressed, brush your hair, and put on your shoes—and, heaven forbid, if you had to think about how you tie your shoes every day. If this were the case, you would probably not get out of the house by noon. Hopefully, you would have a ride because learning to drive a car anew each day might be dangerous. You get my point: 95% of the things we do need to be done on autopilot, without using a lot of energy and thought; otherwise, we would struggle to complete many of our daily tasks.

One problem of living in autopilot mode is that some thoughts and behavioral patterns you engage in simply are not good for you (i.e., excessive sexual fantasy, thinking you are bad, or feeling anxious in social situations). When we don't slow down to analyze what is happening, these patterns continue to guide how you think, feel, behave, and believe.

I should point out here that, when I talk about patterns or habits, I am not just referring to our behaviors. We also have habits related to how we think and how we feel. Yes, even our thoughts and feelings can be put on autopilot. Dr. Dispenza even suggested that we could become addicted to our own emotions. Regarding this, he wrote, "Most of us live in the past and resist living in a new future. Why? The body is so habituated to memorizing the chemical records of our past experiences that it grows attached to these emotions. In a very real sense, we become addicted to those familiar feelings. So, when we want to look to the future and dream of new vistas and bold landscapes in our not-too-distant reality, the body, whose currency is feelings, resists the sudden change in direction (4). It is sad to think about it, but our mind and body can resist change that would be good for us.

My goal in this chapter is to help you challenge the way you think, feel, and act so that you can establish new habits. It will be these habits that will change your life forever, and that will help you reclaim your life as well. The reason for this focus is that, in recovery, your new patterns will eventually become the habits that will lead to sustained improvement. As you act, feel, and think in new ways, you will begin to create new neuropathways. Your brain will be shifting away from addictive habits and will instead start developing new ways of thinking, feeling, and behaving.

Let me illustrate how this happens by sharing a story, as told by Charles Duhigg in his popular book *The Power of Habit*. Here, he tells the story of Lisa Allen, a model candidate in a study by the National Institutes of Health. The institutes were studying former smokers, chronic over-eaters, problem drinkers, obsessive shoppers, and those with other destructive habits. The one thing that everyone had in common was that they had all made remarkable changes in their lives over a short period of time. The researcher's focus was on how the changes were being made (5).

When Lisa was recruited into the study she made significant improvements in her life. Here are some of the key points of Lisa's story, as told by Duhigg. Her husband came home from work one day and told her he was leaving her for another woman. Over the next few months, Lisa's life fell into disarray. She found herself in debt, overweight, depressed, and angry. On a whim, she decided to visit Cairo, Egypt, to see the Pyramids of Giza and the Sphinx. It was there that she decided that something had to change. She made a goal to travel back to Egypt and cross the desert, even though she didn't even know the name of the desert. But, to do that, she would have to give up smoking.

Regarding this transition, Duhigg wrote, "...for reasons (the scientists) we're just beginning to understand, that one small shift in Lisa's perception that day in Cairo—the conviction that she had to give up smoking to accomplish her goal—touched off a series of changes that would ultimately radiate out to every part of her life. Over the next six months, she would replace smoking with jogging, and that, in turn, changed how she ate, worked, slept, saved money, scheduled her workdays, planned for the future, and so on (6).

The researchers found that it wasn't the trip to Cairo that caused the shift; instead, what they found was that, when Lisa focused on changing just one habit, i.e., smoking, it helped her to change other patterns. By focusing on just one pattern—what is known as a "keystone habit"—Lisa taught herself how to reprogram the other routines in her life, as well (7).

The researchers found that, as individuals in their studies began changing one pattern, their brains began to override older pathways. Duhigg described what happened this way: "...when researchers began examining images of Lisa's brain, they saw something remarkable: One set of neurological patterns—her old habits—had been overridden by new patterns. They could still see the neural activity of her old behaviors, but those impulses were crowded out by new urges. As Lisa's habits changed, so had her brain" (8).

What is most exciting about research like this is that we can all be like Lisa. As we intentionally develop new patterns (keystone habits), we will change as well. As you implement a new keystone habit into your life, you, too, can benefit from the cascade of benefits that come from developing new patterns.

Finding Your Keystone Habit

As you consider what habit you would like to begin your change with, there are a few valuable principles to remember as you build new patterns. The following reminders on how to effectively establish new habits were presented in the British Journal of Health in an article titled Making Health Habitual:

1. Decide on a goal that you would like to achieve for your health.

2. Choose a simple action that will get you toward your goal, which you can do on a daily basis.

3. Plan when and where you will do your chosen action. Be consistent: choose a time and place that you encounter every day of the week.

4. Every time you encounter that time and place, do the action.

5. It will get easier with time, and within ten weeks, you should find you are doing it automatically without even having to think about it.

6. Congratulations, you've made a healthy habit! (9)

It is interesting to note that the authors suggested that, in 10 weeks, you should find your new habit will automatically happen. When I read that, I wondered about the old saying that habits are formed in 21 days. As I reviewed the research on habits, I discovered that developing habits is more complex than just giving it a time frame, e.g., 21 days. What researchers have discovered is that more basic habits can be formed in shorter periods of time, e.g., 18–21 days. However, more complex or difficult habits can take longer, up to 254 days (10).

Based on the work of Phillippa Lally and her colleagues, what we now know is that habits are most likely to stick with us once we have engaged in the same behavior for 66 days. In their fascinating article on the development of habits, Lally and her team discovered that roughly 95% of habits become more natural (automatic) around the 66-day mark (11).

If we bring these two ideas together regarding how long it takes to form a habit and starting a keystone habit, we know that, by engaging in the same behavior for 66 days, you will reach the point in which your new actions, thoughts, and emotions can happen automatically. The benefit of doing the same behavior for 66 days is that you will channel your mental energy in ways that will rewire your brain. The added benefit is that if you do this every day for 66 days, it will begin to happen without you giving it any thought. Pretty cool, huh? Finally, as you work on the keystone habit, it will naturally create a trickle-down effect where you will see benefits in other parts of your life, much like Lisa Allen experienced (e.g., more energy, better organization, getting out of debt, etc.). In other words, positive behaviors lead to positive outcomes.

Now that we have discussed ideas on how to establish a new habit, let's review keystone habits that are directly related to building your recovery capital. I provide these examples because they are supported by the research on recovery capital. I have also observed how they have benefitted many of my clients over the years. Please remember that these are just examples. It is more important for you to identify your keystone habit.

My hope is that you have already started thinking about a habit that you want to incorporate into your daily living. Or perhaps you are already doing something daily that is your keystone habit. Either way, as you focus on developing your new habit, you should be experiencing less time thinking about your sexual behavior/s or acting them out. What happens in the change process is that you replace old habits with new ones.

When I present this concept in my groups, I can see the participants' thinking; unfortunately, some of them get stuck because they think that their new habit needs to be something big or grand. The good news is that change actually starts through engaging in small activities (e.g., Lisa Allen gave up smoking and replaced it with running). While recovery may seem complicated, simply starting with small steps can create a foundation for long-term growth and recovery.

Some of the habits my clients have developed include:

- Getting adequate sleep

- Healthy eating

- Exercising on a regular basis (three to five times a week)

- Self-improvement (e.g., reading books, writing in a journal)

- Money management

- And, yes, making their bed (see Admiral William McRaven's book Make Your Bed)

Some of these habits are directly related to items on the recovery capital scale. In many cases, I have watched clients choose a keystone habit that they wanted to develop, which lined up directly with the recovery capital behaviors. What I discovered was that, almost instinctively, my clients were focusing on habits that built their recovery capital. This made a lot of sense, as I believe that we naturally know what we need to do to recover. The challenge is slowing down enough to listen to what our mind is telling us.

For the remainder of this chapter, I am going to explain the benefits of establishing keystone habits from a scientific perspective. However, there is a barrier against developing healthy habits that I would like to address. The issue is related to motivation. Most of us have a difficult time maintaining the motivation to stick with a program to maintain the habit we are trying to form. That is why most people fail to keep their New Year's resolutions.

One way to stay focused on carrying out your new habit is to do it when your energy is high. I believe that most people lose interest in maintaining their new practice because they are trying to do so when they are low on energy. As I will explain, most of us struggle to focus or remain on task when we have little to no energy. Even more concerning is that it is easy to slip back into unhealthy habits when our energy is low. For this reason, there are a couple of principles to remember as you work on developing your keystone habit:

Principle #1: Be Aware of Your Energy Levels

If you are tired or low on energy, you will most likely not feel like doing the activity or event related to your keystone habit. Therefore, if you are aware of this, you can either boost your energy or change the time you start your new habit to a time when your energy is higher (e.g., exercise early in the morning rather than after dinner in the evening). If you feel the need to boost your energy, some examples of how to do this include: 1) taking a short nap; 2) eating a healthy snack; 3) going for a brisk walk.

Principle #2: Reduce the Decisions You Have to Make

As you attempt to establish a new habit, it is best if you reduce the barriers to carry out the activity. Researcher Roy Baumeister discovered that we can experience decision fatigue. Making a decision requires mental energy. The more decisions we have to make, the less energy we have (12). Therefore, if you want to succeed at maintaining your new habit, reduce the number of choices you have to make. For example, if your keystone habit is to report your recovery progress to someone, start by determining who you are going to share your progress with, when you are going to talk with them, and how often you are going to report your progress. The goal is to reduce the number of decisions you have to make.

Let's now review specific habits that can aid in your recovery. I will try to explain the science of why these habits are especially helpful to the recovery process. Remember that you initially should just try one habit but realize that, as you do one of them, the others may naturally start happening as well.

Sleep Habits

How much sleep did you get last night? How has your sleep been this week? Do you sleep well most nights? Your answer to these questions may have more to do with your recovery than you think. Let me explain why. There is substantial evidence that a good night's rest will provide you more energy throughout the day and is especially important when you are dealing with higher levels of stress.

When I examine sleep in the recovery capital scale (I sleep well most nights), around 39% of individuals in our clinical sample reported that they weren't sleeping well. Interestingly, there was a negative relationship between sleeping well and sexual behaviors. Individuals who said that they slept well-reported lower scores on the sexual behaviors inventories that I provided them. In addition, those who were not sleeping well were significantly more depressed (13).

As I contemplated the relationship between sleeping well and recovery, I remembered a book by Dr. Roy Baumeister, *Willpower*, which discusses what happens to individuals when they don't sleep: simply, they run out of energy, which he calls "ego depletion." While there are many ways to deplete our energy, lack of sleep is the primary contributor.

The outcome of depleted energy is not good for anyone, according to Baumeister. Baumeister and his colleagues discovered that when research participants' energy was depleted, "a sad movie made them extra sad. Joyous pictures made them happier, and disturbing pictures made them more frightened and upset. Ice-cold water felt more painful to them than it did to people who were not ego-depleted. Desires intensified, along with feelings. After eating a cookie, the people reported a stronger craving to eat another cookie—and they did, in fact, eat more cookies when given a chance" (14).

Implications from these studies on the recovery process are significant. Baumeister suggests that, if you're trying to resist temptation, you may find yourself feeling the forbidden desires more strongly just when your ability to resist them is down. Ego depletion, he says, creates a double whammy: Your willpower is diminished, and your cravings become stronger than ever (15).

So, if you are one of the 39% of individuals not sleeping well, you might consider developing better sleep hygiene. One way to improve this is to follow these tips, as outlined by the American Alliance for Healthy Sleep:

- Keep a consistent sleep schedule. Get up at the same time every day, even on weekends or during vacations.

- Set a bedtime that is early enough for you to get at least seven hours of sleep.

- Don't go to bed unless you are sleepy.

- If you don't fall asleep after 20 minutes, get out of bed.

- Establish a relaxing bedtime routine.

- Use your bed only for sleep and sex.

- Make your bedroom quiet and relaxing. Keep the room at a comfortable, cool temperature.

- Limit exposure to bright light in the evenings.

- Turn off electronic devices at least 30 minutes before bedtime.

- Don't eat a large meal before bedtime. If you are hungry at night, eat a light, healthy snack.

- Exercise regularly and maintain a healthy diet.

- Avoid consuming caffeine in the late afternoon or evening.

- Avoid consuming alcohol before bedtime.

- Reduce your fluid intake before bedtime (16).

There are many benefits of getting adequate sleep and as you implement the strategies above they will help you increase your overall energy. By improving your sleep habits you will gain strength in other areas. Here's how getting sleep helps. First, as you sleep more, your energy levels will increase. This, in turn, will help you to accomplish your tasks. Second, you will have sufficient energy to combat cravings and temptations. Third, you will have the strength to participate in the activities you desire. Fourth, your body will feel stronger.

As I researched the benefits of getting a good night's rest, I discovered additional benefits, including

- Get sick less often

- Stay at a healthy weight

- Lower your risk for serious health problems, e.g., diabetes and heart disease

- Reduce stress and improve your mood

- Think more clearly and do better in school and at work

- Get along better with people

- Make good decisions and avoid injuries; for example, sleepy drivers cause thousands of car accidents every year

Source: HealthyFinder.gov (17)

Eating and a Balanced Diet

Eating a healthy and balanced diet is not always easy. In fact, if you are like me, you hear the idea of eating healthy and think, "What exactly is a healthy and balanced diet?" I have been taught this most of my life, but I have heard so many versions of what is healthy and what is not healthy that I really don't know anymore. So I went to Google and explored a few websites. I found this definition: "A healthy diet includes a variety of fruits and vegetables of many colors, whole grains and starches, good fats, and lean proteins." I then thought what are "good fats" or "whole grains and starches." Perhaps this shows my ignorance, but I am going to guess that most of us do not think about whether or not we are eating a balanced diet. This is what some people refer to as "eating blindly." The idea is that we have accustomed ourselves to eating what we want and when we want. This form of mindless eating has led the Center for Disease Control and Prevention to declare an obesity epidemic (18).

Perhaps you are wondering how balancing your diet can aid in your recovery. There are many benefits to eating healthy foods. Here are just a few of them:

1. Weight loss
2. Reduce the risk of cancer
3. Diabetes management
4. Heart health and stroke prevention
5. Stronger bones and teeth
6. The health of the next generation
7. Better mood
8. Improved memory
9. Improved gut health
10. Better sleep

If you would like to learn more about the benefits of healthy eating, the website medical news today provides great ideas that are backed by research (19). The key point is that healthy eating habits can go a long way in giving you more energy and can aid you when the battle for recovery intensifies.

Exercise

A common outcome of being stuck in addiction is that it takes a lot of energy. This use of energy often prevents individuals from participating in activities like exercise. Research on addiction and exercise reveals that, prior to seeking treatment, 71% of participants had not participated in exercise six months prior to seeking substance abuse treatment. The researchers defined exercise as "at least 20-minute bouts of moderate-intensity aerobic activity, three times per week" (20).

Interestingly, researchers have also found that consistent exercise aids in blunting cravings (21). In his insightful book *Spark*, Tim Ratey shares a compelling story of the Odyssey House in New York. This inpatient center houses individuals who have been imprisoned, homeless, and whose addictions have turned their lives upside down. Their holistic approach focuses on helping members learn the benefits of exercise. As they progress, some of them run 5-ks and eventually move up to running a full marathon. Director Peter Provet described the benefits: "...exercise can serve as an antidote and as a type of inoculation against addiction." He also believes that, "As an antidote, you're giving the individual an avenue of life experience that most have not had, e.g., the goal of exercise, the feeling of exercise, and challenge of exercise, the pleasure and the pain, the accomplishment, the physical well-being, and the self-esteem" (22).

As we continue to learn more about the benefits of exercise, it is becoming apparent that it is good for us. In addition to helping combat addiction, it has also been helpful in reducing levels of depression, anxiety, ADHD, and stress (23). As I reviewed these findings, it was not surprising to find that individuals who were exercising and maintaining their health reported lower levels of acting out behaviors.

When I address this topic with my clients, I often let them know that they should begin any exercise program with a visit to their doctor to make sure they have proper medical guidance. Once they have medical clearance, I suggest that they start slowly and move up. One client began walking and gradually incorporated running into his training. Soon he had built up his capacity for running and signed up for a 5-k run. Next, he was off to longer distances. The last I heard, he had run a half-marathon.

There are many ways to exercise. If you don't like running, consider biking or swimming. Or perhaps you want to begin your exercise with a nice yoga session. The point is to find what you enjoy doing. If you really want to increase your success in having exercise be your keystone habit, invite someone to join you. Having someone to exercise with often makes it a more enjoyable experience.

Self-Improvement

As I have observed, clients who make the most progress over the years possess a strong desire for knowledge and understanding. Often, they ask me for books and videos, i.e., they want homework between our sessions. They are hungry for change. This is what I refer to as the productivity principle: When individuals engage in positive, productive behaviors, they feel energized, confident, and better about themselves. Productive behaviors lead to positive outcomes.

Some individuals choose to work on recovery by learning as much as possible. By the way, that is what you are doing right now. Good job! As you learn about recovery, you discover so much more about addiction and the recovery process. I believe this is a valuable step to take as you work on your recovery; i.e., knowledge is power.

Some of the key areas I encourage my clients to focus on besides addiction include:

- Emotional regulation
- Family history
- Trauma recovery
- Relationship skill-building

If you want to see my suggested reading list, see Appendix F.

As I type this sentence, I am reminded that my clients who do their best also diversify their learning. Seldom do they just learn about addiction and recovery. Often, they become people who simply love to learn. The idea behind recovery capital is that it should increase the quality of your life. I've had clients change professions, go back to school, and develop a skill that they've wanted to pursue but never felt like they could. The process of recovery almost naturally encourages individuals to live a more full and complete life. You didn't come to this earth without a purpose. You came here to be creative and live a life filled with joy. Obtaining knowledge through learning and skill development will help you find that joy.

Money habits

Whether we want to or not, we all have to deal with money. It's what pays for the roof over our head, the cars we drive, the food we eat, and the rest of our bills. There is no way around the fact that we all need money. In my research conducted with 468 individuals seeking help to stop their sexual behaviors, nearly 75% reported that they worried about money, and 47% reported that they did not meet their obligations promptly (24).

In addition to money being a worry for individuals, it also plays a significant role in relationships. In *For Love and Money: Exploring Sexual & Financial Betrayal in Relationships*, author Debra L. Kaplan quotes an interesting study conducted in 2012 by the American Institute of Certified Public Accountants (AICPA): In their "national telephone survey, financial matters were listed as the most common cause of discord among American couples. Twenty-seven percent of those who are married or living with a partner acknowledged that disagreements over money were the most likely cause of a spat, causing an average of three arguments per month. Financial matters topped the list, beating out children, chores, sex, work, friends, and every other potential bone of contention" (25,26).

Perhaps the survey's most important finding was that "much of a relationship's financial conflict could be traced to a failure to communicate about money matters. Amazingly, 55% of those surveyed admitted that they did not set aside time on a regular basis to talk about financial issues" (27).

Whether you are a spendthrift or a saver, developing a healthy relationship with money can improve your recovery. You can begin by asking yourself a few questions:

1. Do I track my money?

2. Am I intentional in my spending habits?

3. Is there a connection with my sexual habits and my spending habits?

4. Is there a relationship between my spending habits and problems in my relationships? (e.g., conflict over how much money I spend, or do you hide money from your spouse/partner?)

If money is something you are often stressing about, I suggest you take the time to monitor your spending habits and create a financial strategy. Lisa Allen, as previously mentioned, struggled with many compulsive behaviors, yet, as she implemented her keystone habit, she overcame many of them, which included getting out of debt.

Finally, if you want to understand your personal relationship between money and sex more fully, I recommend that you read my colleague Debra L. Kaplan's book, *For Love and Money: Exploring Sexual & Financial Betrayal in Relationships*, which will help you to gain tremendous insight into how money plays a role in many areas of your life, including your sex life.

Suggested Assignment

Because money is such an important issue that we all have to deal with, I suggest that you take a few minutes and write your response to these questions:

Question: What financial habits do I want to form? When I develop healthy financial habits, how will my life be improved?

Make Your Bed

If you watched Admiral William McRaven's graduation address at the University of Texas or if you read his book, *Make Your Bed*, you have likely been moved by his general premise: if you want to change the world...start off by making your bed. As a young Navy SEAL in training, he learned the importance of making his bed. Regarding this, he wrote: "Making my bed correctly was not going to be an opportunity for praise. It was expected of me. It was my first task of the day, and doing it right was important. It demonstrated my discipline. It showed my attention to detail, and, at the end of the day, it would be a reminder that I had done something well, something to be proud of, no matter how small the task" (28).

While making your bed may not be your chosen keystone habit, it demonstrates an important principle of recovery: discipline. When you are in the middle of your addiction, your life is chaotic. By putting structure in your life, you will develop the habits of successful people. The guiding concept of making your bed is to start your day by doing something right. I invite you to consider what behavior you could do first thing in the morning that will help you start your day right. For Admiral McRaven and many other military men and women, they start their day by making their bed. I encourage you to find the habit that gives you the discipline and structure necessary for recovery.

Chapter Summary

As you engage in the recovery process, you will develop healthy habits. It was recommended that you start by developing a single habit, i.e., a keystone habit. As you establish this keystone habit, you will likely experience benefits in other areas of your life. As you create new habits, if you do them for at least 66 days, they will begin to happen automatically. Simple habits may take only 18 days to happen on autopilot, while more complex habits can take up to 256 days.

Based on the recovery capital research, ideas were provided in areas in which you may want to begin developing your habits. Areas discussed include: 1) getting adequate sleep; 2) healthy eating; 3) exercising on a regular basis; 4) self-improvement; 5) money management; and 6) making your bed.

By developing healthy habits, you gain more discipline and feel more confident in your ability to heal and recover.

Chapter Twelve

Creating the Moments that Will Change Your Life

It's never too late—in fiction or in life—to revise.
(Nancy Thayer)

When I asked Terry about his first experience attending the group, he said, "I couldn't believe I was sitting in a room with ten other men listening to them talk about things I promised myself that I would never tell anyone. The first guy described his history of acting out and how he had been clean for six months. He was getting his six-month chip. I thought to myself, 'Holy cow, what am I doing here? I can't tell these guys what I have been doing. Am I going to be asked to share my story, too?' As the evening progressed, I found their experiences were a lot like mine. The only difference was that they talked openly with each other about their challenges. I saw how they freely shared their struggles with each other. Their genuine support of each other impressed me. By the end of the evening, I shared parts of my story with them. That first group experience was when I realized how much help I needed. That night was the beginning of my long journey towards recovery."

When I ask clients to share their experiences with recovery, I often hear stories like Terry's. Often their success stories include broad statements like, "I think my group helped me a lot," or "I had a good therapist." What is often missing in these statements are the moments, i.e., the stories where the change process began.

Usually, as I probe for more information, trying to see if some specific moments or experiences stick out to them, most of my clients have a difficult time identifying one particular event. In most cases, they report incremental changes that occur over time. This supports the idea that change is a process that takes time and consistent effort rather than it being an event.

While I agree that creating lasting change is a process, some experiences are si-lent game-changers that accelerate recovery. In discussions, it is not uncommon for my clients to not recognize these moments. Why? In many cases, it is because they have become so used to their new behaviors that they have shifted out of conscious incompetence and are working on being unconsciously competent (see Chapter 4). While they can readily remember the painful memories associated with their behaviors, their new habits are happening almost automatically.

Terry's story is an example of this process. Initially, he was frightened to attend a group. But as he heard others sharing their stories, he began sharing parts of his struggles. As time progressed, he began to share more and more. What was initially unimaginable became part of his routine. By attending the group, opening up and sharing his story, and eventually becoming accountable with his group, he experi-enced many moments that created change in him.

Terry will tell you that his group played a critical role in his transformation. While I agree, I also suggest that he started down the pathway toward recovery by putting himself into an environment where the change process could happen. This is what I refer to as "creating the moments of change."

Imagine what would have happened if he hadn't attended the group. He wouldn't have seen the value of being with others, neither would he have experienced the power of group—nor would he have seen the benefits of opening up to the group if he had stayed to himself and not engaged with others. Then, when the group was over, he would return home to report that he had just wasted two hours and that he would not be returning. My point is that Terry created the moment by getting in his car, driving to the group, walking in, and opening up his heart to growth and learning. His initial action put him in the right environment where change could happen.

In this chapter, I will discuss some of the most powerful moments that have been shared with me. It's these types of stories that motivate me to keep going, even when I have a client who seems to be stalled in his or her recovery journey. I have come to accept that I can't control when the change will happen, but I believe that, as long as my clients are trying, their moments of change will indeed happen.

How to Create Moments of Change

While there is no formula for creating the exact moments of change, there are three principles that increase the odds of experiencing moments of change for my clients:

1. Place yourself in the right environment

2. Have the right mindset

3. Engage in the work of recovery

Here's an example of how my clients do these three things. When they interact with people actively working on their recovery, they are putting themselves in the right environment. They are learning from others who are succeeding in what works and what does not (e.g., ignoring shame). By simply being around successful people, they observe how others are winning the battle. As they watch others who are succeeding, they develop a similar mindset. They begin to think as successful people think. Finally, as they take action (e.g., call a sponsor in a time of need, practice a relaxation strategy when they are stressed, or surrender when they feel overwhelmed) like others who are successful, they experience what it feels like to succeed. They are creating moments of change.

Jake's experience illustrates this point. When Jake came to my office, he was excited to share with me what had happened to him. I was surprised by how energized he was. For many years, he had struggled in his battle to stop viewing pornography and fantasizing about women. He seemed to be in and out of therapy. He would come for a while, and then I wouldn't see him for a few months. In most cases, when he stopped coming to therapy, he would let me know that he was in a good spot and that he was ready to try on his own. Then, within a few months, he would relapse and return to therapy. We would review his most recent relapse patterns and help him create a new action plan.

After observing this pattern over three years, he came in for a session down and discouraged, asking, "Why can't I overcome this and put it behind me once and for all?" I listened to his concern and then felt like we needed to review the key behaviors associated with recovery capital. As we talked, he realized that he had been doing some of the things related to recovery capital, and, even then, he had only given token efforts to do them. It was at that point that he realized he hadn't fully engaged in as many recovery capital items as he could.

So, when he came into my office excited, I was curious about what had happened. He told me that, during the last session, when I had mentioned that successful people find a sponsor and actively participate in a recovery group, he decided that he would commit to what successful people do. The outcome surprised even him. For the first time, he gave a 12-step group a chance. He had found a sponsor and had already talked with him a few times.

I asked him what made things different this time. Previously, I had talked with him about the importance of finding a sponsor and being accountable to his group. Finally, something kicked in, and he got it. Here's what he shared with me, "I always thought I could just do it on my own. I had attended a group but never really felt comfortable there. Then, when you said, "Successful people don't just attend group, they are actively involved. I realized that I had never really given the group a chance. I had gone through the motions, but I had never really engaged like I am now."

In reviewing Jake's experience, you can see that he was going to group (placing himself in the right environment). Still, he didn't have the right mindset while attending the group, nor did he actively engage in the work of recovery. I have found that when all three things are happening together, moments of change increase.

Over the next few weeks and months, he experienced many moments of change. He started focusing on being in and creating the right environment for recovery. He was attending and participating in groups. Also, he changed what he listened to on the way home from work. Instead of listening to talk radio or music, he shifted to listening to podcasts that discussed recovery, or he listened to motivational audiobooks. Each day, he wanted to learn something new. He began sharing what he was learning with his wife and others.

A few months after making these changes, he began supporting others in recovery. This strengthened his resolve to stay on track and helped him to see his progress. Other areas of his life also improved. He received a promotion at work and ran a half-marathon. He was doing all three of these things, which enabled him to experience many moments of change.

Applying the Flywheel Effect to Your Recovery

For years I have wondered if it is possible to speed up the recovery process. I have pondered how I could help my clients understand what real recovery looks and feels like. I want them to have hope. I want them to realize that their life can be so much better than it has been. Yet I have also seen many people like Jake who make progress and then relapse. They get back up and repeat the same cycle for months and even years. Then, eventually, something happens in their life, and they make tremendous progress over what seems like a short period of time. When this happens, I think to myself, "Why couldn't this have happened earlier?"

As I contemplate the answer to why change takes time, I return to the idea that it takes time to soften a heart. I also understand that change is a process and not an event. When people make sudden changes, in most cases, they haven't developed the habits that lead to sustained healing or recovery. An example of this is what happens to lottery winners after they hit the jackpot. According to multiple studies, about 70% of all lottery winners end up going broke and filing for bankruptcy (1). Even with all their winnings, they go broke because they haven't developed the habits of what financially successful people do.

The books *Changing for Good* by James Prochaska and *Change Anything* by Kerry Patterson suggest that there are stages of change or that change has to be learned. In other words, change requires sustained effort over time. James Collins describes one of the best descriptions of how to gain momentum in the change process in his best-selling book, *Good to Great*.

In writing about the flywheel effect, Collins says, "Tremendous power exists in the fact of continued improvement and the delivery of results. Point to tangible accomplishments—however, incremental at first—and show how these steps fit into the context of an overall concept that will work. When you do this in such a way that people see and feel the buildup of momentum, they will line up with enthusiasm" (2).

The power of the flywheel effect is something that happens ever so slowly in the beginning, but, as commitment and alignment to values occur, the flywheel picks up momentum. Collins, who also discusses companies that went from being a good company to a great company, describes the process this way, "The good-to-great companies tended not to publicly proclaim big goals at the outset. Rather, they began to spin the flywheel—understanding to action, step after step, turn after turn. After the flywheel built up momentum, they'd look up and say, 'Hey, if we just keep pushing on this thing, there's no reason we can't accomplish X'" (3).

The idea of the flywheel can be applied to the recovery process, as Collins uses keywords such as "commitment" and "alignment." When individuals are succeeding in the recovery process, they commit to change and then align with principles that work in recovery. Below are examples of these principles in action.

Aligning with What Works

Samantha was hesitant to seek professional help to discuss her sexual affairs. Yet, she picked up the phone and set up an appointment (Moment of Change #1). As she met with her therapist, she opened up about her sexual struggles with men. She liked the attention. In the first few sessions, she didn't hold back. She talked about things that she had held in secret for years (Moment of Change #2).

Her husband discovered her cheating when he saw a message from another man. He threatened to leave and was constantly talking about divorce. He still didn't know the extent of her behaviors. Over the ten years of their marriage, she had had multiple affairs. She knew that, if he learned the whole truth, their marriage would likely be over. As she considered her options, she decided she would prepare a formal disclosure and tell her husband regardless of the cost (Moment of Change #3).

Over the next few weeks, she did a thorough sexual behaviors inventory (see Appendix D) (Moment of Change #4). This information proved helpful, as she saw patterns that began to develop when her dad left her mom and their family. She had longed for the attention of men. By the time she was in high school, she had learned how to get their attention. This awareness helped her to understand more about herself and her unmet emotional and physical needs (Moment of Change #5).

Eventually, she was prepared to do a formal disclosure with her husband, his therapist, and her therapist. Not knowing the outcome, she read her letter to her husband. While she was afraid of the consequences, she moved forward regardless of the outcome. He was upset and told her he would likely file for divorce. Her response was understanding, "I get it if you feel like that is what you need to do, but I hope you can recognize that I am trying. I want our relationship to work out."

Authors note: Her authentic, non-defensive response was critical. If she had responded defensively, they would likely be divorced today (Moment of Change #6).

During the next few weeks and months, Samantha continued dealing with issues from her childhood that she had never addressed. She uncovered unresolved fears of abandonment, times of self-loathing because of her sexual behaviors, and countless arguments with her mom. As she addressed these issues with her therapist, her confidence grew. She realized why she had been having affairs. This knowledge significantly reduced her need for unhealthy attention (Moment of Change #7).

While it wasn't easy, her relationship with her husband did improve. With the guidance of their counselors, her husband wrote an Impact Letter. The purpose of this letter was for her husband to share how his wife's sexual betrayal had influenced him. After Samantha listened to her husband's letter, she then prepared an Emotional Restitution Letter, which focused on the many ways she had deceived or lied to her husband during their relationship. Usually, this letter reveals the methods used to "gaslight" one's partner.

The term "gaslighting" refers to the ways individuals lie, deceive, or manipulate their partners while hiding their sexual secrets. An example of gaslighting would be telling one's spouse that they are going on a business trip when, instead, they are going on a vacation with their affair partner. Then, the gaslighting continues when the betrayed partners ask about the expenses of the business trip and why the company didn't pay for it, and the betraying partner lies again by saying, "I forgot my business card. My company asked me to submit my expenses to them." Then, when the expenses aren't reimbursed, the betraying partner lies again by making up a lame excuse, "My company is having a hard time financially, and they asked that

I wait a few more weeks to get reimbursed."

Over their 10-year marriage, Samantha had created many lies to cover up her sexual secrets. The emotional restitution letter that she read to her husband brought out many of these lies (Moment of Change #8). My research, with more than 10,000 betrayed spouses, reveals that gaslighting is a significant contributor to the trauma that betrayed partners feel. As a result, I believe that one of the essential elements of couples' recovery is going through the three-step process outlined in this section:

1. Prepare and do a formal disclosure (betraying partner prepares)

2. An impact letter is prepared and read (betrayed partner prepares)

3. Emotional restitution letter is read (betraying partner prepares)

Authors note: If you would like to learn more about the process of doing a formal disclosure, an impact letter, and a letter of emotional restitution, I recommend that you seek professional help from a certified sexual addiction therapist (CSAT). You can find a CSAT in your area by visiting https://sexhelp.com/.

When working with individuals like Samantha, you begin to see their flywheel turning.

As they create more and more moments of change, their flywheel picks up more and more speed. At this point, the resulting momentum continues to improve their quality of life significantly.

As I close out this chapter, I would like to add a few more moments of change that I have observed over the years.

1. Finding a sponsor

2. Reaching out to your spouse before relapsing

3. Attending your first group

4. Having meaningful conversations with your group members

5. Working a 12-step program

6. Talking to your accountability team about a relapse (no secrets)

7. Doing daily activities that support recovery (reading a good book)

8. Making amends to individuals who have hurt

9. Praying more fervently

10. Meditating

11. Serving others

12. Exercising consistently

13. Being financially responsible

14. Avoiding other out of control or addictive behaviors

Chapter Summary

The change process can, at times, be almost undetectable to the individual who has been stuck in addiction. Often, these individuals report that the recovery process takes much longer than they would like it to. However, to those who make lasting change, they discover that they can create moments by 1) placing themselves in the right environment; 2) developing the right mindset: and 3) engaging in the work of recovery.

By aligning with what works, you, too, can create moments of change. Then, over time, your flywheel will start spinning, and progress that seemed slow will pick up speed, and you will experience the power of having multiple small successes as your flywheel to recovery gains momentum.

Chapter Thirteen

How to Establish Meaningful Support for Long-Term Recovery

Please help me find a new way so I can be who I am meant to be.
(Anonymous)

Over the past few years, I have trained therapists all over the world. I invite these therapists to identify someone who has made them feel like he or she matters. I hope that this exercise will help them reflect on how someone made them feel special or understood. Often, as they go through this exercise, they will point to a parent, grandparent, friend, coach, or religious leader as the person who has helped them feel special. I continue this exercise by asking them to think about a specific memory they had with their special person. Quite frequently, this ends up being a tender moment for many participants.

I then ask the therapists to consider how many of their clients have had a special someone in their lives. I ask them how many of their clients currently have someone in their lives who makes them feel like they are important. More often than not, as the therapists think through the list of their clients, they realize that many do not have somebody on their team, i.e., someone who supports them.

We all need someone. Every one of us needs to know that someone genuinely understands and cares about us. My goal is to help these therapists realize that, when our clients have no one to support them, we may be the only person who is trying to understand them. Dr. Daniel Siegel described this notion in his book, *Mind*. He tells a story of when he was a young graduate student, and he had met with a woman for a year and a half. She was preparing to move out of state, thus ending their therapy sessions. He took the opportunity to ask her what exact aspect of the experience had helped her the most.

"Oh, that's obvious," she replied. "Yes," said Dr. Siegel. "I know, but if you had to put words to it, what would you say?" She paused, looking at him with moist eyes, and said, "You know, I've never had this experience before. I've never had this experience of feeling felt by anyone. That's what helped me get better." Feeling felt (1).

When I meet with my clients, I realize that many of them have not had the experience of feeling felt by someone else; if they have, it may have been a long time since they last felt like others were genuinely trying to understand them. This is the reason that my first priority as a therapist is to identify with my client's story. Who are they? How did they end up in my office? What are their main concerns? How are they suffering? If I don't know the answer to these questions, I likely won't understand their deepest challenges, and they won't feel important. It is challenging to address the needs of others when you don't honestly know them and the battles they are facing.

The key idea here is that wholeheartedly seeking to understand someone else can go a long way to build trust and help them realize that they matter. Why do I share this with you? I hope that you will see that you, too, can have more influence on your relationships than perhaps you have felt in the past. You can be in someone's corner when they need it, and you can find others who will be on your team when you need them.

In his book, *Never Split the Difference,* former FBI agent and international hostage negotiator Chris Voss found that even some of the most hardened criminals and terrorists responded when they felt understood. Voss wrote, "It all starts with the universally applicable premise that people want to be understood and accepted. Listening is the cheapest yet most effective concession we can make to get there. By listening intensely, a negotiator demonstrates empathy and shows a sincere desire to better understand what the other side is experiencing" (2).

Voss continued by sharing research from the field of psychotherapy, which found "That when individuals feel listened to, they tend to listen to themselves more carefully and to openly evaluate and clarify their own thoughts and feelings" (3). Perhaps this is one of the key reasons why therapy helps. Therapists are trained to listen and seek a deeper understanding of what their clients are feeling.

In an effort to identify how our clients feel about their families and community support, I reviewed the data from over 450 clients who came to our Addo Recovery Clinics during the first half of 2019. The Recovery Capital Scale, which we administer to clients, asks five specific questions that address how clients feel about the support they receive from their family, significant others, and others in their social network.

Unfortunately, far too many reported that they were not satisfied with the support they felt from family. For example, on one item, we asked individuals to check the box if this statement was true: "I am satisfied with my involvement with my family." In Chart #1, you will see that only about 50% of the client's checked that box, and 53% felt like they had lots of support from their family and friends. You can see the other survey questions and the responses in Chart #1.

Chart #1: Family and Community Support

Survey Question	Not checked (No)	Checked (Yes)
I am satisfied with my involvement with my family	50.6%	49.4%
I get lots of support from friends	46.8%	53.2%
I get the emotional help and support I need from my family	38.2%	61.8%
I have a special person that I can share my joys and sorrows with	29.9%	70.1%
I have a network of people I can rely on to support my recovery	31.6%	68.4%

As I reviewed the responses from the clients coming to our clinics, I began thinking about the 50% of those who were not satisfied with their involvement with family or the nearly 40% who felt like they weren't getting the emotional help and support they needed from their family. Then, I wondered about the 30% who said that they didn't have a special person with whom they could share their joys and sorrows. These results made it clear that many of our clients struggle to create and feel a connection with others.

I began thinking about the reasons my clients and others who took the survey may not have felt close to others. I refer to these as barriers against intimacy and connection. In the next part of this chapter, I address why these barriers exist and how they can be overcome. The chapter concludes with specific strategies that successful clients use to enlist community support in their recovery.

Remove the Biggest Barrier (Shame) So You Can Seek Support

Throughout my career, I have talked with hundreds of clients about their first sexual experiences. Over 50% report that, by the age of 12, they had seen pornography, played doctor, been touched inappropriately by someone else, or engaged in some other sexual activity. These early sexual experiences create a wide range of emotions, i.e., it is common to feel sexually aroused while also feeling embarrassed or ashamed. Unfortunately, many children do not feel comfortable enough to talk with a parent or caregiver about such experiences. As a result, they learn to hide and cover up their true feelings and behaviors.

In other cases, when they did talk with family members, religious leaders, or others about their sexual experience, the given advice proved confusing or not helpful. For example, a common response many clients shared was being told just to stop the behavior and not do it again. Without any explanation of why they should stop or why the sexual experience made them feel the way it did, they felt confused.

In some cases, the responses were damaging. Some individuals have shared with me that they were yelled at, ignored, or made to feel like what they did sexually was evil. Such responses create tremendous shame and shut down any desire to talk about what happened. Once exposed to sexual activity, sexual feelings and curiosities don't just disappear; as a result, those who were shamed usually cover up and hide future sexual behaviors because it was not safe to open up and talk with others about what happened. As a result, they are left to deal with their sexual feelings and desires on their own. This creates the perfect storm for sexual activity to escalate in frequency and intensity.

When secretive sexual behaviors happen week after week and month after month for years, it becomes difficult to open up and share with anyone what has been happening. As a result, relationship connections with others has limitations because those who are acting out do not feel entirely comfortable, letting others genuinely know them. Thus, secrets create barriers against recovery and the development of healthy relationships.

Eventually, hidden sexual behaviors are discovered. Either individuals get caught or they can no longer carry the burden of their secrets. Once the truth is revealed, the person (or people) with whom they wish they could turn to is often so deeply hurt by their disclosure or discovery that emotional support is withheld.

I have been asked many times why people wait so long to talk about their out-of-control sexual behaviors. The answer is shame. The fear of being exposed is scary. The fear of being judged, criticized, made fun of, or rejected is so strong that keeping secrets overrules the idea of seeking help. This is why recovery needs to include shame reduction. When individuals can understand how shame has changed their lives and directly address its negative influence upon them, they often become more willing to reach out and establish meaningful support.

The Influence of Shame on Relationships

Chapter Nine focused on establishing strategies for resolving shame. Now I want to address the specific ways shame hurts relationships and how it prevents individuals from building meaningful support.

When your shame is high, your internal voice is often self-critical and negative. Here's what the voice of shame may sound like, "There is something wrong with me." Or, "I don't belong here or anywhere." In some cases, my clients have reported that they have had those thoughts for most of their lives. What are the consequences, then, of carrying these negative thoughts for so many years?

Eventually, you stop questioning the negative voice and simply accept that what you are thinking is right. At that point, the belief "there is something wrong with me" is so ingrained into how you think that you stop questioning whether it is true or not. Then, as you approach others with the belief, "there is something wrong with me," you will likely fear that others will see your faults, and you will be exposed.

As a result, even though you long for connection, you will likely hold back in your relationships. Or, in a worst-case scenario, if your behaviors are brought to light, you may get angry and lash out. Regarding this, Dr. Daniel Hughes suggested that "When under the conditions of shame, one is not able to hide, but remains exposed to the other, one is likely to lash out in a state of rage (4). Hughes continues by sharing research by Drs. Tangney and Dearing, who wrote, "Individuals of all ages in states of shame are likely to 'shift the blame elsewhere,' externalizing the problem and directing rage at the supposed source of the problem" (5).

In essence, when hidden behaviors are revealed, individuals often lash out at others because of their shame. This is when being critical of others or blaming them for their problems is most likely to happen. This is referred to as gaslighting, i.e., lying, minimizing, and deceiving which are unhealthy forms of engagement that increase trauma symptoms in the betrayed and hurts the relationship satisfaction (6).

An essential reason for reducing shame is that it prevents connections and intimacy from developing. How exactly does it do this? Tangney and Dearing studied the difference between guilt and shame. What they discovered is critically important to understand. They found that individuals who felt guilt had more empathy for others, while those with shame had less empathy (7). This finding suggests that, if your shame is left unaddressed, it will hinder your ability to feel empathy for others. "Empathy is a social and emotional skill that helps us feel and understand the emotions, circumstances, intentions, thoughts, and needs of others, such that we can offer sensitive, perceptive, and appropriate communication and support" (8).

Reread that definition of empathy. Empathy is a skill. When we have it, we have the ability to feel and understand others, which in turn helps us offer sensitive and appropriate support. Usually, when I go over this definition of empathy with my clients, I ask them if they have felt like others have shown empathy for them. They often report that they have felt very little empathy from others. They also tell me it has been hard for them to feel empathy for others.

Many of my clients have told me that it is not easy for them to understand and feel a partner's anger after discovery. They report that they want to run and hide from the intense emotions. When I asked one group of men about why having empathy for their partners was difficult, they taught me a valuable lesson. They said that, when they try and show care or concern for their partner, their efforts are often rejected.

One typical example shared with me is when they say, "I'm sorry," and their partner says something like, "You don't really feel that way or you wouldn't have done what you did." In these situations, they have a difficult time feeling empathy for a partner because their attempts to repair what they have done are rejected, which triggers their feelings of shame (i.e., I'm not enough, I can't do this right).

In this example, my suggestion to the group is to stick with the pain of their partner. I ask them to stop and think about what their partner is really feeling. They are hurt. However, instead of saying, "I am hurt," they show anger. So, what they are saying is, "You have no idea how much you have hurt me, and now I am going to protect myself because I don't want to be hurt again."

By staying focused on a partner's pain, the group begins to develop more empathy for what these partners have been going through. We will often role-play a variety of cases, so they begin to understand the importance of using empathy to help one's partner heal. If you would like to learn more about developing empathy in your recovery, I cover this in my advanced online course (See Resource Section).

Whether or not you have been given empathy throughout your life, it is a skill that will benefit your life, and it will improve your chances of succeeding in your relationships. We all need to give and receive empathy. We all suffer in unique ways, so when we have people who give us empathic responses, we feel heard and understood. When we experience this kind of caring response from others, mentally, we calm down and allow people into our lives. This is how meaningful relationships develop.

To summarize, one of the most significant barriers against finding meaningful support is unresolved: shame. Shame prevents connection. Shame limits your ability to stay present when people in pain are upset. Shame triggers rage and defensiveness. Shame limits your ability to have empathy. The solution, then, is to reduce shame and increase your empathy for others. Empathy helps you feel the suffering of others; it enables you to repair the wounds you have created, and it gives you the best opportunity to succeed in your relationships.

Role-Playing an Empathic Response

Empathy may not come easy for you, especially if you have not had a lot of experience with it throughout your life. The good news is that it can be learned, and you can see positive results when you develop it as a relationship skill. In my relationship-skill-building classes, I help participants increase their empathy by role-playing situations where they wish someone would have had empathy for them.

One of the specific areas I focus on is painful or traumatic memories associated with my clients' first sexual experiences. I will often role-play with them what a healthy response would be from a loved one upon discovery of his or her sexual behavior. Here's an example of what happened versus what could have happened.

Situation: A seven-year-old boy and girl were playing doctor when the young girl's mom entered the room. Enraged, the mom tells her daughter to get dressed and yells at the boy that he is in big trouble. She grabs him by the neck after he quickly gets dressed and marches him to his house. His family is sitting down for dinner. Upon entering the boy's house, the girl's mother speaks loud enough that the entire house hears what the boy was doing. His parents, equally upset, tell their young son to go upstairs to his room, and they will talk about it later.

Response #1: What actually happened.

The boy's parents told him what he was doing was bad and that he should never do that again. They told him he couldn't go over to that girl's house ever again. They also said that he wouldn't be allowed to play with others if that was what he was going to do. They concluded by asking him if he knew that what he did was wrong. He said yes, out of fear, not out of understanding. After that experience, the boy became more reserved. He felt out of place in his own home. He believed that he was a bad boy.

Therapist note: This event influenced this boy for decades. He was young and didn't understand the adults' responses. There is so much that could have been done differently to educate this boy and comfort him. Instead, he was shamed and left alone to deal with something he didn't understand.

When I hear stories like this, I know that one way to help a client heal is to go to that specific memory or situation and role-play the event using an empathic response.

Response #2: An empathic response

Mom: Son, how are you doing? I would feel a little scared. (Notice mom trying to identify what the boy might be feeling.)

Boy: Yeah. I was scared, Mom.

Mom: Can you help me understand what happened?

Boy: I was playing at Jenny's house, and she told me about a game called doctor. She said we had to take off our clothes to play.

Mom: Then what happened?

Boy: We took off our clothes. Jenny told me that I should be the doctor, and she would be the patient. She was just going to lay down when Jenny's mom came into the room and found us.

Mom: What happened next?

Boy: I quickly got dressed while she yelled at me and told me I was in big trouble and that I would never be allowed to play with Jenny again.

Mom: I bet that made you feel sad. You like playing games with Jenny.

Boy: I did, but I can't play with her anymore.

Mom: Do you know why Jenny's mom was so upset?

Boy: Because we were doing something bad.

Mom: Did you know what you were doing was bad?

Boy: No! I felt it might be bad, but I didn't know.

Mom: Son, you are not a bad boy. You are a really good boy. I am glad to be your mom. You make me happy, and I love the way you are.

Boy: But I can't be friends with Jenny anymore because I did something bad.

Mom: Son, you are just learning about these things. You didn't know what you were doing was bad. Can I tell you why I think Jenny's mom was so upset?

Boy: Yes.

Mom: First, our bodies are special, and we want to protect them. Your body is yours. Jenny's body is hers. When you are young, it is normal to be interested in how boys and girls are similar and different. However, because your body is so special, it is something that we don't share with anyone, including Jenny.

Boy: I see. Jenny's mom was mad because we weren't protecting our bodies.

Mom: Right, she was trying to protect her daughter. Would you like me to talk with Jenny's mom about what happened? And would you like to speak with Jenny about what we have talked about?

Boy: Do you think it would help so I can be friends with Jenny again?

Mom: We can try.

Authors note: This example illustrates how a loving and kind mom helped her son work through the experience that made him feel like he was a bad boy. Notice how she began with questions, which would help her to understand what had happened. Then, she validated her son by telling him he was a good boy. This is critical because he was already starting to believe that he was a bad boy. Finally, his mom educated him about his normal curiosities and helped him to understand the importance of protecting his body. As he got older, his mom could have taught him about healthy sex and it's importance in relationships.

Moments such as this can influence a person's approach to relationships. When we are fortunate enough to have someone who shows us empathy, we do not get stuck in the adverse event. Instead, it becomes a memory of an event that happened rather than a life-altering experience.

Usually, when I role-play situations like this one with clients, they begin to see the power that empathy could have had upon their experience. They also realize how empathy would have helped them in relationships with others. Empathy is a healer and enhances our ability to feel connected with others. The good thing is we can all develop our empathy skills, which will make us better in relationships with others. As you go through your recovery journey, learning to give and receive empathy from others will be a valuable skill to have.

Utilizing Family and Community Support

While a therapist can provide substantial support during the recovery process, research shows that there are more effective options. In 2007, Moos and Moos, in studying the influence of family and community resources on the recovery process, found that clients gained little from individually focused addiction treatment when it failed to mobilize family and community resources (9). Researchers studying long-term recovery outcomes found that family and community support was more important than any individually focused treatment with those who were dealing with severe addiction (10). While this is not surprising, it is an essential reminder that, if you want to succeed in recovery, your chances significantly improve when you enlist family, friends, and other community members in your recovery efforts.

The reality is that most people who begin recovery don't have the type of re-lationships where they feel comfortable enough to say, "Hey, I need some help. I feel like my life is getting out of control, and I have been doing some pretty crazy things. Could you please help me?" Instead, many people feel quite the opposite about seeking help from others. They don't want to burden others with their prob-lems, or they feel like no one cares.

I have often wondered how different our world would be if we all had someone to turn to in our times of need. Imagine being able to share with someone your challenges and know that that person was genuinely concerned about you and your well-being. What would it be like knowing that you wouldn't be judged but, instead, would be given love and support? This may sound like a fantasy world, but this is what healthy people do in relationships.

For individuals who are married or in a committed relationship, you will probably not receive empathy from your partner as he or she deals with your betrayal. That person is dealing with his or her own feelings and should not be expected to provide empathy and support in the beginning part of the recovery process. This can come with time, as you develop empathy for your partner's pain and trust increases in your relationship. As you both work toward healing and recovery, emotional connection can increase in your relationship as you both learn to see each other's suffering.

As you work toward recovery, you will want to find others who truly understand you. You will want to find people who can show you empathy even when you are struggling. I have found that those in the community who are most capable of helping throughout the entire journey are:

- Accountability teams (group support)
- A sponsor
- A spiritual leader
- A supportive family member
- A close friend

Learning to utilize community support is not easy; yet, community support has consistently been found to be among the most useful resources for individuals who succeed in recovery. If you are like many of my clients, you may feel resistance to the idea of reaching out for support. The idea of attending a group, finding a spon-sor, or talking with someone else can feel overwhelming. If this is a barrier for you, let me share some of the ways others in your community can aid in your recovery and what support can be like.

Accountability Teams

An accountability team is a group of individuals who are experiencing similar challenges. They can provide you excellent support during your vulnerable moments. They can also give you a reality check when you need to talk through something you are going through at home, at work, or in other areas of your life. Accountability teams support each other beyond relapses. A network of people provides you with the strength to keep going. They allow you to feel like you are not alone. I have seen accountability teams who dine together, attend sporting events of another group member's children, and give each other birthday gifts. In summary, accountability team members become friends.

If you do not know where to start finding an accountability group, look up one of the following organizations:

Group	Link
Sex Addicts Anonymous	https://saa-recovery.org
Sexaholics Anonymous	https://www.sa.org
Sex and Love Addicts Anonymous	https://slaafws.org/meetings
S.A. Lifeline Foundation (spiritual)	https://salifeline.org/#blog

These four organizations focus on the 12-step program and also encourage participants to have a sponsor. If you have never been to a meeting, your first visit may feel uncomfortable; remember, however, each member of the group also had his or her first meeting, too. An accountability group can provide you with extra support when you have no one else to turn to. Finally, some of the organizations listed above have online support groups if you are not able to make it to a meeting in your area.

Finding and Utilizing a Sponsor

Finding a good sponsor is critical in your recovery. This person will support you when you need someone to talk to. He or she can call you out when you are minimizing or rationalizing certain behaviors. This person may even reach out to you if you haven't been in contact in a while.

When I work with individuals, I encourage them to share three things with their sponsor [note: this model was originally created by Dr. Patrick Carnes and can be found in his works (11)]:

1. If they relapsed (note that a relapse should be a specific behavior or thought, e.g., viewing pornography, visiting a massage parlor, allowing a fantasy to

replay over and over in one's mind, etc.)

2. If they have slipped (a slip is defined by the individual; examples include visiting a website that usually leads to relapse, intentionally driving by a place where you acted out in the past, looking at someone in a sexual way and allowing that thought to linger in your mind).

3. Positive behaviors. Some people call these "dailies." A daily is something that helps prevent a slip or relapse. Examples include reading a good book, visiting a friend, doing an act of service, attending a meeting, calling your sponsor.

At the beginning of recovery, I usually recommend that clients reach out to their sponsor daily. This type of accountability helps sustain progress and helps prevent multiple relapses.

A good sponsor can also help you to avoid certain pitfalls. For example, a sponsor may begin seeing specific patterns in your behaviors and can point them out to you (e.g., They might say, "It seems like most of your relapses are happening late at night. Let's come up with a plan you can use at night").

If you have a good sponsor, he or she will also become a good friend. You will learn to use this person's brain when yours has been hijacked. A sponsor will know a lot about your life and your challenges and support you and guide you through the recovery process. As you make progress in your recovery, you, too, can help others.

A Spiritual Leader

Over the years, I have had the privilege of meeting with and training many religious leaders from various denominations. The most common question they have for me is, "How can I best help those who seek my help?" Many have enlisted my support and other professionals to educate themselves about sex addiction.

A good spiritual leader can provide significant support throughout your recovery efforts. Some of the ways a religious leader can help include:

- Give spiritual guidance and help you work through the repentance process

- Provide you spiritual support (e.g., spiritual readings, praying for you)

- Consistent accountability (being accountable with a religious leader can help during stressful times)

- Provide support to your partner, if you are married, while also providing help to you

- Enlist someone in your congregation to help you (often spiritual leaders know others who you can turn to for additional support)

- Provide you additional support resources in your area (e.g., 12-step groups in your area, a therapist that they know and trust)

A Supportive Family Member

Over the years, I have received mixed responses from clients when discussing whether a family member could be a part of his or her recovery team. Some of them feel comfortable talking with their family members about their sexual addiction, while others wouldn't dare share with their family what they have been doing. Those who do speak with their family members still need to learn how to best utilize their family for support.

Unfortunately, many of the clients I have worked say they can talk with their family about their struggles, but few are asking for help when they need it the most. If you have family support, are you doing the following?

1. Telling your family members what you need help with and when (e.g., I need to call someone while on business trips so that I don't hire an escort).

2. Asking your family member to call you if they haven't heard from you in a few days.

3. Reporting to your family member any slips, relapses, and positive activities you are engaging in.

4. Calling your family member when you are triggered.

If you have a family member who is willing to support you but isn't doing any of the steps listed above, you might consider sharing this list with that person and asking him or her to support you.

A Close Friend

Sometimes the best support comes from a best friend. While you may not have thought about using a friend to support your recovery efforts, I can tell you that many of my successful clients find that their friends are helpful. One client said to me that his friend was supportive but not intrusive. His friend would simply ask him how the battle was going. This question let my client know that his friend was following up on him—not in an intrusive way but in a way that helped my client feel that someone was watching over him.

If you are afraid of being judged by your friend, the following story may be helpful. I was talking with a client about the potential people he could enlist to be on his recovery team. He identified a friend to talk to and set up a time for them to talk. When he revealed to his friend what he was struggling with, his friend said that he, too, was struggling with the same challenge. They became a part of each other's support team. When you start talking to others about your sexual behaviors, you may be surprised at how many are going through something similar to you.

As I have reviewed the literature on what successful people do, I am reminded that recovery is not a solo experience. Individuals who try to achieve recovery on their own struggle to gain traction because they are flying solo. In contrast, when secrets are brought out into the light, they often melt away. I encourage you to develop your recovery team.

In a training I attended by the late Mark Laaser, I learned a valuable lesson about having a whole team to support your recovery. Dr. Laaser, also a recovering sex addict, shared this story with us: "A few years into my recovery, I found myself having a really difficult day. So I pulled out my list of people who could support me. I called the first guy. No response. I called the second person on my list. No answer. And so it went...person three...four...five...six...seven. Finally, the eighth person on my list responded." His point was that having one person or two may not be enough on really difficult days. He had at least 16 people on his list. Successful people build their recovery team and learn to trust them throughout their journey to recovery. I invite you to create your support team.

Chapter Summary

It is easy to think, "I can stop viewing pornography, hiring escorts, or engaging in random hookups on my own." However, researchers have discovered that having a team to support your recovery is one of the best things you can do to maintain sobriety (12). One of the primary reasons people avoid seeking help is due to shame. When shame is high, a person will hide behaviors and often get upset or angry when caught. One of the most effective ways you can overcome shame is to develop empathy for others. This, in return, will increase your relationship skills and help you remain comfortable when reaching out for support.

As your relationship skills increase, you will feel more comfortable reaching out for support. I have watched individuals, as they progress in their recovery, turn to a sponsor, call a friend, or reach out to a family member when in need. Mind you, these relationships don't happen overnight; gradually, however, successful people develop a network of people who can support their recovery. They realize that there is no need to fly solo.

Support Resources (found at https://bit.ly/treating-sex-addiction — under Chapter 13)

- Accountability for those Working Recovery (Video)

https://utahcoalition.org/project/accountability-working-recovery-sup-porting-others-recovery/

- A Dialogue with Your Sponsor (Video)

Chapter Fourteen

Loving Your Way Through Addiction Recovery

In order to be loved, we have to love, which means we have to understand.
(Thich Nhat Hanh)

As I listened to Sara's story, it was hard for me to hold back the tears. Her husband had died in the act of cheating on her. She didn't get to say good-bye. She didn't get to see him become the man he told her he wanted to be. When others asked about how he died, she had no idea what to say to them. She tried to protect his reputation and the memories others had of him, but she felt like she was living a lie.

As we talked, it was clear that she had loved him and that he had attempted to give her love, even through his addiction. She shared with me the difficult times they had had with his addiction. Through it all, she had tried to forgive him and see his goodness. On the other hand, he couldn't love himself. She said he had been extremely critical of his behaviors and periodically would tell her that she should move on because he couldn't stop. Then, he would reverse-course and express a heartfelt regret and tell her he needed her. They had been on this roller coaster for years. He would do well for months at a time, and then he would disappear into a sexual trance. By the time he came out of the trance, he had violated her trust and broken her heart. She had picked herself up so many times, and each time she tried her best to move on. She had loved him through everything, and now he was gone.

As I listened to her story, I found myself questioning a core assumption that I had made throughout my career. I believed that if my clients had someone who loved them, they would heal and recover. Sara's experience with her husband made me question this long-held belief.

Eventually, I realized that my assumptions were wrong. I had been thinking about recovery and love the wrong way. Here's how my belief has changed. I now believe that being loved can increase one's desire to recover, but it can never replace the importance of loving and accepting oneself. I am not talking about a narcissistic form of love. I'm talking about a genuine love that comes with understanding who one really is and then living up to that potential. In order to heal, we must learn to love better, and the first step is to love ourselves better.

When we love ourselves, we will naturally love others. This principle was taught in the New Testament. When Christ was asked which commandment was the greatest in the law, he answered, "Thou shalt love the Lord thy God with all thy heart, and with all thy soul, and with all thy mind. This is the first and great commandment. And the second is like unto it, Thou shalt love thy neighbor as thyself" (1).

What would the world be like if we loved our neighbors the same way we love ourselves while in our shame? Imagine this conversation with your neighbor: "I was thinking about you the other day, and I decided that you're useless. I'm pretty sure that everybody thinks you're a waste. You are a loser." Most people would never say something like this to their neighbor, and yet they speak this way to themselves all the time.

Jesus expected that we would love ourselves and others. This type of love begins with compassion for self and then extends to others. I believe that this type of self-love after a long history of living with toxic shame is the most critical step you will take in your journey to recovery. I want you to learn to love your way throughout the recovery process—both yourself and those around you. This will increase your opportunities for finding and creating genuinely intimate and loving relationships.

I often think about Sara's husband. He had a loving wife, but he hadn't learned to love his way through addiction recovery. I wish I could have met him. I would like to have helped him see himself through a different lens, one where he didn't see himself as broken or helpless or hopeless. Instead, I would like for him to have seen himself being the loving man he truly was meant to be. Yes, he got lost, but his true identity was never completely gone. Sara said he would try and succeed for months and sometimes years at a time. He wanted to heal, but he never wholly believed it was possible for him. Due to this belief, he had never reached out to anyone besides his wife for support. She was very patient, and he was much better than he realized, but his fears had prevented him from seeking specialized help for his compulsive sexual behaviors.

If I could sit down with him today, I would seek to understand how he thought and felt about himself. I would want him to feel understood and not judged. I would want him to feel like he could share his challenges with me. I would want him to know that help was available to him. I would do this by sharing with him the principles of what successful people do in recovery. Specifically, I would want him to understand the power of building recovery capital (see Chapter 1). I would want him to learn emotional regulation skills (see Chapter 10). Together, we would help him create a recovery plan (see Chapter 4). We would focus on helping him develop healthy habits (see Chapter 11) and develop more meaningful support (see Chapters 6 and 13). Most importantly, we would address his shame (see Chapter 9) and help him develop self-compassion (see Chapter 7). By learning to do these things, he would see his true worth and value.

I believe that, had he learned these skills; he would have eventually come to love himself. Also, he would have been more capable of loving others. He would have seen Sara and attempted to be more aware of her needs. He would also be better at understanding the needs of others and responding to help them. He would have been loving his way through addiction recovery.

I know the idea of loving self and others through recovery may sound difficult and perhaps even strange, but for me, it is the answer to long-term healing. I almost left this chapter out of this book because it sounds odd, "love your way to recovery." However, after meeting with client after client and seeing the positive influence this idea had on them, I realized I couldn't leave this chapter out. Love will combat shame, improve your most important relationships, reduce loneliness, and help you feel more connected with others. Love is a powerful tool you can include in your journey to recovery, but it will need to be the right kind of love.

Let me explain what I mean when I say the right kind of love. Love, true love, is not a sexual exchange between two people who hardly know each other. Nor is love found in sexual videos found online for self-gratification. Love is a tender interaction between two committed people who value each other and seek to bring the other joy. This type of love is built on principles of trust and honesty, service and sacrifice, and kindness and compassion for the other.

Another way to explain what love is and what love is not is by explaining the difference between love and lust.

The Difference Between Love and Lust

A challenge that many of my clients face is that while having an affair or engaging in other sexual activities outside of their primary relationship, they experience physical and emotional feelings that parallel love. These emotions can be confusing to them and others. After all, how can they love their spouse and this new person?

If we explore the physiological differences between love and lust, we may find the answer.

When I talk with clients who are confused by their feelings, I try to explain to them the difference between love and lust. According to researchers the primary chemicals associated with love are oxytocin and vasopressin. These neurochemicals are associated with attachment and are different from those involved with lust (testosterone-induced dopamine and norepinephrine)(2). Understanding the difference between being "in love" and "in lust" can be explained by the extent the neurochemicals that are released into the body. An individual who has oxytocin and vasopressin flowing through their body will desire social bonding and connection. They will seek to nurture and comfort the one they love. Conversely, individuals with high levels of the lust hormones testosterone and norepinephrine may be unable to experience social bonding. They will seek out sexual contact, but never allow attachment to occur (3).

In a committed relationship, two individuals will actually receive both the love hormones and lust hormones. This is a crucial point to make because some people do not believe that any lust is healthy. The lust neurochemicals testosterone-induced dopamine and norepinephrine are what bring excitement and sexual pleasure to our relationships. Furthermore, when the lust hormones are released, they can also increase the presence of the love hormones oxytocin and vasopressin which strengthens the bond in relationships. The critical difference between individuals who attach and those who don't in relationships is the neurochemical balance. Individuals trapped in addictive tendencies have elevated dopamine and norepinephrine levels, which dampen the release of the love hormones. (4)

I have observed that individuals who have affairs do feel both love and lust hormones. While the lust hormones may be more dominant, they do desire to bond and connect with their lover. However, when their secrets are discovered, and their primary relationship is on the line, their infatuation comes to a screeching halt. Suddenly, they are facing a very stressful decision. Should I leave with my lover or stay with my spouse who I have been married to for years. While I have seen this decision go both ways, those who attempt to repair their marriages often realize that they were blinded by lust while having their affair.

As individuals continue in their recovery efforts, they shift away from lust and towards love. They recognize others' suffering (compassion) and feel their pain (empathy). This happens when they attend 12-step groups and hear about the challenges and difficulties of those in their group. It also happens when they attempt to repair the hurt and pain that their behaviors created for their spouse and others (making amends). As their compassion and empathy increases, they will naturally increase their levels of oxytocin and vasopressin. If we looked at the transition from lust to love from a neurochemical view, we would see an increase in the bonding chemicals, oxytocin and vasopressin and a decrease in the lust based neurochemicals.

Now that I have discussed what love is and what love is not, let's turn our attention to the role of self-love in the healing and recovery process.

Self-Love

When leading a recovery group, I will often ask the participants this question: "How many of you feel like you are good at loving yourself and others? Most group members respond that they have not been good at giving and receiving love. I will then ask: "Why do you think you struggle with love in relationships?" While I have received many responses to this question, the most common answers are 1) Shame, I don't love myself; and 2) I didn't have a good example; I feel like I was never taught. This is when I ask, "If you could learn how to be more loving, would you be interested?" The universal answer is yes. Everyone wants love. As Thich Nhat Hahn said, "We all need to love and to be loved" (5).

One of the challenges we face in our society today is that many of us did not see a successful relationship while growing up. To illustrate this point, I invite you to consider this question: "While growing up, how effective were your parents at teaching you to have a healthy marriage?" I typically ask my clients to give their parents modeling of a healthy relationship a score between (10 being outstanding and 0 not good at all). Rarely, do I get more than 50% who give their parents a score above five. I would say the average rating would probably be a 3 or 4. As a society, we are not modeling healthy relationships. This means that, if we are going to improve in our relationships, we have to learn how to do better than the models we experienced growing up.

What score between 0 and 10 would you give your parents' modeling of a healthy relationship?

This chapter provides ideas that you can use to love and connect on a deeper level with the people who matter the most to you. I hope that these strategies will help you realize that love is a choice you can make every day. You can learn to love your way to recovery.

Powerful Principles for Loving Your Way Through Addiction Recovery

Josh looked at me and asked, "What if I try and she rejects me? I'm not sure I can deal with her rejection again." Josh had been working hard on his recovery for a few months and was making good progress. Before starting therapy, he had had multiple affairs during his 10-year marriage to April. He finally realized the hurt and pain he had created for her and their children. Now, he was genuinely trying to save his marriage and his family.

It had been nearly a year since he had disclosed his behavior to April, and I had been working with him for three or four months. I could tell he was discouraged. When I inquired what was wrong, he said, "I thought we would have a better relationship by now, but I think it's getting worse, not better." He felt emotionally distant from April and didn't know what to say or do to make things better.

According to April's therapist, she, too, was making good progress, but she wasn't ready to forgive and move on. She was afraid to trust him again because he had been so good at hiding his behaviors. She thought she knew who he was, but after discovering his infidelity, she had to re-evaluate everything she thought she had known about him. She felt like she didn't know who he was anymore. She had stopped monitoring all of his behaviors and being critical of him. She was also sleeping better and talking with a friend when she needed support.

While they were making good individual progress, their relationship was not moving forward. They were stuck. This is a common occurrence for couples as they work on their recovery. I have observed that two people can work on their individual healing, but that does not necessarily mean that they will know how to repair their relationship. This was the case with Josh and April.

As we talked about their interactions, it was clear Josh wanted a better relationship with April, but he wasn't sure she could ever forgive him. He also wondered if she had stopped loving him and was just staying in the relationship for the sake of their children. For many years, he had felt inadequate in his relationship with April because she didn't know about his sexual secrets. He felt like she would have never married him had he disclosed to her the depth of his involvement with pornography before their marriage. Then, when he cheated on her, he believed that, if April knew everything, she would leave him and take the children with her.

The feelings of being inadequate and unlovable were not new to him. While growing up, he wasn't close to either of his parents. When he was eight or nine years old, he found his dad's porn stash in the garage. It didn't take long before he was sneaking magazines out of the garage and viewing them while his parents were gone. He learned to hide his sexual behaviors (i.e., primarily viewing pornography and masturbation) from his parents, even though he didn't know how they would respond.

He told me that he believed his parents were so busy with their problems that they didn't have time to parent. He described intense fighting and conflict between his parents. After leaving home, he learned that his parents were cheating on each other. They eventually divorced.

Josh had never really connected with his parents, and now he felt like he was going to lose his wife and children. It was one thing he had told himself would never happen to him. His fears were coming true. He had cheated like his parents, and he was not going to have the relationship he wanted to have with his children.

Can you feel Josh's worries?

I could, but I knew something that Josh didn't. April hadn't made her decision about whether she would stay or leave their relationship. She was trying, but he couldn't see her efforts due to his fears. No, she wasn't ready for a closer relationship, but she did want to see how he responded to therapy. She was watching to see if he would find a sponsor, attend a group, and follow through on these commitments he had made. She also was looking for consistency. Most importantly, she was hoping he would be more aware of how his actions had hurt her. Knowing that these things mattered to her, I had hope for them.

Helping Josh be patient with the healing process was not easy. When April would tell him that she wasn't ready for a closer relationship, he interpreted that to mean that she wouldn't ever want to be with him again. I invited him to focus on the things he could control instead of on whether April was going to forgive him.

He gave me a challenging look as if to say, "What are the things I can control?"

This was the opportunity I was looking for. I said, "You can have much more influence in your relationship than you think — everything you do and say matters. You can be positive. You can lift April and your children by smiling and saying kind things to them. You can find ways to serve the members of your family."

"But will it work?" he asked.

"Does it matter? You will be a better man if you do these things."

This was a significant turning point for him. He realized that he had been worrying so much about losing his family that the fear had nearly paralyzed him. When April was upset at him, or he felt emotionally distant from her, he would get upset and fight with her, or he would pull away and sulk; neither of these responses was helping their relationship get any better. As we reviewed the patterns of conflict in their relationship, he began to see that he had focused solely on her responses to him. He had been playing the victim role. She didn't want to connect, so he had pulled away. In the victim role, he wasn't thinking about how he had hurt her through his actions.

This awareness helped us turn the attention in therapy to how he could respond when April was upset. He realized that he needed to focus on his recovery and learn how to react differently to her when she was angry. As we reviewed their patterns for fighting, he had questions about how to respond when April was upset. He told me that, when she was angry, he didn't know what to do or say. I took this opportunity to help him understand that there were principles that, when applied, could help him respond more effectively to April. These principles, when used in relationships, lead couples to have a better understanding of each other. I explained to him that if he applied the ideas, he would be better at loving his way through recovery.

In the next part of our discussion, I outlined the principles that I have found to be effective in helping individuals develop better relationship skills. These relationship principles, at a minimum, help my clients feel better about themselves, and, in best-case scenarios, they improve the odds that their relationship can make it.

Principle #1: Develop a Compassionate Mindset

In Chapter 7, I wrote how compassion is a key ingredient to recovery. While self-compassion is essential for recovery, compassion for others is equally important for healing relationships. The first principle of loving your way to recovery is to develop a compassionate mindset.

Here's an example from the conversation that I had with Josh.

Josh said he didn't know what to say to April when she was upset. When I asked him how she acted when she was angry, he said, "She starts asking me question after question. Why did I lie? Did I really want to be with her? Why wasn't she enough? Did I like having sex with the other women more than with her?"

When I asked him how he responded to all of her questions, he told me that he would just shut down and listen to her until she was done. When she finished talking, she would ask, "What do you have to say?" His response always was, "I'm sorry." That wasn't enough for her. She would say something like, "If you were sorry, you wouldn't have done it in the first place." Josh didn't know what to say to that, so he just didn't say anything at all.

I then shared with Josh what I tell all of my clients about the word "sorry." The word sorry by itself doesn't mean anything. I asked Josh what made him say he was sorry. He responded by saying, "I'm sorry for hurting her. I'm sorry for lying to her." Then, he told me that he had said those exact things many times over the past few months. It didn't matter. She would still get upset at him.

I shared with him a valuable lesson on this topic that I learned from Janice Abrams Spring, in her book *How Can I Forgive You*. She wrote, "An apology is more than a simple 'I'm sorry,' though that's a fine way to begin. It's also a way of saying that you take responsibility for your actions, care deeply about the pain you caused, and intend never to repeat the transgression" (6).

I asked Josh to pause and reflect on the hurt he created through his actions and the lies he had told. The purpose of this reflection was to allow him to feel April's suffering. Usually, I don't do this exercise with clients in the early part of their recovery because their shame is too high. However, as they make progress and develop the capacity to feel the pain they have created without becoming emotionally overwhelmed (this is called "shame resiliency"), I want them to be with their partner's pain. This is how compassion develops. The Latin root of the word, compassion, is pati, which means "to suffer." The prefix, com-, means "with" (7). I tell all of my clients that, by increasing their levels of compassion, they are choosing to love.

After explaining the Latin definition of compassion to Josh, I asked him to think about his last argument with April. I wanted him to think about how he could have had compassion for her at that moment. I began role-playing with him. I would play her, and he would try a compassionate response. When he got stuck, I would step in and offer suggestions.

Here's a short example of a role-play where Josh showed compassion for his wife:

Me [playing his wife]: Why did you lie to me all these years? If you didn't want to be with me, why didn't you just tell me?

Josh: There's no good excuse. I became a liar — someone you couldn't trust. I broke promises to you. You deserved better.

Me: You're right. I do deserve better. You're a liar.

Josh: I don't know what to say. I just told her I had lied to her. What do I say here?

Me, helping Josh: I regret my decisions every day. I deceived you, and you didn't deserve that. I am just starting to understand in a small way how much I hurt you.

Therapist note: In my example, I reiterated the deception and tried to acknowledge the pain. This is called "witnessing the pain."

We went back to the role-play.

Me: You don't care about how much you hurt me. If you did, you wouldn't have done what you did.

Josh turned to me and said, "I don't know what to say when she tells me I don't care about how much I hurt her." I asked him, "What's the truth?" He said, "I feel bad every day. I hurt the person I love the most." I replied, "Then, just tell her your truth."

Josh: I know my actions made it seem like I didn't care about hurting you, but every day I regret how much pain I have put you through.

After Josh's last response, I found myself having a hard time being angry with Josh. He was genuine, and I could feel it.

Here are a few things to notice that happened during this role-play:

- Josh didn't get defensive. It would have been easy for him to argue back. Instead, he chose to accept what she was saying to him. Even though he didn't agree with everything she said, he did acknowledge what she was feeling.

- He owned his mistakes and didn't blame her.

- He acknowledged his lies and deceit

- He tried to witness her pain. Initially, when I accused him of not caring about her pain, he didn't know what to say. When I asked him just to tell her his truth, his honest response was, "I feel bad every day." This is something April would need to hear if she was going to believe he was changing.

For more information on seeking genuine forgiveness, see https://bit.ly/treating-sex-addiction under Chapter 14.

Principle #2: Love Is a Choice: Make It Each Day

Every day, we make decisions that influence how we interact with others. Often the way we treat those closest to us is based on the patterns we've created over months and years. When these patterns are positive and healthy, we create meaningful bonds with others. When these patterns are unhealthy, we disconnect from the relationship.

Recently, I was working with a couple who had been married for 15 years. As we discussed their marriage and reviewed the interaction patterns they had established together, we identified a few events that occurred ten years earlier in their relationship that had created a cascade of negative interactions. Unfortunately, none of those events had been resolved. As we explored the unhealthy patterns that they had developed from 10 years earlier, the negative beliefs they held toward each other were evident. The wife had come to believe that all her husband wanted was sex. Her husband, on the other hand, had come to believe that his wife was controlling. The beliefs they held toward each other had been creating a lot of fights and influencing how they saw each other for more than a decade.

I couldn't help but feel bad for them. They had both been suffering from loneliness, discouragement, and disappointment in their relationship. They had discussed divorce many times and probably would have carried through with it if it had not been for their children and their religious beliefs.

After helping them identify the core beliefs they held about each other, I asked them if they liked each other. They both looked at me and said, "yes." When I asked them to share how they were showing each other that they cared for their partner, they sheepishly told me that they were not doing that very much. I then kindly said, "If you like each other, you sure aren't acting like it." They shook their heads and agreed with me.

This discussion provided me with the opportunity to discuss a powerful idea shared by Dr. Barbara Fredrickson in her book Love 2.0. Fredrickson suggests that, in all of our relationships, there are micro-moments where we can feel a positive resonance with others. She believes that love is not unconditional but, instead, is something that we create moment by moment in our relationships (8). These special moments include critical elements that most of my clients do not currently have in their life. They include:

- Eye contact

- A friendly smile

- Healthy touch

- Being in the present moment

You may have noticed how similar this list is to the attachment model we explored in Chapter 2 on what children need in their infancy to thrive and develop a secure bond. Fredrickson's research on positive resonance in relationships supports the idea that the basic needs of attachment never really leave us. Therefore, if we want to thrive in life and our relationships, we need to learn to create as many micro-moments of love in our day-to-day interactions. Love is a choice which we need to learn to make every day.

Fredrickson offers a few suggestions for how couples can do that. She wrote, for example, "Couples who regularly make time to do new and exciting things together—like hiking, skiing, dancing, or attending concerts and plays—have better-quality marriages. These activities provide a steady stream of shared micro-moments of positivity resonance" (9).

Single people also need to establish micro-moments of connection in their lives.

While talking with an individual female client, I discovered that she spent most of her weekends alone. Her roommates were often gone each weekend, so she had the apartment to herself. While she liked time to herself after a busy week at work, by the time Sunday came around, she felt incredibly lonely and isolated.

As we discussed the idea of creating positive interactions with others during the weekend, she realized that her isolation came from an unhealthy relationship in which she had been deeply hurt. This negative experience had caused her to isolate herself from others so that she wouldn't get hurt again. This awareness, however, helped her recognize the critical need for her to reach out and bond with friends from her past. She also began focusing on developing new friendships. For her, the idea of creating micro-moments with others changed her outlook on relationships. She found that simple actions like giving a compliment to someone, calling an old friend just to say hi, or inviting a group of friends over for a game night helped her combat her loneliness.

Here is a short list of ways you can create micro-moments of love.

- Provide someone a service (e.g., visit a grandparent, help someone in need, volunteer at your local food bank)

- Give attention to someone by asking them questions about their life

- Write a letter to someone who has had a positive influence on your life and then ask to meet with them and read your letter to them.

- Smile at others while making eye contact with them

- Take a meal to a friend who is sick

- Read a book to a child

- Invite friends to an activity and express to them how much you appreciate them

- If you are married, do something kind for your partner that you know he or she would appreciate

- Call a friend on their birthday or anytime and let them know how much they have blessed your life

The power of creating micro-moments of love can be life-changing for you and others around you. I have learned this lesson from many people over the years. One particular story illustrates how others have taught me the value of loving others through simple acts of service.

A few years ago, I needed help installing a new microwave above the stove in my house. I asked a neighbor to look at my electrical outlets and give me feedback. When he looked at my situation, he said, "You will need a new outlet. I can install one up here in the cupboard in a jiffy." An hour later, we had a new microwave above our stove. As he was leaving, he said something to me that has changed my life. I expressed to him my appreciation for his help, and he replied, "There isn't another place I would have rather been." He was so genuine. At that moment, his kindness and acts of service made me want to be a better man.

Love is a choice. Choose to make it every day, and your life will be better.

Principle #3: Create a Safe Environment

Have you ever been in a situation where you didn't feel safe? How did you respond? Most likely, you prepared to protect yourself, or you quickly fled. Why do we react this way? We are designed to fight, flee, or freeze when threatened. We are biologically wired to assess our environment for safety, and only if we determine we are safe will we choose to bond or connect with others.

Regarding this process, Dr. Stephen Porges, an expert on the fight/flight response, wrote, "Only in a safe environment is it adaptive and appropriate to simultaneously inhibit defense systems and exhibit positive social engagement behavior" (10). Dr. Porges revealed that our first instinct is to protect ourselves. Once we have had time to assess our environment, if we determine that it is safe, we can choose to connect with others.

This is a critical piece to understand if you want to create love in your relationships. When the people around us feel safe in our presence, they will likely relax and socially bond with us. Conversely, if individuals cannot determine if we are safe, they will almost always choose to protect themselves and avoid bonding with us. Remember, our initial instinct is to protect ourselves. Therefore, even in committed relationships, if our partner can't determine whether he or she is safe with us, that partner will likely turn to his or her natural instincts of pulling back (flight) or lashing out (fight).

When someone feels safe in our presence, their mind relaxes. This allows them to open up and share their thoughts and emotions with us. Even their nonverbal body language indicates that they feel safe in our presence. For example, they will genuinely smile at us, maintain eye contact, and make gestures toward us that show they are interested in a connection. We all read the nonverbal cues given to us by others, so we know when someone is open to connecting with us or if they are holding back.

The key principle to understand is this: Safety is at the foundation of all healthy human connection. Simply said, if we want to connect with others, we have to create a safe environment where others feel safe in our presence. When safety exists, a connection can happen; when safety is absent, the natural outcome is to protect oneself through the fight, flight, or freeze response.

When we feel safe with others, we become more aware of their needs, and they become aware of ours. This form of syncing together is referred to as "attunement." In safe relationships, we learn to attune to each other. Attuned people can finish each other's sentences or pick up on subtle cues that their loved one needs something. Attuned people help their friends without even being asked. People who are attuned to the needs of others have a mindset that allows them to look outside of themselves. When we become that kind of person, we will have developed a high relationship IQ, and others will feel more safe and secure in our presence.

When our relationship IQ is high, we understand how to give and receive in relationships. Others feel understood by us. We almost intuitively know how to meet their needs. This is a skill and can be developed. In addition to giving to others, individuals whose relationship IQ is high also let others into their life. When they need help or assistance, they reach out for support. They are not afraid to say, "I need help." You will notice that throughout this book, I have emphasized the importance of being open and letting others in to help you. By being aware of others' needs and reaching out when you need help, you are increasing your relationship IQ.

When I talk with my clients about this idea, I emphasize that nobody has a market on being kind and caring. We make this choice every day. Nobody can stop us from creating a safe environment in our relationships. Some people respond to this idea by saying, "But my partner is always yelling at me since s/he discovered my sexual behaviors." My response is to let them know that their response to that anger can still be loving. I realize that this is not easy, but it is possible. I have observed many clients who have chosen to listen and show empathy for their partner's pain rather than get angry and defensive. By staying present with their partners suffering, they make more rapid progress. The change in their relationships don't happen overnight; eventually, however, they show their partner through their loving behavior that they genuinely want a better relationship.

They learned that, instead of turning to their shame and responding with anger, they could listen intently and validate the pain that their partner described. They learned to acknowledge the pain they created instead of listing off their partners' faults.

These responses provided an environment for their partner to feel heard and understood. When I have talked with betrayed partners throughout my career, most of them have expressed a strong desire for their partner to understand their pain genuinely. When my clients learn to show this type of care, they are creating a safe environment for their partner to be heard and felt.

If you would like to learn how to understand your partner's pain more effectively, I have created a short audio recording titled, Opening Your Heart to Your Partner's Pain. You can find this recording at https://bit.ly/treating-sex-addiction under Chapter 14.

Below are some strategies that I have found to be useful for creating safety in relationships

Strategy #1: Be Consistent and Predictable

One way to create a safe environment is to be predictable. Dr. Stephen Porges found that, when individuals are trying to determine if someone is safe to connect with, even the slightest of changes can cause them to pull back. Regarding this, Porges wrote, "Slight changes in the biological movements that we see can shift a neuroception from 'safe' to 'dangerous.' When this shift occurs, the neural systems associated with prosocial behavior are disrupted, and the neural systems associated with defensive strategies are triggered" (11). This explains why 90% of the betrayed partners that I have surveyed over the years report that, when they are around their partner, they are constantly trying to read his/her emotions (12).

Below is a list of specific ways to be predictable in your relationships:

- Be where you say you are going to be.

- Do what you say you are going to do. If you have to break a commitment, give a clear explanation of why.

- Avoid spontaneous changes.

- Strive to be emotionally consistent. Avoid shifting from anger to love and back to anger.

- Make and keep commitments (i.e., I will be home at 6:00 p.m.; I will mow the lawn this weekend).

Strategy #2: Show Commitment

If you have hurt someone through your sexual actions, that person will likely question your commitment. One way to rebuild trust is to show commitment by working on your recovery without that person asking you to do it. Additional ways to show commitment include: 1) being patient with their recovery process; 2) verbally expressing your commitment to the relationship; and 3) develop your non-defensive listening skills, which means you can listen to them without getting upset.

Strategy #3: Be Honest and Trustworthy

At the core of connection is honesty and trustworthiness. In the past, you may have broken the trust of your partner. However, your past behavior does not mean that's who you are. You were dishonest in the past, but you can now commit to being honest and truthful. I have observed how powerful complete honesty and truthfulness can be in the healing process. In my work, I have watched couples heal when the betraying partner writes an "emotional restitution" letter. This letter acknowledges the ways that they lied, deceived, and manipulated their partner. While it can take months to prepare couples for this form of disclosure, it often has a powerful healing effect.

Things to remember when it comes to being honest:

- A lie is any communication given with the intent to deceive.

- If I make a commitment, I keep my promises.

- Speak the honest truth regardless of the consequences.

Strategy #4: Create an Environment Where Others Feel Loved

If you have ever been around someone who made you feel like you were the most important person in the world, you have met someone who knows how to make others feel loved. Most of us have had at least one person in our lives who loved us this way. I would invite you to think about the things that person did to make you feel loved and make a list of the things they did for you. The memories and experiences that you have with this person can be the template you use to show others love.

Creating a safe environment is at the foundation of all healthy relationships. When we understand the importance of safety and apply the four strategies listed above in our relationships, trust can be restored, and healing becomes possible.

Principle #4: Lift Others Through Your Loving Kindness

I often wonder if we could sit with another person and listen to their life story, how we would interact with them. Early in my career, I had an experience that has changed my approach to therapy and how I see others. I was a graduate student in Lincoln, Nebraska, doing an internship at Lutheran Family Services. While there, my supervisor asked me if I would be willing to meet with individuals who were getting ready to be released from prison. Anxious to get as much clinical experience as I could, I agreed to meet with as many prisoners as possible.

I soon learned that they were changing my whole approach to therapy and how I saw my clients. They all came from difficult backgrounds. One man, in particular, had spent over half his life in prison. As I listened to his story and the challenges he faced in his childhood, I wondered how I would have turned out if I had grown up in his home. What happens to children when they are physically and emotionally abused, given drugs at a young age, and live in poverty, wondering where their next meal is going to come from?

Each of the prisoners I met with taught me a valuable lesson, the most important of which is that I should seek to understand the whole story of the person sitting in front of me. Since those early experiences, I have found that the best work I do as a therapist begins when I try to understand my client in a nonjudgmental way. Everyone has a story that needs to be heard and understood.

My experience at the prison also taught me the importance of trying to "see" each person I meet with, by keeping an open mind. As I listened to their stories, I gained a deeper appreciation for their challenges. I have since realized that, when I approach people with an open and loving mindset, our experiences together become rich and rewarding.

Since my initial experience with the prisoners, I have learned that those who practice loving kindness meditations develop a deeper awareness for others. Researchers, who study the brains of Buddhist monks that practice loving-kindness meditations, discovered several impressive outcomes.

Below are some of the benefits of practicing loving-kindness:

- Compassion meditation, it seems, resets the brain so that it is always prepared to respond to another's suffering (13)

- Compassion meditation can nudge you toward the positive end of the outlook dimension; it strengthens connections between the prefrontal cortex and other brain regions important for empathy (14).

- Compassion meditation also likely facilitates social intuition (15).

As you heal from addictive behaviors, practicing loving-kindness can significantly increase your relationship skills. The loving-kindness meditation is not complicated; in fact, it is easy to do. Here are the steps for loving-kindness meditation. First, start with yourself and repeat the following four statements for three to five minutes:

May I feel safe.

May I feel happy.

May I feel healthy.

May I live with ease.

Practice doing this simple meditation for a few days and then transition to someone else that you care about. Simply, change your meditation to

May (name of person) feel safe.

May s/he feel happy.

May s/he feel healthy.

May s/he live with ease.

By doing these meditations, you can increase the empathy you feel for others and increase your level of self-compassion. In addition, your social intuition will increase, which means you will be more likely to see the needs of others around you. The benefits of loving-kindness meditations (LKM) extend into other areas as well. Researchers have found that meditation can reduce depression, anxiety, stress, anger, and addictive cravings (16,17).

Principle #5: Express Gratitude

If you are in the early stage of recovery, the idea of expressing gratitude as a way to love your way through recovery may sound ridiculous. However, as you gain more traction in your recovery, you will begin to feel like a new person. As you grow in your recovery, you will feel more awake and alive. These feelings will bring a renewed sense of gratitude. You might call your change a rebirth.

Regarding this idea, Dr. Patrick Carnes wrote, "Sex addicts in recovery can go through a second adolescence and emerge with a new sense of innocence" (18). Many of my clients express a new excitement for life. While most would never want to go back to their darkest moments, many of them are grateful for what they have learned about themselves and others as a result of their addiction.

The idea of using gratitude in recovery has scientific backing. In an interesting journal article, "Does Gratitude Promote Recovery from Substance Misuse?" Gila Chen identified gratitude as a positive emotion that increases personal recovery capital. Regarding the power of gratitude, she wrote, "The prospects for successful recovery are dependent on personal and social resources including character traits and attitudes, material resources and relationships. In this context, gratitude has been empirically highlighted consistently as a valuable positive emotion and attitude, building lasting and beneficial personal and social resources and helping to maintain interpersonal relationships, improve quality of life and promote more adaptive coping strategies rather than resorting to negative strategies such as substance misuse. Gratitude enables the individual to develop the personal arsenal of strengths necessary to conduct a sober and productive life" (19).

Expressing gratitude has many benefits. Dr. Martin Seligman, the founder of positive psychology, in his book, Flourish, revealed specific strategies that can increase your happiness by raising your well-being and lowering depression. Both of these strategies are directly related to expressing gratitude. I encourage you to do both of these exercises as you work toward recovery. They will improve your life in many ways.

Exercise #1: The Gratitude Visit

Dr. Seligman outlined the exercise this way:

Close your eyes. Call up the face of someone who is still alive who years ago did something or said something that changed your life for the better. Someone who you never properly thanked. Someone, you could meet face to face next week. Got a face? Gratitude can make your life happier and more satisfying. When we feel gratitude, we benefit from the pleasant memory of a positive event in our life. Also, when we express our gratitude to others, we strengthen our relationship with them (20).

Here's how to carry out the gratitude visit. First, recall a memory or an experience you had with the person you identified above. Second, write a letter of gratitude to this person with specific examples of how he or she blessed your life. The letter should be around 300 words in length. Third, plan to deliver the letter in person. Ask the person if you could meet with them without telling them why. Fourth, say to the person you would like to read a written a letter to them. Ask that person to let you read that letter. When you are done, you can discuss it together.

Dr. Seligman said this about those who completed this exercise: "You will be happier and less depressed one month from now" (21).

Exercise #2: What Went Well (3 Blessing Exercise)

In Dr. Seligman's write-up for this exercise, he suggested that we don't take time to reflect on the good things that happen in our lives. In this exercise, the goal is to help you find more happiness by focusing on what went well today. This exercise has also been found to increase levels of happiness and decrease depression (22).

Here are the steps to doing the what went well exercise. First, commit to trying this exercise each day for at least one week. Second, every night, take 10 minutes to write down what went well today and why. You can use a journal or computer, but make sure you have a physical record of what went well each day and why it went well. Seligman suggested that it may feel awkward writing about what went well, but after one week, he claims you will see the benefits (23).

I would like to add a third gratitude exercise that I have found helpful in my work with clients.

Exercise #3: The 100 Things to be Grateful For

Happy people tend to find the good in life, even during challenging times. The purpose of this exercise is to help you build a list of 100 things that you are grateful for. This list will take time to create and can grow beyond 100 things, if you choose. Much like the what went well exercise, the primary focus is to help your mind focus on the good things happening in your life.

Here are the steps you will take to build your list of 100 things you are grateful for. First, think of one thing you are grateful for. It could be a family member, your job, a good book you read, or music you enjoy listening to. Second, once you have identified what you are grateful for, write it down. Then write down why you are grateful for that person or thing. Third, as you build your list of 100 things you are grateful for and why you are thankful for these things, review your list at least once a week. This will remind you of what you are grateful for and why. Fourth, when you identify a person you are grateful for, write that person a note letting them know that you are grateful for them.

Dr. Martin Seligman has found that practices like the three exercises listed above can significantly improve your level of happiness and well-being. As you learn to create more positive emotions, you will find more joy in life. As you cultivate gratitude in your day-to-day life, you will be on your way to recovery and an increase in your life satisfaction.

Chapter Summary

Love is powerful. It can heal you and those you care about the most. You can love your way toward addiction recovery. By applying the five principles outlined in this chapter, you will be more loving: 1) develop a compassionate mindset; 2) remember that love is a choice, and you can make it every day; 3) create a safe environment so others can connect with you; 4) lift others through your acts of loving-kindness; and 5) express gratitude each day. As you apply these principles in your life, you will be happier, and you will find more joy in your life.

Support Resources (found at https://bit.ly/treating-sex-addiction — under Chapter 14)

- The Biology of Love: Touch and Oxytocin

Thank You

Dear Reader,

It is intimidating writing a book on a complex subject like sexual addiction. During the past 25 years, I have had the privilege of meeting incredible people, just like you. I wrote this book with you in mind. I envisioned you sitting in my office. I could imagine you reaching out for the first time to get help. Or, I imagined you as a person who has been seeking help for months or years but is still looking for solutions. Regardless of why you picked up this book, I applaud you for letting me share with you what I have learned over the past 25 years about sexual addiction and its treatment.

I have tried, throughout this book, to share real-life stories and examples of the recovery process. I hope that these examples have given you hope that recovery is possible. My deepest desire is that you will experience an improvement in the quality of your life. As I have said throughout this book, recovery is not just about sobriety, it is about having a significant improvement in every aspect of your life.

Most important, if I could have one wish for you, it would be that you find more meaningful connections and better relationships.

May you be blessed as you move towards your healing and recovery.

Best regards,

Dr. Kevin B. Skinner, LMFT, CSAT-S

P.S. As a reminder, you can visithttps://bit.ly/treating-sex-addiction for support material for each chapter in this book.

References and Notes

Introduction:

1. American Society of Addiction Medicine (2019). Definition of addition. Retrieved from https://www.asam.org/resources/definition-of-addiction.

2. Ibid

3. Laudet, A. B., & White, W. L. (2008). Recovery capital as prospective predictor of sustained recovery, life satisfaction, and stress among former poly-substance users. Substance Use & Misuse, 43(1), 27–54. DOI: 10.1080/10826080701681473.

Chapter One:

1. White, W., & Cloud, W. (2008). Recovery capital: A primer for addictions professionals. Counselor, 9(5), 22-27.

2. Baumeister, R. F., & Tierney, J. (2012). Willpower rediscovering our greatest strength. London: Allen Lane.

3. Cacioppo, J. T., & Patrick, W. (2009). Loneliness: human nature and the need for social connection. New York: W.W. Norton.

4. Matthews, D. A., & Larson, D. B. (1995). The faith factor: An annotated bibliography of clinical research on spiritual subject, Vol. 3. National Institute for Healthcare Research, Rockville, MD.

5. Morjaria, A., & Orford, J. (2002). The role of religion and spirituality in recovery from drink problems: A qualitative study of Alcoholics Anonymous members and South Asian men. Addiction Research & Theory, 10, 225–256.

6. Moos, R. H., & Moos, B. S. (2007). Protective resources and long-term recovery from alcohol use disorders. Drug and Alcohol Dependence, 86, 46–54.

7. Kaskutas, L. A., Bond, J., & Humphreys, K. (2002). Social networks as mediators of the effects of Alcoholics Anonymous. Addiction, 97(7), 891–900.

8. Retrieved from https://ncphp.org/wp-content/uploads/2017/06/Relpase-

declines-after-5-years.pdf

Chapter Two:

1. Brown, V. B. (1981). Human intimacy: Illusion & reality. (Pg. 1) Parliament Publishers. Salt Lake City, Utah

2. Johnson, S. (2019). Attachment theory in practice: Emotionally focused therapy (EFT) with individuals, couples, and families. The Guilford Press. New York: New York

3. Ibid

4. Porges, S. W. (2011). The polyvagal theory: Neurophysiological foundations of emotions, attachment, communication, and self-regulation. New York: W.W. Norton.

5. Ibid

6. Ibid

7. Ibid

8. Retrieved from https://www.ncbi.nlm.nih.gov/pmc/articles/PMC4798868/

9. Johnson, S., (2019). Attachment theory in practice: Emotionally focused therapy (EFT) with individuals, couples, and families. The Guilford Press. New York: New York

10. Retrieved from https://www.cdc.gov/violenceprevention/childabuseandneglect/acestudy/index.html

11. Bigras, N., Daspe, M.-È., Godbout, N., Briere, J., & Sabourin, S. (2016). Cumulative childhood trauma and adult sexual satisfaction: Mediation by affect dysregulation and sexual anxiety in men and women. Journal of Sex & Marital Therapy, 715(April), 1–20.n Retrieved from http://doi.org/10.1080/0092623X.2016.1176609

12. Daigneault, I., Hébert, M., & McDuff, P. (2009). Men's and women's childhood sexual abuse and victimization in adult partner relationships: A study of risk factors. Child Abuse & Neglect, 33(9), 638–647. Retrieved from http://doi.org/10.1016/j.chiabu.2009.04.003

13. Godbout, N., Dutton, D. G., Lussier, Y., & Sabourin, S. (2009). Early exposure to violence, domestic violence, attachment representations, and marital adjustment. Personal Relationships. Retrieved from http://doi.org/10.1111/j.1475-6811.2009.01228.x

14. Retrieved from https://www.cdc.gov/violenceprevention/childabuseand-neglect/acestudy/aboutace.html

15. Retrieved from https://www.ncbi.nlm.nih.gov/pubmed/19840693

16. Skinner, K. B. (2019). Preliminary findings on the relationship between adverse childhood experiences (ACEs) and sexual compulsivity. Unpublished data.

17. Harris, N. B. (2018). A deepest well.

18. Ibid

Chapter Three:

1. Duke University. (2008, October 16). Early Exposure To Drugs, Alcohol Creates Lifetime Of Health Risk. ScienceDaily. Retrieved December 24, 2019 from www.sciencedaily.com/releases/2008/10/081016124244.htm

2. Skinner, K. B. (2019). Pornography Use Study. Unpublished data

3. Squire, L. R., & Kandel, E. R. (1999). Memory: From mind to molecules. New York: Scientific American Library; see also Church, D. (2007). The genie in your genes: Epigenetic medicine and the new biology of intention. Santa Rosa, CA: Elite Books, p. 94.

4. Wolynn, M. (2017). It didnt start with you: how inherited family trauma shapes who we are and how to end the cycle. NY, NY: Penguin Books, an imprint of Penguin Random House LLC.

5. Dispenza, J. (2015). You are the placebo: making your mind matter. Carlsbad, CA: Hay House, Inc.

6. Ibid

Chapter Four:

1. Broadwell, M. M. (1969). Teaching for learning (XVI). The Gospel Guardian. Retrieved from wordsfitlyspoken.org.

2. https://en.wikipedia.org/wiki/Four_stages_of_competence

3. Flower, J. (1999). In the mush. Physician Executive, 25(1): 64–66. PMID 10387273.

4. https://en.wikipedia.org/wiki/Four_stages_of_competence

5. White, W., & Cloud, W. (2008). Recovery capital: A primer for addictions professionals. Counselor, 9(5), 22-27.

6. https://utahcoalition.org/project/accountability-working-recovery-support-ing-others-recovery/

7. Dispenza, J., & Amen, D. G. (2015). Breaking the habit of being yourself: how to lose your mind and create a new one. Carlsbad, CA: Hay House.

Chapter Five:

1. Gollwitzer, P., & Sheeran, P. (2006). Implementation intentions and goal achievement: A meta-analysis of effects and processes. Advances in Experimental Social Psychology 38: 69–119.

2. Patterson, K. (2014). Change anything: the new science of personal success. London: Piatkus.

3. Gollwitzer, P., & Sheeran, P. (2006). Implementation intentions and goal achievement: A meta-analysis of effects and processes. Advances in Experimental Social Psychology 38: 69–119.

4. Klein, G. (2017). Sources of power how people make decisions. Cambridge, MA: MIT Press.

5. Ibid

6. Ibid

7. Ibid

Chapter Six:

1. https://utahcoalition.org/project/accountability-working-recovery-support-ing-others-recovery/

2. Skinner, K. B. (2019). Results from Trauma Inventory for Partners of Sex Addicts (TIPSA). Unpublished data.

3. Laudet, A. B., & White, W. L. (2008). Recovery capital as prospective predictor of sustained recovery, life satisfaction, and stress among former poly-substance users. Substance Use & Misuse, 43(1), 27–54. doi: 10.1080/10826080701681473

4. Ibid

5. BN Publishing. (2008). Alcoholics Anonymous big book. Charleston, SC.

6. Retrieved from https://blogs.psychcentral.com/addiction-recovery/2012/12/honesty-in-addiction-recovery/

7. Wilkes, P. (2012). The art of confession: renewing yourself through the

practice of honesty. New York: Workman Pub. Co.

8. Ibid

9. Retrieved from https://blogs.psychcentral.com/addiction-recovery/2012/12/honesty-in-addiction-recovery/

10. Laudet, A. B., & White, W. L. (2008). Recovery capital as prospective predictor of sustained recovery, life satisfaction, and stress among former poly-substance users. Substance Use & Misuse, 43(1), 27–54. doi: 10.1080/10826080701681473

11. Ibid

12. Corley, M. D., & Schneider, J. P. (2012). Disclosing secrets: An addicts' guide for when, to whom, and how much to reveal. Tucson, AZ: Recovery Resource Press.

13. Ibid

14. Ibid

15. Ibid

16. Retrieved from https://dearpeggy.com/results.html

Chapter Seven:

1. Germer, C. K. (2014). The mindful path to self-compassion: Freeing yourself from destructive thoughts and emotions. Kbh.: Nota.

2. Ibid.

3. Skinner, K. B. (2019). Data from Assessing Pornography Addiction. Unpublished data

4. Retrieved from https://www.tennessean.com/story/money/2015/01/23/buffalo-face-lifes-storms/22187351/

5. Ibid

Chapter Eight:

1. Butler, M. H., Pereyra, S. A., Draper, T. W., Leonhardt N. D., & Skinner, K. B. (2018) Pornography use and loneliness: A bidirectional recursive model and pilot investigation, Journal of Sex & Marital Therapy, 44(2), 127-137, DOI: 10.1080/0092623X.2017.1321601

2. Ibid

3. Cacioppo, J. T., & Patrick, W. (2009). Loneliness: human nature and the need for social connection. New York: W.W. Norton.

4. Ibid

5. Mikulencer, M., & Shaver, P. R. (2018). Attachment in adulthood. New York: The Guilford Press.

6. Rubenstein, C. & Shaver, P. (1982). In search of intimacy. New York: Delacorte. Steffick, D. E. "Documentation on affective functioning measures in the Health and Retirement Study," Documentation Report no. DR-005. Ann Arbor: University of Michigan, Survey Research Center, 2000. Retrieved from hrsonline.isr.umich.edu/docs/userg/dr-005.pdf.

7. Cole, S. W., Hawkley, L. C., Arevalo, J. M., Sung, C. Y., Rose, R. M., & Cacioppo, J. T. (2007). "Social regulation of gene expression in human leukocytes," Genome Biology 8: R189.

8. Cacioppo, J. T., & Patrick, W. (2009). Loneliness: human nature and the need for social connection. New York: W.W. Norton.

9. Ibid

10. Ibid

11. Hạnh Nhất, & Chödzin Sherab. (2011). True love: a practice for awakening the heart. Boston: Shambhala.

12. McLaren, K. (2013). The art of empathy: a complete guide to lifes most essential skill. Boulder, CO: Sounds True, Inc.

13. Hạnh Nhất, & Chödzin Sherab. (2011). True love: a practice for awakening the heart. Boston: Shambhala.

14. McLaren, K. (2013). The art of empathy: a complete guide to lifes most essential skill. Boulder, CO: Sounds True, Inc.

15. For related definitions, see Baron-Cohen, Zero degrees of empathy, 11, and Gordon, Roots of empathy, 30.

16. McLaren, K. (2013). The art of empathy: a complete guide to lifes most essential skill. Boulder, CO: Sounds True, Inc.

17. Retrieved from https://www.medicalbag.com/home/lifestyle/laughter-therapy-shown-to-boost-immune-function-in-cancer-patients/

18. Ibid

19. Hughes, D. A. (2007). Attachment focused family therapy. W.W. Norton & Company. New York New York.

20. Ibid

21. Field, T., Diego. M., Pelaez, M., Deeds, O., & Delgado, J. (2012). Depression and Related Problems in University Students. College Student Journal 46, 193-202.

22. Figueiredo, B., Canario, C., Tendais, I., Pinto, T.M., Kenny, D., & Field, T. (2018). Couples' relationship affects mothers' and fathers' anxiety and depression trajectories over the transition to parenthood. Journal of Affective Disorders. 238:204-212.

23. Hernandez-Reif, M., Ironson, G., Field, T., Hurley, J., Katz, G., Diego, M., … Burman, I. (2004). Breast cancer patients have improved immune and neuroendocrine functions following massage therapy. Journal of Psychosomatic Research, 57(1), 45–52. doi: 10.1016/s0022-3999(03)00500-2

24. Retrieved from https://greatergood.berkeley.edu/article/item/why_physical_touch_matters_for_your_well_being

25. Retrieved from http://pediatrics.med.miami.edu/touch-research

26. Berscheid, E. (1985). "Interpersonal attraction," in Lindzey, G., & Aronson, E. eds., The handbook of social psychology. New York: Random House.

Chapter Nine:

1. Wilkes, P. (2012). The art of confession: renewing yourself through the practice of honesty. New York: Workman Pub. Co.

2. Thomas Nelson. (2015). The Bible: King James Version. Nashville.

3. Ibid

4. Hawkins, D. R. (2014). Power vs. force: the hidden determinants of human behavior. Carlsbad, CA: Hay House, Inc.

5. Dispenza, J., & Amen, D. G. (2015). Breaking the habit of being yourself: how to lose your mind and create a new one. Carlsbad, CA: Hay House.

6. Ibid

7. Szegedy-Maszak, M. (2005). Mysteries of the Mind: Your unconscious is making your everyday decisions." U.S. News & World Report. Also see: Kappas, J. G. (1999). Professional hypnotism manual. Knoxville, TN: Panorama Publishing Company.

8. Shapiro, F. (2014). The role of eye movement desensitization and reprocessing (EMDR) therapy in medicine: Addressing the psychological and physical symptoms stemming from adverse life experiences. The Permanente Journal, 18(1): 71-77. DOI:10.7812/TPP/12-098.

9. Kolk, B. A. van der. (2015). The body keeps the score: mind, brain and body in the transformation of trauma. London: Penguin Books.

Chapter Ten:

1. Leach, J. (1994). Survival psychology. New York University Press

2. Goleman, D. (1996). Emotional intelligence. New York: Bantam Books

3. Damasio, A. R. (1999). The feeling of what happens: Body and emotion in the making of consciousness. Orlando, FL: Harcourt Brace

4. Goleman, D. (1996). Emotional intelligence. New York: Bantam Books

5. LeDoux, J. (1996). The emotional brain. pg. 214. Simon and Schuster. New York: New York

6. Ibid

7. Ibid

8. Lehrer, J. (2009). How we decide. pg. 37. Houghton Mifflin Harcourt. New York: New York.

9. Goleman, D. (1996). Emotional intelligence. pg. 28. New York: Bantam Books

10. Siegel, D. J. (2007). The mindful brain. W. W. Norton & Company. New York: New York. (The mindful brain…287–288 Kindle)

11. Kabat-Zinn, J. (2003). Coming to our senses: Healing ourselves and the world through mindfulness. New York: Hyperion Press

12. Boyce, B. (2011). The mindfulness revolution. pg. 3. Shambhala Publications, Inc.: Boston, Massachusetts

13. Siegel, D. J. (2010). The mindful therapist. Norton. New York: New York

14. Wegner, D. M. (1994). White bears and other unwanted thoughts. pg. 2. The Guilford Press. New York: New York

15. Siegel, D. J. (2010). The mindful therapist. pg. 55. Norton. New York: New York

16. Neff. K. (2011). Self-compassion. pg. 123. Harper Collins. New York: New York

17. Ibid

Chapter Eleven:

1. Cloud, W., & Granfield, R. (2008). Conceptualizing recovery capital: Expansion of a theoretical construct. Substance Use & Misuse, 43 (12–13), 1971-1986. DOI: 10.1080/10826080802289762

2. Laudet, A. B., & White, W. L. (2008). Recovery capital as prospective predictor of sustained recovery, life satisfaction, and stress among former poly-substance users, Substance Use & Misuse, 43(1), 27–54. DOI: 10.1080/10826080701681473

3. Dispenza, J., & Amen, D. G. (2015). Breaking the habit of being yourself: how to lose your mind and create a new one. Carlsbad, CA: Hay House.

4. Szegedy-Maszak, M. (2005). "Mysteries of the Mind: Your unconscious is making your everyday decisions." U.S. News & World Report. Also see: Kappas, J. G. Professional hypnotism manual (Knoxville, TN: Panorama Publishing Company, 1999). My first exposure to this concept was in 1981 when I studied hypnosis with John Kappas at the Hypnosis Motivation Institute. Back then, he stated the subconscious was 90% of the mind. Recently, scientists are estimating that it's about 95 percent. Either way, it is still a lot.

5. Duhigg, C. (2014). The power of habit: Why we do what we do in life and business. New York: Random House Trade Paperbacks.

6. Ibid

7. Ibid

8. Ibid

9. Polak, L. (2013). Making health habitual. British Journal of General Practice, 63(607). doi: 10.3399/bjgp13x662966

10. Lally, P., van Jaarsveld, C. H. M., Potts, H. W. W., & Wardle, J. (2010). How are habits formed: Modelling habit formation in the real world. Euro J Soc Psychol., 40:998–1009. [Google Scholar]

11. Lally, P., & Gardner, B. Promoting habit formation. Health Psychol Rev. In press: DOI: 10.1080/17437199.2011.603640. [Google Scholar]

12. Baumeister, R. F., & Tierney, J. (2012). Willpower: Why self-control is the secret of success. London: Penguin Books.

13. Skinner, K. B. (2019). Unpublished findings from sexual addiction recovery capital scale (SARCS)

14. Baumeister, R. F., & Tierney, J. (2012). Willpower: Why self-control is the secret of success. London: Penguin Books.

15. Ibid

16. Retrieved from http://sleepeducation.org/essentials-in-sleep/hcalthy-sleep-habits

17. Retrieved from https://healthfinder.gov/healthtopics/category/everyday-healthy-living/mental-health-and-relationship/get-enough-sleep#the-basics_2

18. Retrieved from https://www.cdc.gov/obesity/strategies/index.html

19. Retrieved from https://www.medicalnewstoday.com/articles/322268.php

20. Abrantes, A. M., Battle, C. L., Strong, D. R., Ing, E., Dubreuil, M. E., Gordon, A., & Brown, R. A. (2011). Exercise preferences of patients in substance abuse treatment. Mental Health and Physical Activity, 4(2), 79–87. doi:10.1016/j.mhpa.2011.08.002

21. Ratey, J. J., & Hagerman, E. (2008). Spark the Revolutionary New Science of Exercise and the Brain. Boston: Little Brown & Company.

22. Ibid

23. Ibid

24. Skinner, K. B. (2019). Unpublished findings from sexual addiction recovery capital scale (SARCS).

25. Kaplan, D. L. (2013). For love and money: Exploring sexual & financial betrayal in relationships. Tucson, AZ: publisher not identified.

26. American Institute of CPAs (AICPA). (2012). AICPA survey: Finances causing rifts for american couples. Retrieved from http://www.aicpa.org/press/pressreleases/2012/pages/ finances-causing-rifts-for-american-couples.aspx.

27. Kaplan, D. L. (2013). For love and money: Exploring sexual & financial betrayal in relationships. Tucson, AZ: publisher not identified.

28. McRaven, W. H. (2017). Make your bed: little things that can change your

life --and maybe the world. New York: Grand Central Publishing.

Chapter Twelve:

1. Retrieved from https://brandongaille.com/22-lottery-winners-bankrupt-statistics/

2. Collins, J. C. (2009). Good to great: Why some companies make the leap ... and others don't. New York, NY: Collins.

3. Ibid

Chapter Thirteen:

1. Siegel, D. J. (2017). Mind: A journey to the heart of being human. New York: W.W. Norton & Company.

2. Voss, C., & Raz, T. (2017). Never split the difference: Negotiating as if your life depended on it. London: Random House.

3. Ibid

4. Hughes, D. A. (2011). Attachment-focused family therapy. New York: W.W. Norton.

5. Tangney, J., & Dearing, R. (2002). Shame and guilt. New York: Guilford

6. Skinner, K. B. (2019). Unpublished findings gaslighting and PTSD symptoms in betrayed partners.

7. Tangney, J., & Dearing, R. (2002). Shame and guilt. New York: Guilford

8. Ibid

9. Moos, R.H., & Moos, B.S. (2007). Protective resources and long-term recovery from alcohol use disorders. Drug and Alcohol Dependence, 86, 46-54.

10. Cloud, W., & Granfield, R. (2008). Conceptualizing recovery capital: Expansion of a theoretical construct. Substance Use & Misuse, 43(12-13), 1971–1986. doi: 10.1080/1082608080228976

11. Carnes, P. (2015). Facing the shadow: Starting sexual and relationship recovery: a gentle path to beginning recovery from sex addiction. United States: Gentle Path Press.

12. Cloud, W., & Granfield, R. (2008). Conceptualizing recovery capital: Expansion of a theoretical construct. Substance Use & Misuse, 43(12-13), 1971–1986. doi: 10.1080/1082608080228976

Chapter fourteen:

1. Thunder Bay Press. (2000). The Holy Bible: King James Version. Matthew 22: 36-39; San Diego, CA.

2. Tancredi, L. R. (2010). Hardwired behavior: what neuroscience reveals about morality. Cambridge: Cambridge University Press.

3. Ibid

4. Ibid

5. Hạnh Nhất, & Chödzin Sherab. (2011). True love: a practice for awakening the heart. Boston: Shambhala.

6. Spring, J. A., & Spring, M. (2006). How can I forgive you?: the courage to forgive, the freedom not to. New York, NY: Harper Collins.

7. https://www.quora.com/What-are-the-roots-of-the-word-compassion

8. Fredrickson, B. (2014). Love 2.0: how our supreme emotion affects everything we feel, think, do, and become. New York: Plume.

9. Ibid

10. Porges, S. W. (2011). The polyvagal theory neurophysiological foundations of emotions, attachment, communication, and self-regulation. New York: W. W. Norton.

11. Ibid

12. Skinner, K. B. (2019). See https://bit.ly/treating-sex-addiction. Unpublished data.

13. Fredrickson, B. (2014). Love 2.0: how our supreme emotion affects everything we feel, think, do, and become. New York: Plume.

14. Ibid

15. Schreiner, I., & Malcolm, J. P. (2008). The Benefits of Mindfulness Meditation: Changes in Emotional States of Depression, Anxiety, and Stress. Behaviour Change, 25(3), 156–168. doi: 10.1375/bech.25.3.156

16. Ortner, C. N. M., & Zelazo, P. D. (2014). Responsiveness to a mindfulness manipulation predicts affect regarding an anger-provoking situation. Canadian Journal of Behavioural Science / Revue Canadienne Des Sciences Du Comportement, 46(2), 117–124. doi: 10.1037/a0029664

17. Marlatt, G. A., & Bowen, S. (2006). Mindfulness Meditation as a Treat-

ment Intervention. PsycCRITIQUES, 51(36). doi: 10.1037/a0003649

18. Keane, H. (2002). Whats wrong with addiction? Melbourne: Melbourne University Press.

19. Chen, G. (2017). Does gratitude promote recovery from sub-stance misuse?, Addiction Research & Theory, 25:2, 121-128, DOI: 10.1080/16066359.2016.1212337

20. Seligman, M. E. P. (2013). Flourish: a visionary new understanding of hap-piness and well-being. New York: Atria.

21. Ibid

22. Ibid

23. Ibid

Appendix A:

Family History/Genogram

Below is a sample Genogram of Jonathan's family. His story was told in Chapter Seven. In the top you can see the legend. You will notice that addiction was common in both his family and his wife Stephanie's family. Other challenges such as anxiety, depression, and alcohol abuse were included. This example can serve as model for you to evaluate your family history and the key issues that your family has dealt with. The primary purpose of included a Genogram is to help you understand how your family history may be influencing you now.

The Treating Sexual Addiction online support class for this book provides has a copy of this Genogram along with questions for you to start working on your own. I encourage you to explore your families patterns so you have more insight into how your past may be influencing you now.

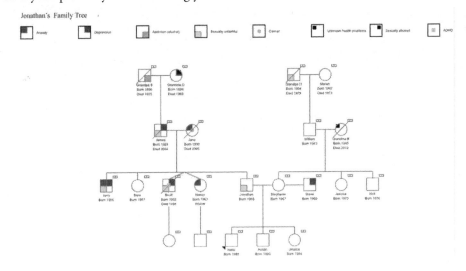

Questions for your Family History/Genogram:

Your Family

Questions for Mom's side of the family:

1. List physical health issues (i.e. diabetes, cancer, etc.)

2. List any addictions for each family member

3. List mental health issues (i.e. depression, anxiety, etc.)

4. List, if any, abuses that occurred

Questions for Dad's side of the family:

1. List physical health issues (i.e. diabetes, cancer, etc.)

2. List any addictions for each family member

3. List mental health issues (i.e. depression, anxiety, etc.)

4. List, if any, abuses that occurred

Note: if you have questions you can review the example of Jonathans family tree.

Appendix B

Outlining Your Recovery Plan

In Chapter Four, we discussed the importance of building a recovery plan. This appendix provides an outline of what a solid recovery plan could look like.

My Recovery Plan

As you develop your recovery plan, it may be helpful to break down your strategy into different steps. First, identify what you are going to change. Second, review the areas for improvement. Third, list as many items as you feel are relevant to change for your successful recovery. Third, identify short-term steps, midterm steps, and long-term steps you will put into your recovery plan.

Here's an example (You can find a copy of this to fill out at https://bit.ly/treating-sex-addiction

Under Appendix B)

First step: What am I going to change?

- End my affair
- Stop flirting with people

Second step: Additional areas to change and improve upon

- Build my recovery capital (review assessment results)
- Deal with my childhood issues with my parents
- Improve my relationship skills
- Increase my awareness so that, when I am vulnerable, I have a plan
- Be more effective at dealing with stress (reduce my anger)

- Understand and work through my shame
- Build a recovery team

Short Term (Action Steps)

What am I going to change?

- End my affair?

Why am I going to change it?

- I have seriously hurt my spouse and other family members. I also want to change to be a better person.

How am I going to change it?

- I am going to completely cut off any contact with the other woman/man. If there is any attempt by _____, I will avoid any contact and call friend (Matt).

Who can help me change it?

- I will talk with my therapist
- I will develop a support team (I need to work on getting this team together)

When am I going to start?

- I meet with my therapist next Monday.
- I will talk with my friend about being a support person for me.
- Things that will help me do these things:
- Improve my relationship with my wife and children. I need to listen more and try to understand them
- Reduce my shame; Dr. Skinner suggested I reread Chapter Nine
- Learn how to better deal with stress (read Chapter 10 and practice the C.O.A.L approach
- Attend a 12-step group

Behaviors and thoughts I have to avoid:

- No flirting
- When lustful thoughts come I need to identify them

- No pornography

Note: You will want to repeat this process for each of the issues in step two.

Midterm Recovery Plan

What am I going to change?

- Continue to stay away from affair partner
- Talk with my accountability team
- Find and talk with my sponsor

Why am I going to focus on these things during the middle part of recovery?

- I have to be consistent
- I need support and accountability

How am I going to change it?

- I will need to make sure I attend group and keep reaching out until I find my support team. So the answer is consistency. Don't quit trying.

Who can help me change it?

- My friend Matt has been with me through the thick and thin of my challenges. I will tell him what is happening and ask him for long-term support. I will let him know that I am including others to round out my recovery team.

When am I going to start?

- These things should already be happening in the midterm. If they aren't, I will talk with my therapist and identify the barriers.

Additional issues to focus on in the midterm recovery plan

- Work through childhood issues (e.g., Mom's anger at me, rejection at school, negative self-beliefs)
- Develop better relationship skills: How? Read books recommended by Dr. Skinner
- Focus on reducing shame: How? Review Chapter Nine, read Healing from the Shame That Binds You

Long-Term Recovery Plan (be specific)

- Build a better relationship with my wife and children (How?)

- Develop empathy for my wife suffering.

- Spend more time with my children

- Increase compassion for self and others (per Dr. Skinner's recommendation)

• Be more productive and focused at work

- Spend less time browsing the web

- Include others in my projects

- Set a goal to finish a project each day

• Develop stress reduction (what Dr. Skinner calls emotional regulation skills)

- Use Headspace app to practice mindfulness

- Practice breathing three minutes each day just focusing on breathing

- If I'm not making progress, I am going to consider neurofeedback as suggested by Dr. Skinner for individuals who are anxious. (See Dr. Skinner's suggestions for dealing with ADHD and other mental health topics at this link: https://bit.ly/treating-sex-addiction)

Appendix C:

Five Things To Do Before You Relapse

It is important to make a plan if you want to change your life. The five things list is designed to help you have a plan for the times when you feel overwhelmed with cravings. You will be more prepared to respond to difficult moments when you have a plan in place. The five things list should be reviewed often. One of my favorite assignments to give my clients is to have them write down their five things list with their non-dominant hand each day for 7 to 10 days.

Your five things list should include using as many senses as possible.

Here are a few examples of what your five things list could look like:

1. Acknowledge the craving and give it a name.

2. Leave the room, if possible be in a room with others

3. Contact a friend or family member

4. Avoid any digital device until I have talked with someone

5. Play the piano

The purpose of this list is to have specific things you commit to do when the temptation comes. If you have been through your list and still feel the cravings, I would encourage you to go through the list again. If your list includes talking with a friend or family member, you will want to be specific with them about the craving you are having (e.g. I am alone and struggling to avoid calling someone I have hooked up with before).

Be careful to avoid putting things on your list that you are not willing to do.

This list should be things that you commit to yourself and others that you will do before relapsing.

When my clients commit to doing their five things list they usually make great progress.

Your Five Things to do Before You Relapse List

1.

2.

3.

4.

5.

It is usually best to include one item that requires some kind of physical move-ment away from the place where they cravings began. It is also good to have some form of accountability on your list.

Appendix D:

Sexual History Timeline

The sexual history timeline is designed to help you explore all of the sexual experiences you have had throughout your life. This exercise will help you see patterns, identify specific time frames when your sexual behaviors began, increased in intensity, and changed. The timeline is broken up into different periods of time. You may have little to know sexual experiences in one time frame and a lot in other time frames. Be as specific as possible about your age, what the sexual experience was, and how many times it happened during that specific time frame.

Example:

Age: Five

Sexual experience: My friend introduced me to pornography and we started touching each other.

Frequency: It only happened one time.

Age:

Birth   Five (5)

|——|

Age:

Sexual Experience:

Frequency (amount of times it happened):

Six (6)   Eleven (11)

|——|

Age:

Sexual Experience:

Frequency (amount of times it happened):

Twelve (12)   Seventeen (17)

|————————————————————————————————|

Age:

Sexual Experience:

Frequency (amount of times it happened):

Eighteen (18)   Twenty-Five (25)

|————————————————————————————————|

Age:

Sexual Experience:

Frequency (amount of times it happened):

Eighteen (26)   Present

|————————————————————————————————|

Age:

Sexual Experience:

Frequency (amount of times it happened):

Note: It is common to have multiple sexual experiences during the same range of time (e.g. masturbation begins, exposed to pornography, first sexual experience, etc). If this is the case, you can find a downloadable copy of this exercise in the free support content area

Appendix E:

Key Life Inventory

All of us have key life events that alter our lives for good or bad. In this assignment, your task is to identify the significant events that have changed your life. Take into account big events like the death of a loved one, to moving, to your first sexual experiences. Other things you might include: moving, parents fighting, a parent with mental health challenges or substance abuse problems, or being bullied on a playground. Write down as many experiences as you can think of for the next few minutes. Once you are done, place your experience on the timeline.

Event: **Age:**

_____

_____

_____

_____

_____

_____

_____

_____

_____

_____

_____

_____

_____

Now place each of the events above on the timeline below:

Timeline:

Review: Please respond to the following questions in your journal

Now that you have identified key life events you have experienced, what sticks out to you the most? Identify any common themes between the events and then identify the events that had the biggest impact on your life.

Appendix F:

Recommended Readings and Other Resources

Other Resources by Dr. Kevin B. Skinner

1. Treating Pornography Addiction: The Essential Tools for Recovery

2. Treating Sexual Betrayal: The Essential Tools for healing

3. Strengthening Recovery Through Strengthening Marriage: Healing from Pornography Addiction (With Geoff Steurer)

4. Finding and Creating True Intimacy (Audio Series)

5. Rebuild Your Relationship after Sexual Betrayal: A Couples Guide to Healing

Dr. Skinner's Websites:

1. https://www.humanintimacy.com

2. https://www.drkevinskinner.com

3. www.bloomforwomen.com

4. www.addorecovery.com

Addo Recovery Clinics and Partners (Found throughout the United States and Canada).

Outpatient clinics for treating sexual compulsivity and sexual betrayal. If you are looking for support in your area we may have a specialist near you. Contact Addo Recovery at: 855-229-2336

Recommended Readings by Category:

Sexual Addiction

1. Facing the Shadow (By Dr. Patrick Carnes)

2. Out of the Shadows (By Dr. Patrick Carnes)

3. Sex Addiction 101: A Basic Guide to Healing from Sex, Porn, and Love Addiction (By Robert Weiss)

4. Always Turned On: Sexual Addiction in the Digital Age (By Robert Weiss and Jennifer Schneider)

5. Letting Go: The Path of Surrender (By David R. Hawkins)

Couples Work after Discovery of Sexual Betrayal

6. Courageous Love: A Couples Guide to Conquering Betrayal (By Stefanie Carnes)

7. Disclosing Secrets: An Addicts Guide for When, to Whom, and How Much to Reveal   (By M. Debrah Corley and Jennifer P. Schneider)

Family History (Book on how your past influences your present behaviors)

8. It Didn't Start with You (By Mark Wolynn)

9. A Deepest Well (By Nadine Burke Harris)

Emotional Regulation (How to address stress and stay connected with others)

10. Emotional Intelligence (By Daniel Goldman)

11. True Love (By Thich Nhat Hanh

12. The Mindfulness Workbook for Addiction: A Guide to Coping with the Grief, Stress and Anger that Trigger Addictive Behaviors) (By Rebecca Williams and Julie Kraft)

Trauma Recovery

13. The Body Keeps the Score (By Bessel van der Kolk, M.D.)

14. Getting Past Your Past (By Francine Shapiro)

Relationship Skill Building

15. The Seven Principles for Making Marriage Work: A Practical Guide from the Country's Foremost Relationship Expert (By John Gottman and Nan Silver)

16. The Relationship Cure: A 5 Step Guide to Strengthening Your Marriage, Family, and Friendships (By John Gottman)

17. Love 2.0: Finding Happiness and Health in Moments of Connection (By Barbara Fredrickson)

18. Hold Me Tight: Seven Conversations for a Lifetime of Love (By Susan Johnson)

19. Love Sense (By Susan Johnson)

My Favorite Books

20. The Power of Moments: Why Certain Experiences Have Extraordinary Impact (By Chip and Dan Heath)

21. The Seven Decisions: Understanding the Keys to Personal Success (By Andy Andrew)

22. Grit: The Power of Passion and Purpose (By Angela Duckworth)

23. Spark: The Revolutionary New Science of Exercise and the Brain (By John Ratey)

Online Courses

Treating Sexual Addiction: (Advanced Recovery Class—Online)

Would you like more hands one support in your recovery efforts? Dr. Skinner has prepared an advanced class you can take online. This course addresses important questions like:

- How can I model my recovery after what successful people are doing?

- Why is it so hard to quit?

- Why do I feel like nobody understands me?

- What can I do on days when I don't want to quit?

- How can I more effectively respond to my spouse/partner?

If you are looking for extra support, Dr. Skinner's advanced online course will provide you guidance throughout your journey to recovery. This advanced course goes beyond what Dr. Skinner covered in his book. If you are looking to move beyond your addiction and reclaim your life, this class will provide you the tools to succeed.

Learn more about the Advanced Class today!

https://www.humanintimacy.com/course/treating-sexual-addiction

Made in the USA
Monee, IL
10 April 2024

56214263R00143